SHAKESPEARE'S SERIAL HISTORY PLAYS

Shakespeare's Serial History Plays provides a re-reading of the two sequences of English history plays, *Henry VI – Richard III* and *Richard II – Henry V*. Reconsidering the chronicle sources and the staging practices of Shakespeare's time, Grene argues that the history plays were originally designed for serial performance. He charts the cultural and theatrical conditions that led to serial productions of the histories, in Europe as well as in the English-speaking world, and looks at their original creation in the 1590s and at modern productions or adaptions, from famous stagings such as the Royal Shakespeare Company's 1960s *Wars of the Roses* through to the present day. Grene focuses on the issues raised by the plays' seriality: the imagination of war, the emergence of character, and the uses of prophecies and curses through the first four; techniques of retrospection, hybrid dramatic forms, and questions of irony and agency in the second.

NICHOLAS GRENE is Professor of English Literature at Trinity College, Dublin. He is an authority on both Renaissance and Irish drama and his books include *Synge: a Critical Study of the Plays* (1975), *Shakespeare, Jonson, Molière: the Comic Contract* (1980), *Bernard Shaw: a Critical View* (1984), *Shakespeare's Tragic Imagination* (1992), and *The Politics of Irish Drama* (Cambridge University Press, 1999).

D1393763

SHAKESPEARE'S SERIAL HISTORY PLAYS

SHAKESPEARE'S SERIAL
HISTORY PLAYS

NICHOLAS GRENE

CAMBRIDGE
UNIVERSITY PRESS

PUBLISHED BY THE PRESS SYNDICATE OF THE UNIVERSITY OF CAMBRIDGE
The Pitt Building, Trumpington Street, Cambridge, United Kingdom

CAMBRIDGE UNIVERSITY PRESS
The Edinburgh Building, Cambridge CB2 2RU, UK
40 West 20th Street, New York, NY 10011-4211, USA,
477 Williamstown Road, Port Melbourne, VIC 3207, Australia
Ruiz de Alarcón 13, 28014 Madrid, Spain
Dock House, The Waterfront, Cape Town 8001, South Africa

http://www.cambridge.org

First published 2002

Printed in the United Kingdom at the University Press, Cambridge

Typeface Baskerville Monotype 11/12.5 pt.   *System* LATEX 2$_\varepsilon$ [TB]

A catalogue record for this book is available from the British Library

Library of Congress Cataloguing in Publication data
Grene, Nicholas.
Shakespeare's serial history plays / Nicholas Grene.
p.   cm.
Includes bibliographical references and index.
ISBN 0 521 77341 5
1. Shakespeare, William, 1564–1616 – Histories.
2. Great Britain – History – 1066–1687 – Historiography.   3. Historical drama,
English – History and criticism.   4. Kings and rulers in literature.   5. Middle Ages in literature.
6. Cycles (Literature)   I. Title.

PR2982 .G74   2002
822.3'3 – dc21   2001037482

ISBN 0 521 77341 5 hardback

For Philip Edwards

Contents

Illustrations

Plates 1, 3, 9 courtesy of Department of Early Printed Books, Trinity College Dublin Library; plates 2, 6, 7, 11–14, by permission of Shakespeare Centre Library, Stratford; plate 3 by permission of the *Radio Times*; plate 4 by permission of graphic designer Andy Williams, Royal Shakespeare Company; plate 5 by permission of BBC Worldwide Ltd; plate 8 by permission of photographer Laurence Burns; plate 10 by permission of BBC Information and Archives; plate 15 by permission of photographer Matthias Horn.

Acknowledgements

I acknowledge gratefully two terms' leave of absence from Trinity College, Dublin: the first in 1993 when this book was started, and the second in 2000 when it was finished. I also had the substantial benefit from Trinity College of a grant from the Arts and Social Sciences Benefaction Fund to support my research in 1993, and assistance from the Provost's Academic Development Fund towards the cost of the book's illustrations. I am very appreciative of an Andrew Mellon Fund Fellowship which I held in 1994, making possible a valuable period at the Huntington Library. Some of the material used in the first chapter was first tried out as a paper at the Huntington Library Renaissance Literature Seminar, and at various times subsequently in lectures at the Universities of Tokyo, Cape Town and Chicago.

A number of people over the years have helped me with suggestions for lines of research, answers to queries, assistance in tracking down specific items: Paolo Bosisio, Edward Burns, Jean-Michel Déprats, Joan FitzGerald, Sophia Grene, Peter Holland, David Scott Kastan, Dennis Kennedy, Felicia Londré, Richard McCabe, Tina Mahony, Valeria Marinelli, Andrew Murphy, Stephanie Nelson. I want to thank especially Sandra O'Connell who first made me aware of the production *Schlachten!*, and did so much to enable me to make use of it in this book. I am grateful to John Rowland of the Trinity College Audio Visual Media Services and to Brendan Dempsey of the Photographic Centre for their help in preparing the illustrations.

Shakespeare's histories have been a long-term shared interest with my father, David Grene; although we see the plays differently, I know that my ideas on the subject have been greatly influenced by his thinking. My mother, Marjorie Grene, read the book in draft form and it has gained throughout from her quick eye for misplaced commas, stylistic solecisms, fudged and muddled argument. The remaining infelicities are all my own. The book is dedicated to Philip Edwards who was my teacher in Trinity College in 1965–6, my colleague and head of department at the University of Liverpool 1974–9. Since then I have continued to enjoy the encouragement and stimulus of his friendship, the inspiration of his work.

Chronology of major serial productions / adaptations

Date	Plays/title	Company/theatre	Director/producer
1864	*Richard II – Richard III*	Weimar Court Theatre	Franz von Dingelstedt
1906	*Richard II – Richard III* (without 1 *Henry IV*)	Shakespeare Memorial Theatre, Stratford	F. R. Benson
1935	'The Ten Chronicle Plays of William Shakespeare'	Pasadena Playhouse	Gilmor Brown and others
1951	*Richard II – Henry V*	Shakespeare Memorial Theatre, Stratford	Anthony Quayle, John Kidd, Michael Redgrave
1951–3	1–3 *Henry VI*	Birmingham Repertory Theatre	Douglas Seale
1960	*An Age of Kings*	BBC Television	Michael Hays, Peter Dews
1963	*Wars of the Roses*	Royal Shakespeare Company, Stratford	Peter Hall and John Barton
1964	*Richard II – Henry V*	RSC, Stratford	Peter Hall, John Barton, Clifford Williams
1965	*Il gioco dei potenti*	Teatro Lirico, Milan	Giorgio Strehler
1975	*Henry IV – Henry V, Merry Wives*	RSC, Stratford	Terry Hands
1977	*Henry V,* 1–3 *Henry V*	RSC, Stratford	Terry Hands
1978	*Kings*	Carcassonne	Denis Llorca
1978–9	*Richard II – Henry V*	BBC TV Shakespeare	David Giles, Cedric Messina
1982–3	*Henry VI – Richard III*	BBC TV Shakespeare	Jane Howell, Jonathan Miller
1986–7	*Henry IV – Henry V*	English Shakespeare Company	Michael Bogdanov
1987–8	*Wars of the Roses*	English Shakespeare Company	Michael Bogdanov
1988	*The Plantagenets*	RSC, Stratford	Adrian Noble
1999	*Schlachten!*	Deutsches Schauspielhaus, Hamburg; Salzburg	Luk Perceval
2000–1	*This England: the Histories*	RSC, Stratford	Steven Pimlott, Michael Attenborough, Edward Hall, Michael Boyd

Note on the texts

For the eight history plays with which this book is concerned, I have used the New Cambridge Shakespeare editions as follows:

King Richard II, edited by Andrew Gurr
  (Cambridge University Press, 1984).
The First Part of King Henry IV, edited by Herbert Weil and Judith Weil
  (Cambridge University Press, 1997).
The Second Part of King Henry IV, edited by Giorgio Melchiori
  (Cambridge University Press, 1989).
Henry V, edited by Andrew Gurr (Cambridge University Press, 1992).
The First Part of King Henry VI, edited by Michael Hattaway
  (Cambridge University Press, 1990).
The Second Part of King Henry VI, edited by Michael Hattaway
  (Cambridge University Press, 1991).
The Third Part of King Henry VI, edited by Michael Hattaway
  (Cambridge University Press, 1993).
King Richard III, edited by Janis Lull
  (Cambridge University Press, 1999).

For other plays of Shakespeare cited in the text, except where otherwise stated, I have used the Peter Alexander text of the *Complete Works* (London and Glasgow: Collins, 1951).

Quotations from the First Folio are taken from:

Charlton Hinman (ed.), *The Norton Facsimile of the First Folio of Shakespeare* (New York: Norton, 1968).

I have quoted source materials wherever possible from:

Geoffrey Bullough (ed.), *Narrative and Dramatic Sources of Shakespeare* (London: Routledge & Kegan Paul, 1960–2), vols. III–IV.

For chronicle passages that Bullough does not include I quote from:

Edward Hall, *The union of the two noble and illustre famelies of Lancastre &
Yorke* (London: Richard Grafton, 1548).
Raphael Holinshed, *The third volume of Chronicles*, 2nd edn (London,
1587).

Introduction

In 1965, when I was still at school in Belfast, I watched the BBC Television broadcast of *The Wars of the Roses*, John Barton and Peter Hall's Royal Shakespeare Company adaptation of the three parts of *Henry VI* and *Richard III*. I was amazed. It was partly the acting: Peggy Ashcroft playing Queen Margaret from handsome battlefield trophy to vengeful harridan; the gentle, gaunt, shambling David Warner as King Henry; and Ian Holm's brilliant, baby-faced Richard of Gloucester. But it was also the sheer grip of the narrative as it built from episode to episode, battle to battle, from one tense council-table confrontation to another. I had never heard of the *Henry VI* plays, much less read them. I had no idea how heavily they had been condensed and adapted by Barton and Hall, nor yet how celebrated this production had been. The one Shakespeare history play that I did know, and know well, was *1 Henry IV*, because it was a prescribed text for A-level, and we had spent months of class time reading and re-reading it We were well taught. We were shown the unity of the play, focused on the theme of honour. The central figure was Prince Hal, flanked by Hotspur who overvalued honour – 'By heavens, methinks it were an easy leap / To pluck bright honour from the pale-faced moon' – and Falstaff who thought it a mere scutcheon. Between these polar opposites Hal had to get the balance right. The play's dramatic structure was equally shapely, rising through the mid-point of Hal's interview with his father, to the climactic culmination of his duel with Hotspur at Shrewsbury. Because it was called the *First Part of Henry IV*, we must have been aware that there was a *Second Part*, but no one suggested we read it. Come June, there would be no questions on *2 Henry IV*, no marks for knowing it; *1 Henry IV* was our set text, end of story.

Critical times have changed since 1965, and my awareness of Shakespeare's history plays has changed with them. Still, those two early experiences of the histories must have stirred in me some curiosity that has resulted, however belatedly, in this book. Were Shakespeare's

1

histories designed to have anything like the effect on their original audience that the television *Wars of the Roses* had had on me? What was
the relationship of an individual play such as *1 Henry IV*, with all its formal autonomy, to the plays that preceded and followed it in sequence?
When I started to think about these issues, I was concerned primarily
with intentions. Had Shakespeare pre-planned a series of four plays on
the reigns of Henry VI and Richard III, another series devoted to the
time of Richard II, Henry IV and Henry V, or did he just keep adding
on sequels as he went along? I have tentative answers to offer to these
questions in my first chapter. But with so much undecidable in the matter
of Shakespearean intentions, I became preoccupied with broader issues.
I wanted to explore what was involved in the enterprise of serialising
the chronicles in the 1590s, how the sequences of plays were shaped up
out of their narrative sources, and how that enterprise may have been
related to theatre practices of the time. I was equally interested in the
much later theatrical opportunities afforded by the plays as they have
been given serial productions or adaptations in the modern period, that
phenomenon of which *Wars of the Roses* was only the best-known example.
My object has been to bring together these two sorts of evidence, and
use that as the basis for a reconsideration of the two history play series.

The initial section of my book seeks to tell the story of these serial histories, in Chapter 1 attempting to reconstruct the theatrical market-place
conditions out of which they arose, the indications of sequential design
or otherwise in their treatment of the chronicle sources, the formal interrelationship of the plays themselves. The second chapter moves on to an
overview of modern serial productions, beginning in the mid nineteenth
century and flourishing in the twentieth, with their intellectual and cultural contexts. The frame of reference in both these chapters is limited.
In looking at sources, for instance, I have concentrated more or less
exclusively on Hall and Holinshed, the two main chronicles on which
Shakespeare drew, ignoring many other materials he may have used.
My focus is on how the plays were quarried out of their source texts,
the ways their serial continuum resembles or differs from the ongoing
historical rhythms of the chronicles. Equally my account of the plays
in performance does not claim comprehensiveness. I have looked only
at productions or adaptations of more than two of the plays as a series, and not with even emphasis at all of these. Although I have tried to
reconstruct the effect of earlier stagings from reviews, prompt-books, eye-
witness accounts, with performance there can be no substitute for being
able to watch for oneself. Accordingly the bias of detailed illustrations

throughout this book is tilted towards the modern productions that I have been able to see, or those where a full visual record on film or video can be recovered.

Among readers of the book, there may be those who might have preferred a more thoroughgoing study of the source material, or those who believe the book would have been better based exclusively in performance analysis. I have decided to combine the two in order to explore the phenomenon of the plays' seriality both in its origins and in its changing theatrical manifestations. This is a text-centered book, often concerned with close reading. The object of such an approach, however, is not to revert to an old-fashioned principle of the autonomy of the text, the canonical integrity of the Shakespearean plays in and for themselves. Rather the opposite: I hope to show how the plays, themselves constructions from the chronicles, are open to continuous reconstruction on the stage.

The aim of the two main sections of the book, devoted to the two history play series, is to re-read them in the light both of my reconstruction of their Elizabethan origins and of their latter-day theatrical redactions. Given this perspective, it would have made no sense to work my way forward a play at a time. Instead I have followed a number of themes and interpretative issues thrown up by attending to the plays as series. So with the *Henry VI – Richard III* sequence, concerned as it is with wars, foreign and domestic, I have looked in Chapter 3 at how those wars are imagined, how and if that imagination changes from play to play according to a developing pattern of theatrical representation. With the through-casting of characters in the series, there is also the question of the ways these individual figures may be progressively characterised, the acting opportunities they provide for 'building a character': this is the subject of Chapter 4. Prophecies and curses are tropes frequently used in the earlier set of histories to shape up the dramatic narrative to come: Chapter 5 is centred on how they function, and what sort of causalities they imply.

The second group of plays, *Richard II – Henry V*, is formally more independent, more loosely connected, in my view. Yet, as they succeed one another in a continuing chronological sequence, they grow into a series if only retrospectively. It is the retrospective mode that I consider in Chapter 6 – the uses made of looking back, both at an imagined past in *Richard II* and, in the later plays, at the previously represented theatrical action. The mode of the history play notably shifts in the *Henry IV* plays, with the introduction of a hybrid history form capable of including comedy. Chapter 7 is concerned with the effects of this multi-strand, multi-mode genre upon the linear historical narrative represented by the series. The last chapter is devoted to the transformation of Prince Hal into Henry V, and the questions of change and identity entailed by that transformation enacted over a sequence of three plays.

There is a problem for anyone writing on Shakespeare of how to deal with the huge and ever-increasing body of scholarship and interpretation. In this book I have tried faithfully to acknowledge my critical debts, to credit the sources for any specific ideas or information borrowed. In other cases, however, I have given references only to material that comes directly in the line of my argument. I have nowhere cited a book or article just to demonstrate that I have read it. I have adopted this policy the more readily because the book is intended not only for Shakespearean specialists but for students who may prefer a text less laden with scholarly citation. I hope that such a light armour of annotation will not appear either ignorant or arrogant.

The approach in this study is intended to be open-ended and exploratory, rather than thesis-led. With such a book, even more than with other works of interpretation, the proof of the pudding must be in the eating. But, in the context of modern critical analysis of Shakespeare's history plays, it may have something to recommend it by way of new departure. Writing on the histories over the last fifty years has been dominated to an extraordinary extent by reaction to just one book: E. M. W. Tillyard's *Shakespeare's History Plays*. It is not just that Tillyard's conception of all eight plays as a single integrated vision of English history reflecting the 'Tudor myth', the 'Elizabethan world order', was for a time very influential on scholars and theatre directors. In fact the argument of the book was quite soon challenged, then repeatedly contested, and has come to be all but discredited. More significantly, Tillyard set the terms of a debate that has continued to run and run. Ways of looking at the histories may have changed with the impact of new historicism, cultural materialism, and feminism, but the political and social configurations underpinning the histories remain the compelling critical consideration. Interpretation of the history plays has been preoccupied, not to say obsessed, with ideology. This book makes no claim to be an ideology-free zone: a good deal of attention is necessarily given to the political implications of the plays and their several serial representations. But starting from the fact of their seriality as a changing theatrical manifestation across time may provide a different sort of entry to the issues, may allow us to see the histories from another angle. That, at least, is what I hope the book can achieve.

PART I

The story of the histories

CHAPTER ONE

Serialising the chronicles

How to tell the story of the histories in their own time? Shakespeare's ten history plays, a whole section of the First Folio, getting on for a third of the complete corpus, were all but one of them written and produced in the 1590s; after 1600 there is only the much later collaborative *Henry VIII*. In this Shakespeare's practice reflects/dominates that of his theatrical contemporaries. There hardly was any such thing as an English history play in the professional theatre before 1590; there was a marked falling off in the genre after the turn of the century. Of an estimated 150 plays dealing with the history of England in the period 1562 to 1642, nearly 80 are dated in the one decade of the 1590s.[1] Felix Schelling who supplied these figures, writing in his 1902 book on *The English Chronicle Play*, supplied also a traditional explanation for the phenomenon, one way of telling the story of the histories:

It was in the very nature of things that the popularity of the Chronicle Play should find its origin in the burst of patriotism and the sense of national unity which reached its climax in the year 1588 and stirred England to meet and to repulse the Spanish Armada.[2]

By the opposite end of the twentieth century critics had grown more sceptical of a historically inevitable 'nature of things', and the ideological sky over interpretations of the period had darkened. The post-Armada period was no longer read as one of euphoric patriotism, and Shakespeare's history plays were often construed rather as a contribution to a radical historiography reflecting the political unease of the time.[3] Times change and change the way we tell the story.

However it is told, the story of the emergence of the Elizabethan history play is necessarily bound up with the story of Shakespeare's emergence as a dramatist. The first two known allusions in print to Shakespeare's presence in the London theatre (Nashe's *Pierce Pennilesse* and Greene's *Groatsworth of Wit*) are both from 1592, and both refer to what were already evidently the very successful *Henry VI* plays. Greene's envious attack on the 'upstart Crow, beautified with our feathers' was originally interpreted as evidence of Shakespeare's beginnings in the theatre as an adapter of other men's plays. For Edmond Malone, the Greene attack clinched his view that the anonymously published texts known as the *First Part of the Contention* and *The True Tragedy of Richard Duke of York* were the early unadapted versions of the plays by other dramatists which, when re-written by Shakespeare, became *2 Henry VI* and *3 Henry VI*.[4] However, the bibliographical work in the 1920s which established *1 Contention* and *Richard Duke of York* as merely reported texts of the equivalent *Henry VI* plays allowed for a different view of Shakespeare's beginnings in the theatre.[5] When Shakespeare was no longer to be seen as a hack 'fixer' who advanced to writing his own solo plays, the *Henry VI – Richard III* series could be read instead as being all his own, a tetralogy of premeditated design.[6] This chimed well with the influential Tillyard conception of the grand narrative of the two tetralogies as a whole.[7] For a time, from the 1940s on, textual scholarship and critical interpretation together sustained a unified idea of the histories as a single massively planned enterprise with which Shakespeare began his career.[8]

By the 1980s, however, grand narratives were decidedly unfashionable, and the editors of the Oxford Shakespeare comprehensively dismantled the monolithic version of the histories. In their 1986 edition the plays were once again held to be collaboratively written, not composed in chronological sequence, and were re-named to correspond to the titles by which they were (allegedly) first known in the theatre. So in the Wells and Taylor *Complete Works*, the reader no longer finds the sequence of *1 Henry VI, 2 Henry VI, 3 Henry VI*, familiar from the Folio on, but *The First Part of the Contention, Richard Duke of York*, and only then *1 Henry VI*.[9] Underlying this revised version of the early history plays were the editorial principles giving new authority to theatrical evidence, even if it was from reported texts or so-called 'bad' quartos. They were the same principles which produced, most controversially, the editorial decision to have a character called Oldcastle in *1 Henry IV* who then in *2 Henry IV* turns into Falstaff, to reflect the name-change which appears to have been forced on Shakespeare between the two plays.[10] Where previous editors and critics had constructed an early Shakespeare in control of a planned series of history plays, reflected in the sequential march of reign after reign of the Folio text, the Oxford edition posited happenstance histories derived from unstable texts created by the arbitrary contingencies of theatre.

The object of this chapter is to concentrate on the two series of Shakespeare's history plays, leaving out the non-serial *King John* and the later *Henry VIII*, and to frame the story of the histories in the 1590s somewhat differently. I want to begin by relating the emergence of Shakespeare's multi-play history series to the vogue for two-part plays following on from the spectacular success of *Tamburlaine*, to show how the fashion for history plays may have arisen as much in response to the market dynamics of the theatre as to the political atmosphere of England in the aftermath of the Armada. It is in such a context that I situate the *Henry VI – Richard III* plays. Starting with a recapitulation of the facts and problems associated with the *Henry VI* plays, I want to come at what was involved in this first extended effort of serialising the chronicles for the stage. I shall be attending less to the issue of whether Shakespeare planned and wrote them all in chronological order as one ideologically integrated creation, but rather to the issue of how the narrative continuum of his major source, Hall's *Union of the two noble and illustre famelies of Lancastre & York*, was shaped into the set of four plays. I want to examine particularly how far that shaping was designed with serial production of the plays in mind, and what evidence there may be, internal or external, that they were produced as a series in the theatre of the time. The evidence on this appears to me to be different for each sequence. It might seem logical to suppose that if Shakespeare had succeeded in creating one series of four plays on English history, then the second set of such plays would certainly have been pre-planned, and that has been the common assumption. Yet in my view the *Richard II – Henry V* plays are much less clearly written for serial production; in their formal distinctness and the weakness of the links between them, they suggest a set of individual compositions only incrementally accumulating into a series. This, at least, will be my story of the histories in the 1590s.

TAMBURLAINE AND THE TWO-PART PLAY

The principle of sequels and series, the marketing strategy of selling people more of what they liked the first time, is fundamental to any number of different entertainment industries: the Barsetshire chronicles, the Forsyte saga, soap operas, television mini-series, the latest Hollywood success number 2, 3 or 4 coming soon to a cinema near you. It seems so fundamental that it is hard to imagine anyone having first invented it. But as far as the English Renaissance stage goes, the credit has to go to Christopher Marlowe with *Tamburlaine*. There does not seem to be a single example of a two-part play certainly performed in the London professional theatre before *Tamburlaine* in 1587–8. There has been a great deal of argument as to whether Marlowe planned both parts of *Tamburlaine* in advance; the Prologue to *2 Tamburlaine*, if we take it literally, suggests rather a cash-in sequel:

> *The generall welcomes* Tamburlain *receiv'd*
> *When he arrivèd last vpon our stage,*
> *Hath made our Poet pen his second part*[11]

But in the wake of *Tamburlaine* two-part plays, sequels and series, planned and unplanned, are everywhere. There are records of well over forty titles which have more than one part in the period up to 1616.[12]

Many of these plays survive in title only. Some of those that are extant involve companion plays rather than sequels, such as *A Knack to Know an Honest Man*, a quite unrelated work that served as follow-up to *A Knack to Know a Knave*.[13] This was in all probability the relationship also of Shakespeare's *Love's Labour's Won*, which we only know from Francis Meres' *Palladis Tamia*, to his *Love's Labour's Lost*. But whether the plays were actual narrative continuations of one another or merely designed to hook on to a previous title, the underlying market principles were the same: to build quickly on any theatrical success. Philip Henslowe's *Diary* supplies detailed evidence of how such two-part plays were commissioned, and brings out the speed with which sequels were delivered. So, for example, a play called *Black Bateman of the North* was ordered by Henslowe from four of his regular authors, Henry Chettle, Robert Wilson, Michael Drayton and Thomas Dekker, in May 1598. It was in production by mid-June; within weeks Chettle and Wilson were getting advances on a second part which was finished by 14 July (Henslowe, 89–93). This sort of pattern is replicated numerous times in the *Diary*: a first part is bargained for, delivered and produced, and if it goes down well, or even in some cases if it looks promising, a second part is demanded almost immediately. Not all two-part plays were unpremeditated, however; in some cases two parts were ordered in advance. To take just one instance, in October 1599 Henslowe bought from Wilson, Drayton, Anthony Munday and Thomas Hathway the script of the 'first pte of the lyfe of Sr Jhon Ouldcastell' and paid them an advance on a second part, which was duly delivered in December (Henslowe, 125, 129).

Two cases of two-part titles are especially interesting as they suggest developments leading from the two parts of *Tamburlaine* to the three parts of *Henry VI*. The first is the anonymous *Troublesome Raigne of John, King of England*, published in 1591, either the source play for Shakespeare's *King John* or some sort of pirated version of Shakespeare's play itself.[14] Two things are significant about it from my point of view here. One is the fact that it was published in two separate parts, even though it seems very unlikely that it was ever performed as two plays. Here was a canny publisher exploiting the vogue for the two-part play and selling one play as two. The other is the sales pitch of the prologue to the play addressed to the 'Gentlemen Readers':

> *You that with friendly grace of smoothed brow*
> *Have entertaind the* Scythian Tamburlaine,
> *And given applause unto an Infidel:*
> *Vouchsafe to welcome (with like curtesie)*
> *A warlike Christian and your Countreyman.*
> (Bullough, IV, 84)

Here we see a bid for the *Tamburlaine* market made on behalf of a play drawn from the English chronicles. It may well have been the need for readily available and continuing narrative materials as well as patriotic fervour that sent playwrights to English history to find subjects of *Tamburlaine*-like audience appeal.

The other play that is significant for my argument is the *First part of the Tragicall raigne of Selimus* published anonymously in 1594, but sometimes attributed to Greene. There does not seem ever to have been a second part to *Selimus*, but Greene, or whoever, clearly planned that there should be one. The events which the play dramatises concern the murderous take-over of the Turkish Empire by Selimus in the year 1512, and the playwright left himself the eight remaining years of Selimus's reign to make the substance of a second part – a Part II which, the conclusion to Part I promises the audience invitingly, 'shall greater murthers tell'.[15] One of the pieces of evidence often used by scholars as an indicator that the second part of *Tamburlaine* was an unpremeditated sequel is the fact that Marlowe had run through most of his source material in Part I, and had to pad out his 'Return of Tamburlaine' with whatever dubiously relevant matter he found to hand.[16] The author of *1 Selimus* had learned that lesson: if you want to have a sequel, plan ahead and economise on your narrative accordingly.

Let me then put a hypothesis. Shakespeare in the early 1590s saw the market possibilities that had opened out from the enormous success of the two-part *Tamburlaine*. In theatrical conditions that demanded readiness with a quick sequel to follow up on a popular play, it was important to have the narrative option of a continuation. English chronicles afforded whole stretches of storystuff nearer home than the plains of Scythia. In the long, messy and war-torn reign of Henry VI, Shakespeare mapped out the materials for not just a two-part play but a whole set of three plays, with the possibility of expansion into four by following the chronicle into the reign of Richard III. It has often been remarked that, if the vogue for English history plays was inspired by patriotic afflatus after the Armada, then the time of Henry VI, in which England went down to disastrous defeat to France and carved herself up in a bloody set of civil wars, was hardly the most obvious subject to choose. But if the primary requisites were a plentiful and continuing stock of Marlovian blood and battles, then you could not do better than the Wars of the Roses. Some critics have been reluctant to countenance the idea of a planned trilogy/tetralogy by Shakespeare because there was no precedent for such a thing at that date. Clifford Leech is a representative example: 'It is not easy to credit that Shakespeare or anyone else can have felt sufficiently sure of his hold on the public, at the beginning of the last decade of the sixteenth century, to plan three consecutive plays covering a single dramatic action.'[17] It may be hard to credit, but it may nonetheless be true. Shakespeare, even this early in his career, may have been setting trends rather than merely following them. But before going on to look at what was involved in this first serialisation of the fifteenth-century English chronicles for the stage, it is necessary to consider the knotty tangle of facts and problems that surround the production of the *Henry VI* plays. My concern is not to attempt a definitive solution of those problems but to establish a balance of probabilities between the available interpretations of the facts.

HENRY VI: FACTS AND PROBLEMS

Facts first. A play Henslowe called 'harey the vj' was given fifteen performances at the Rose Theatre from 3 March 1592 (when it was marked 'ne') to 19 June 1592, shortly before all the London theatres were closed because of the plague (Henslowe, 16–19). It was apparently very successful at least to judge by its high box-office takings in comparison to other plays performed that season. Thomas Nashe in *Pierce Penilesse his Supplication to the Divell*, a work entered in the Stationer's Register on 8 August 1592, made reference to the theatrical impact of Talbot, hero of *1 Henry VI*:

How would it have ioyed brave *Talbot* (the terror of the French) to thinke that after he had lyne two hundred yeares in his Tombe, hee should triumphe againe on the Stage, and have his bones newe embalmed with the teares of ten thousand spectators at least (at seuerall times), who, in the Tragedian that represents his person, imagine they behold him fresh bleeding? (Chambers, *ES*, IV, 239)

Finally, Robert Greene, in his *Greenes Groats-worth of Wit, bought with a million of Repentaunce*, included in his bitter attack on the actors a parody of a line from *3 Henry VI* making unmistakable the identity of the specific actor/playwright attacked:

there is an upstart Crow, beautified with our feathers, that with his *Tygers heart wrapt in a Players hide*, supposes he is as well able to bumbast out a blank verse as the best of you: and being an absolute *Iohannes fac totum*, is in his owne conceit the onely Shake-scene in a countrie. (Chambers, *ES*, IV, 241-2)

Greene died on 3 September 1592, and the *Groatsworth of Wit* was supposedly written on his deathbed.

The problems that arise from these facts are complicated by the publication in 1594 of *1 Contention* and in 1595 of *Richard Duke of York*, the latter identified as having been played by Pembroke's Men, while the company that performed Henslowe's 'harey the vj' was Lord Strange's Men. So against any simple notion that Shakespeare singlehandedly planned and wrote the three parts of *Henry VI* in chronological order, there have to be set the following problematic points:

1. *1 Henry VI* (assuming that it was Shakespeare's play performed at the Rose in spring 1592) was played at a different time and with a different company from the two other parts which had some sort of independent existence as a two-part play.
2. Given that *3 Henry VI* was sufficiently well known by September 1592 for Greene to be able to parody the line 'O tiger's heart wrapped in a woman's hide' (1.4.138), and that the theatres had by then been closed since June, it seems likely that it had been produced by or before 1592, and thus (if Henslowe's 'ne' indicates a new play) *before 1 Henry VI*.
3. If Greene's attack is interpreted as a charge of plagiarism against Shakespeare, then some parts of the *Henry VI* plays may originally have been by other playwrights.

Setting the case out like this, with all its ifs and maybes, suggests how difficult it is to determine for sure how these three plays came to be created theatrically.

Disintegrative interpreters, such as the Oxford editors, and John Dover Wilson before them, build into their arguments for non-chronological composition the enigmatic mark 'ne' in Henslowe's *Diary*.

There is evidence that, although Henslowe was often careless about the titles of plays in his *Diary*, he always identified the second or third parts of multi-part plays to distinguish them from first parts.[18] Therefore, the disintegrators argue, it follows that 'harey the vj' must have been *1 Henry VI* not either of the other two plays and, with a first production ('ne' = 'new') in March–June 1592, was a 'prequel' to *2* and *3 Henry VI* which are assumed to have been performed in 1591–2, early enough to make plausible the easy familiarity of Greene's allusion to the 'tiger's heart'. Further internal evidence has also been produced to support the hypothesis of a 2–3–1 sequence for the plays. It has been remarked that, whereas *1 Henry VI* shows a detailed awareness of the later two parts, *2* and *3 Henry VI* do not seem to require knowledge of the first part: in particular, there are no references back in *2 Henry VI* to Talbot, hero of *1 Henry VI*, a sign, it is claimed, that the historically earlier play was only written later.[19] Those scholars who argue against the plays being composed in chronological order tend also to favour multiple authorship and a lack of theatrical coherence to the series as a whole. In this view, the Folio texts of the *Henry VI* plays are a trilogy reshaped by Shakespeare out of what was originally a collaborative two-part play reflected in the theatrical texts *1 Contention* and *Richard Duke of York*, followed by the prequel *1 Henry VI*.

Michael Hattaway, the editor of the *Henry VI* plays in the New Cambridge Shakespeare series, has preferred the simpler explanation that the three parts were written in 1–2–3 order and by Shakespeare (*1 Henry VI*, Introduction, 36). To my mind, the most compelling arguments in favour of this view are those of structural design, which I will be discussing shortly. But it is worth pointing out that all the pieces of evidence that have been used by the disintegrative school are susceptible of other explanations. So, for instance, Henslowe's enigmatic 'ne' need not necessarily mean 'new', that is a play which is being produced for the first time: it has also been interpreted as meaning newly licensed.[20] 'harey the vj' in March 1592 may only have been 'ne' to Henslowe, coming into the repertoire of the Rose for the first time as the revival of a play already performed elsewhere in a previous season. This might well be consistent with Nashe's peculiar reference to the 'ten thousand spectators at least (at severall times)' who had watched Talbot *redivivus* on the stage. Nashe has been generally assumed in this phrase to be totting up the audiences who would have seen the play in its recent run at the Rose. But it is equally possible that his 'at severall times' refers to earlier productions of the play as well. It is true that there is no record of such earlier productions, but the theatrical records that have survived from this time are so limited and fragmentary that no safe conclusions can be drawn from their absence.

It is obvious that at some point in time the two later parts were separated from *1 Henry VI* to surface as the texts *1 Contention* and *Richard Duke of York*. This may well have happened (as has been plausibly conjectured) in the period 1592–4 when the theatre companies, prohibited from playing in London because of plague, toured the provinces. In such circumstances, with limited personnel and without their prompt-books, it is quite likely that the actors might have put together the reported texts of an improvised two-part play such as we find in *1 Contention* and *Richard Duke of York*. This, however, by no means rules out the existence of an earlier complete trilogy of which the provincial texts would have been a truncated version. From what evidence is extant, it seems likely that there was considerable fluidity in the composition of the playing companies at this time, and it may well be that in a division of resources the newlyformed Pembroke's Men acquired the right to play the later two parts of a *Henry VI* trilogy while *1 Henry VI* went elsewhere. This is conjecture, but it is a conjecture that reasonably covers the known facts.

The issue of authorship is the hardest to prove or to disprove. The inclusion of the three *Henry VI* plays in the Folio is the strongest single piece of evidence for Shakespeare's sole authorship. Against that, the disintegrative case is one based on elaborate stylistic analyses involving tests of vocabulary, metre, speech-patterns and other variables.[21] For all the alleged objectivity of such tests, a great deal of the initial suspicion of multiple authorship of the plays has its source in Greene's attack, which has been assumed to be an accusation of plagiarism. But the 'upstart Crow' passage can also be read another way. Greene's indignation is at the presumption of an actor writing plays, at Shakespeare's pretensions to be 'as well able to bumbast out a blanke verse as the best of you', 'you' being (most likely) Marlowe, Peele, Nashe, university-educated authors like Greene himself. But the upstart crow may have been 'beautified with our feathers' in so far as he was imitating their style rather than actually taking over their plays: *1 Henry VI* in particular is indeed heavy with the influence of Marlowe. And the 'Johannes fac-totum' may have offended his envious colleagues by literally doing everything, not only as Jack-of-all-trades turning his hand to playwriting as well as acting, but writing a whole trilogy of plays of his own, not collaborating with others as the common theatrical practice was. Greene may have been reacting to the quite unprecedented spectacle of the actor/playwright Shakespeare having three plays produced as a series in the theatre to phenomenal success, witness Nashe's ten thousand spectators new embalming Talbot with their tears, witness a readership for Greene's own pamphlet able to pick up the parody on an isolated line of the tortured Richard Duke of York. It is to the planning and production of such a three-part *Henry VI* series, with *Richard III* beyond it, that I want now to turn.

HENRY VI – RICHARD III: PLANNING AND PRODUCTION

Where did Shakespeare – or Shakespeare and collaborators – start dramatising Hall's chronicle of the reign of Henry VI? If we are to believe those who argue that *1 Henry VI* is a prequel to the other two plays, the answer is 1444 with the conclusion of the negotiations conducted by Suffolk for the marriage of Henry to Margaret of Anjou. This is the starting-point of *1 Contention* as it is of *2 Henry VI*. Turn to a copy of the *The Union of the two noble and illustre famelies of Lancastre & Yorke* and try to imagine a playwright, looking for dramatisable material, diving into the fat folio volume at this particular point. It is the twenty-second year of the reign of Henry VI; the marriage of Henry and Margaret supervenes upon his earlier betrothal to the Earl of Armagnac's daughter; the war with France, continuing for many years, has been intermitted but not concluded by the peace of Tours; there is an ongoing narrative of longstanding court rivalries, between the Cardinal of Winchester and the Duke of Gloucester, between the Dukes of York and Somerset. None of these strands of what Hall calls the 'the troubleous season of King Henry the sixt' are easy to follow even if you have read through the chronicle from the start of the reign, but for a theatre audience introduced to the events of 1444 *in medias res* they would have been almost completely unintelligible.

From the point of view of the available source material for *1 Contention/2 Henry VI* what the play omits is as significant as where it starts. In the play the war with France is effectively over. There is just one exchange between the King and Somerset in which the Hundred Years War is ended in three lines:

> KING HENRY Welcome, Lord Somerset. What news from France?
> SOMERSET That all your interest in those territories
> Is utterly bereft you: all is lost.   (*2 Henry VI*, 3.1.83–5)

And that's that. This is the more remarkable given the fact that the war was continuing through the period of the chronicle covered by the play, and that this is the section containing the heroic last stand of Talbot

Kynge Henry the.vi.   Fol.Cxliiii.

rouergne with a puiſſaunt army, whiche ſodainly toke the Earle of Ar=
minacke, at the Iſle in Iordayne, and his yongeſt ſonne, and bothe his
doughters, and by force obteined the countreis of Arminacke, Louuer=
gne, Rouergne and Moulleſſon, beſide the cyties of Seuerac and Ca=
denac, and chaſed the Baſtarde of Arminacke out of his countrey, and
conſtituded gouernor of all thoſe ſeigniories, ſit Theobald de Walper=
gne, bailif of Lyon. So by reaſon of this infortunate chaunce, the ma=
riage concluded was differred, yea, and ſo longe differred, that it neuer
toke effect, as you ſhall heare more plainly declared.

¶ The.xxii.yere.

Hus, while Englande was vnquieted, & Fraũce ſore
vered, by ſpoyle, ſlaughter, & burnynge, all chriſten= The.xxii.
dom lamented the continuall deſtruccion of ſo no= yere.
ble a realme, and the effuſion of ſo muche Chriſten
bloude, wherfore, to appeace the mortall warre, ſo
longe contineuynge betwene theſe two puyſſaunt
kynges, all the princes of Chriſtendom, ſo muche
labored and trauailed, by their orators & Ambaſſa=
dors, ẏ the froſtie hartes of bothe the parties wer ſomwhat mollified, &
their indurate ſtomackes gretly aſſwaged. So there was a great diete
appointed, to be kepte at the citee of Tours in Tourayne, where, for the
kyng of Englande appered, William de la Pole erle of Suffolke, doc=
tor Adame Molyns, keper of the kynges priuie ſeale, and Robert lorde
Roos, and diuerſe other: And for the Frenche kynge were appoynted,
Charles Duke of Orleaũce, Lewes de Burbon erle of Uandoſme, and
greate Maſter of the Frenche kynges houſholde, ſir Piers de Breſell
Stewarde of Poytou, and Barttam Beauriau, Lorde of Pricignye.
There were alſo ſente thither, Ambaſſadors from the Empire, from
Spayne, from Denmarke, and trom Hũgary, to be mediators betwene
theſe twoo princes. The aſſemble was greate, but the coſte was muche
greater, in ſomuche that euery patte, for the honor of their Prince, and
praiſe of their countrey, ſet furth themſelfes, aſwell in fare, as apparell,
to the vttermoſt poynt and higheſt prike. Many metynges were had, &
many thynges moued to come to a finall peace, and mutuall concorde.
But inconcluſion, for many doubtes and greate ambiguittes, whiche
roſe on bothe parties, a finall concord coulde not be agreed, but in hope
to come to a peace, a certain truce aſwell by ſea as by land, was conclu=
ded by the cõmiſſioners, for.xviii.monethes, whiche afterwarde, agayne
was prolonged, to the yere of oure Lorde.M.iiii.C.xlix.if in the meane
ſeaſon it had not been violated & broken, as here after ſhalbe declared.

In the treatyng of this truce, the Earle of Suffolke, extendyng his
cõmiſſion to the vttermoſte, withoute aſſent of his aſſociates, imagened
in his phantaſie, that the nexte waye to come to a perfite peace, was to
moue ſome mariage, betwene the Frenche kynges kynſewoman, and
Kyng Henry his ſouereigne: & becauſe the Frenche kyng had no dough=
ter

Plate 1 Edward Hall, *The union of the two noble and illustre famelies of Lancastre & Yorke*
(London: Richard Grafton, 1548)

at Bordeaux in 1453. Why are none of the French wars included in
1 Contention/2 Henry VI? The most plausible answer is that they have
already been dealt with in the first play of the series. The lack of any
reference to Talbot in *1 Contention/2 Henry VI*, used as an argument that
it was written before *1 Henry VI*, is in fact one of the most telling pieces of
evidence for the opposite case. No English popular dramatist finding in
the chronicle the story of Talbot's valiant death, outnumbered and surrounded, reunited with his son who insists on dying with him, could possibly have wanted to leave it out. But it only makes sense if Shakespeare,
planning ahead for a series of plays on the reign of Henry VI, took the
decision to concentrate the French wars in the first of that series, and
therefore moved back the death of Talbot, stage antagonist of Joan of
Arc, from its historical date of 1453 to an implied date of before 1430
when Joan was captured at Compiègne. Geoffrey Bullough remarked
on the liberties taken with chronology in *1 Henry VI*; he called it 'not
so much a Chronicle play as a fantasia on historical themes' (Bullough,
III, 25). That very gathering together of materials from disparate parts
of the history, concentrating events which took place twenty years apart
into a single narrative sequence, is one of the clearest signs of a master
design for serialising the chronicle.

One of the difficulties in convincing those who resist such a concept
of a master design for the history play series is that it is so without
precedent, so unparalleled in the theatre of the time. It is interesting to
look, therefore, at the record of one comparable series from late in the
1590s, concerned with then recent French history. All we know about
these plays comes from the entries in Henslowe's *Diary*. On 29 September
1598, Henslowe bought from Dekker and Drayton a play he identified as
'firste syvell wares in france', implying that he knew more episodes were
coming: as we have seen, Henslowe consistently distinguished between
first and second parts of plays, where there was more than one part. Sure
enough, with the first part in production in mid-October, he took delivery of a second part from Drayton and Dekker on 3 November, and paid
an advance for a third part on 18 November which was completed on 30
December. There was a still further advance to Dekker on 20 January
1599 for an additional play, the 'firste Intreducyon of the syvell wares
of france' (Henslowe, 98–103). The Henslowe references to the lost *Civil
Wars of France* represent intriguing evidence that a three-part historical series was planned by dramatists contemporary with Shakespeare, though
no doubt with the model of his history series before them. The *Diary*
entries show also that playwrights did sometimes go back and produce a

play on an earlier section of historical narrative, as Shakespeare is alleged to have done with *1 Henry VI*.[22]

However, the cases are significantly different. It seems possible that Dekker and Drayton's sequence on the *Civil Wars in France* may have been a dramatisation of Antony Colynet's *True History of the Civil Wars of France* published in 1591.[23] That polemically Protestant work is organised as a set of annals for the main period covered, 1585 to a right-up-to-date October 1591. Colynet organised his history in books, with a book devoted to each year, apart from one book at the beginning supplying an account of the origins of the war before 1585. It is easy to see how Dekker and Drayton might have started their series where the history's main narrative starts, and divided up the period into three planned parts. When the completed series was popular, as it presumably must have been, they then might well have gone back to Colynet's introductory Book I for a prequel. It is exactly because Hall's *Union* is *not* organised like that, because there are *no* divisions in his chronicle which would have thus warranted starting in the middle and going back later, that the theory of a non-chronological order of composition for the *Henry VI* plays remains so unlikely when we focus on the playwright at work on dramatising his source.

The organisation of the source materials for the set of plays on the reigns of Henry VI and Richard III suggests that it was a series, planned as a series, planned indeed for serial production. This is clearest in what one could call the seeding of characters early on in the sequence who are going to be essential later in the narrative. The Temple Garden scene (*1 Henry VI* 2.4) is a case in point, one of the parts of the play which nobody seems to doubt is by Shakespeare. In this scene an audience is not only prepared for the Wars of the Roses, which are not going to break out as such until towards the end of *2 Henry VI*, but introduced to what is going to be the main cast of characters in that war. The Folio stage direction reads '*Enter Richard Plantagenet, Warwick, Somerset, Poole* [= Suffolk], *and others*' (F, *The first part of Henry the Sixt*, TLN 926–7). The four characters identified in the direction are the essential figures for the civil strife to come: Richard Plantagenet, presently to be reinstated as Duke of York, whose claim to the throne will be the main source of the war; Somerset his principal Lancastrian enemy; Suffolk who is to be a dominant figure in the factions of the 1440s; and of course Warwick the Kingmaker. Shakespeare in this scene imagines his characters as much of an age, quarrelsome young men at the Inns of Court in the Temple: we never in fact learn what they were originally quarrelling about. However, if we assign this scene a notional date of 1425 (the historical date of the

death of Mortimer, which takes place in the next scene), the Earl of
Suffolk would have been twenty-nine and already a successful soldier
in France, the Duke of Somerset twenty-two, Plantagenet fourteen and
Warwick minus three: he was not born until 1428. Such discrepancies
in the ages, the fact that Plantagenet's ambitious designs on the throne,
prepared for in this scene, did not emerge until a generation later, are
of no consequence to Shakespeare. The brilliantly invented scene, with
the formal plucking of the roses in the garden, besides supplying the
audience with a simple way of identifying the opposing sides from then
on, gives them a formal introduction to the figures who are going to
dominate the action not just of the current play but of its two sequels.

We can see more precisely in the following scene how Shakespeare took
a hint from his source to build the character of Richard as key protagonist
for a whole stretch of the series. Still smarting from Somerset's Temple
Garden insults to his nobility – he has been called 'yeoman' on the
grounds that his father lost his rank when executed for treason – he goes
to see his dying uncle Mortimer in the Tower and is told about the Yorkist
claim to the throne. The source for this is the following passage in Hall:

Duryng whiche season, Edmonde Mortimer, the last Erle of Marche of that
name (whiche longe tyme had been restrained from his liberty, and finally waxed
lame) disceased without issue, whose inheritaunce discended to lorde Richarde
Plantagenet, sonne and heire to Richard erle of Cambridge, beheded, as you
have heard before, at the toune of Southhampton. Whiche Richard within lesse
then .xxx. yeres, as heire to this erle Edmond, in open parliament claimed the
croune and scepter of this realme, as herafter shall more manifestly appere.
(Bullough, III, 47)

No scene of a meeting with Mortimer, no hint of the feud of York and
Lancaster beginning at this point, only a chronicler's pointing before and
after. But Shakespeare wants York established from the start of his saga
as the ambitious nobleman with the grievance of his claim to the throne,
and he develops that figure powerfully through *2 Henry VI* with a series
of long soliloquies in which he emerges as the strong man of the power
game. It is the sense of the weight of this figure, as it has been built up
over two plays, which gives the scene of his torture and death in the first
act of *3 Henry VI* its climactic significance.

Apart from York, the key continuing characters of the *Henry VI –
Richard III* plays are King Henry, Queen Margaret and Richard of
Gloucester. In each case he brought them in early and kept them coming
back: Margaret quite unhistorically and improbably, but absolutely true

to character, as a vengeful prophetess lurking round the court in *Richard III*, Henry in the same play as a corpse and then a ghost. Richard, though, is the most remarkable and the most significant case. We first see Richard humping his back into battle at the end of *2 Henry VI*; he there dispatches Somerset, one of the key characters introduced in the Temple Garden scene. In point of fact, Richard would have been a child of three at this stage, younger than Rutland whose pathetic death as a young boy provides one of the gruesome incidents of the Battle of Wakefield in *3 Henry VI*. In Hall we never hear of Gloucester as any sort of active participant in events until 1471, close to the end of the action dramatised by Shakespeare in *3 Henry VI*. What Shakespeare did was to read Richard back into the chronicle, and to show the psychologically plausible emergence of the later hunchback tyrant handed down in the chronicles from Sir Thomas More's history of Richard. If we compare the technique of seeding York in *1 Henry VI* for his crucial role in *2* and *3 Henry VI*, then the early introduction of Gloucester is a strong piece of evidence of Shakespeare's plan for a Richard III play to follow the *Henry VI* series.

Shakespeare read on in the chronicle beyond the point he was currently dramatising; he worked in and worked up the characters he would need for later episodes. But he also developed a structure in which no one play was complete in itself, each part required a narrative sequel. It is the Scheherezade technique to keep the audience narrative-hungry. The series has a spectacular beginning with the funeral of Henry V whose catastrophic early death is the precipitating cause of so much that follows: the loss of France which he had so heroically won, the court factions fighting for power round the hapless figure of the infant Henry VI who will tear England apart. It has an equally definitive closure with the defeat of Richard III, and the reconciliatory union of the houses of Lancaster and York represented by the accession of Henry Tudor. But, in between, no single play comes to a point of narrative rest, much less a formal conclusion. *1 Henry VI*, Act 5 scene 3 has an incident completely without warrant from the chronicle where the Earl of Suffolk captures Margaret of Anjou on the battlefield, is totally infatuated with her and, being married himself, decides to arrange a marriage with the young King. Back in England he sells the idea to Henry, overturning the much more suitable marriage alliance to the Earl of Armagnac's daughter that is already in place. The play ends with Suffolk back off to France:

> Thus Suffolk hath prevailed, and thus he goes
> As did the youthful Paris once to Greece,

> With hope to find the like event in love,
> But prosper better than the Trojan did.
> Margaret shall now be queen, and rule the king:
> But I will rule both her, the king, and realm.
>
> (5.5.103–8)

As Hattaway quite rightly puts it, 'the lines act as a kind of commercial for the second part of the play' (5.5.107–8n). Come back for the next instalment.

The principle of continuous action operates between all four plays. *2 Henry VI* takes up where *1 Henry VI* leaves off with the return of Suffolk from France and the marriage of Henry and Margaret. *2 Henry VI* concludes with the first battle of St Albans, the actual beginning of the Wars of the Roses. The Yorkists have triumphed and determine to press home their advantage:

> YORK ... the king is fled to London
>   To call a present court of parliament.
>   Let us pursue him ere the writs go forth.
>   What says Lord Warwick? Shall we after them?
> WARWICK After them! Nay, before them if we can.   (*2 Henry VI*, 5.3.24–8)

3 Henry VI begins with the York party actually entering the Parliament-house:

> WARWICK I wonder how the king escaped our hands.   (*3 Henry VI*, 1.1.1)

The narrative liaison between *3 Henry VI* and *Richard III* is if anything even more striking. The last of the Henry VI plays ends with the king dead and the apparently definitive triumph of the house of York. But it is only apparently definitive, as signalled by the aside of Richard of Gloucester in the concluding scene as he kisses the baby son of his brother King Edward IV:

> To say the truth, so Judas kissed his master
> And cried 'All hail!' when as he meant all harm.
>
> (*3 Henry* VI, 5.7.33–4)

Richard III is still to come. Shakespeare in fact elides some twelve years of history from the death of Henry VI in 1471 to the sickness and death of Edward IV in 1483, in order to achieve the narrative bridge of Henry's funeral cortege at the beginning of *Richard III* allowing the action to start up where *3 Henry VI* left off. *Richard III* has a much more unified structure as a freestanding play than any of the *Henry VI* plays, but an audience

who has not followed through the sequence will have great difficulty in figuring out the several Edwards and Henrys whose murders are so often made the bones of contention through the action.

The *Henry VI – Richard III* plays were thus planned as an interlocking series with a narrative rhythm building across the parts rather than in the individual plays. What is more, they would almost certainly have been performed as a series in the 1590s. We have of course no detailed production records for Shakespeare's own company, but there is significant evidence in Henslowe of the pattern of production for other plays with more than one part. There are periods of the *Diary* when Henslowe entered up day-by-day takings from his theatres so that we know exactly what was in the repertory, which plays were performed on which days. From those sections we can see the way two-part plays were produced. When a second-part sequel was introduced into the repertory, it was performed on its own maybe a couple of times. Thereafter, once its novelty value had worn off, it was produced the day following its Part 1 predecessor. So, for example, there was a new production of a *1 Hercules* on 7 May 1595, followed by a new play *2 Hercules* on 23 May. The plays were then performed together on successive days on 27 and 28 May, 12 and 13 June, 1 and 2 September, roughly once a month through the season (Henslowe, 28–31). This was the pattern of performance also with better-known plays: the two parts of *Tamburlaine*, hardy perennials, were still being performed in the 1594–5 season, in all seven performances of the two parts together (Henslowe, 26–33).[24] *The Spanish Tragedy*, one of the great sellers of the period, had a prequel written for it which Henslowe calls 'spanes comodye donne oracioe', 'comodey of doneoracio', or 'comodey of Jeronymo', and which appears on its own in the Rose repertory on 23 February 1592. After 13 March, however, it is played ahead of *The Spanish Tragedy* for the rest of the season (Henslowe, 16–18). It obviously did not catch on – and if it was the very feeble *1 Jeronimo* published in 1605 one can imagine why not[25] – and it disappears from the *Diary* after June 1592, while *The Spanish Tragedy*, variously revamped with 'additions', goes on pulling them in for years to come.

Strangely enough, this evidence of serial production of two-part plays in Henslowe appears to have been neglected when it comes to considering Shakespeare's multi-part history series.[26] Much of the scholarly debate about the *Henry VI – Richard III* sequence has turned on whether it was a planned tetralogy of plays devised as such by Shakespeare from the beginning. But even if the disintegrators are right and the series did originate as an improvised and collaborative two-part play with a prequel added on, then the texts that we find in the Folio (revised texts as the disintegrative thesis has it) are plays intended for serial performance. The second and third parts of *Henry VI* may have been split off as *1 Contention* and *Richard Duke of York*, but at some point they were (re)united with *1 Henry VI* and would then have been performed by the Chamberlain's Men, in all probability with *Richard III*, as a sequence over four playing days. Such a production at least would be consistent with the Henslowe companies' practice in the case of two-part plays. It would fit with the design of the plays shaping the chronicle into a serial with a continuing narrative line across the parts, requiring an audience to have the last episode fresh in their minds in order to understand the next. It would have been to such a serial production of the *Henry VI* – *Richard III* plays that the final Chorus of *Henry V* referred:

> Henry the Sixth, in infant bands crowned king
> Of France and England, did this king succeed,
> Whose state so many had the managing
> That they lost France and made his England bleed,
> Which oft our stage hath shown – and for their sake,
> In your fair minds let this acceptance take.
>
> (*Henry V*, Epilogue, 9–14)

Think how much you loved our great *Henry VI* – *Richard III* series: we hope you like this play as much.

RICHARD II – *HENRY V*: AN INCREMENTAL SERIES

'It is not easy to credit', said Clifford Leech, 'that Shakespeare or any-one else can have felt sufficiently sure of his hold on the public, at the beginning of the last decade of the sixteenth century, to plan three con-secutive plays covering a single dramatic action.' I have argued that this is just what he did – not just three plays but four. The oddity is that it was in the second half of the decade, towards the end of the 1590s, with the great success of the *Henry VI* – *Richard III* series behind him, that Shakespeare seems to have become uncertain of his hold on the public when it came to planning another such sequence. At least the features of the earlier set of plays which show that they were planned ahead as a single interlocking, mutually dependent series are much less clearly there in *Richard II* – *Henry V*. Continuing characters are not so obviously seeded early on in the narrative; each play has its own distinctive formal character marking it out from the others; and each has an independent structure with a conclusion that does not require a sequel. *Richard II*, *1 Henry IV*, *2 Henry IV*, *Henry V* are separate and distinct entities by comparison with the one sweep of action which is *Henry VI – Richard III*. I want to look at the various features of discontinuity in the second history sequence as a means of puzzling out why Shakespeare should not there have repeated his earlier formula for serialising the chronicles.

It looks as though Shakespeare, having brought the action of his first history series down to the conclusive conclusion of Bosworth Field, went back to the start of Hall's *Union* in search of a new subject, though he soon switched to Holinshed (which he had already consulted for the earlier plays) as his main source. It is Hall who begins his chronicle just where Shakespeare begins *Richard II*: in 1398 with the challenge to the Duke of Norfolk (Mowbray) by the Duke of Hereford (whom Shakespeare, unlike the chroniclers, calls Bullingbrook). This is the starting-point for the course of events leading on to the deposition and murder of Richard II by Henry IV, which Hall places as 'the beginnyng and rote of the great discord and devision' of the Wars of the Roses (Hall, fol. ii v), a division only to be healed at last, in the chronicle's master narrative, by the union of the houses of York and Lancaster. It was of course Tillyard's main thesis in *Shakespeare's History Plays* that both Shakespeare's tetralogies were an acting out of that master narrative, God's curse on England for Henry IV's usurpation visited on the country in the horrors of civil war, and at length providentially exorcised at Bosworth.

Shakespeare's play *Richard II*, though it does gesture forward towards later history, has an autonomy of action quite unlike any of the previous history plays. In *Richard II*, for the first time, Shakespeare developed a structure and style specifically for the one history play. The *Henry VI* plays chronicle the successive rise and fall of ambitious contenders for power, Somerset, Suffolk, York, Richard of Gloucester, with each of those curves arced from play to play. Even *Richard III*, which has more of a shape of its own than the *Henry VI* plays, represents in the dastardly career of Richard the culmination of an action begun in *3 Henry VI*. But *Richard II* is structured with a new classical elegance around the interdependent rise and fall of Richard and Bullingbrook, the dynamics of power so fitly represented in the image of the balances. Henry's accession, Richard's death, give the play an ending which is a shapely and conclusive close to its particular action. In style too *Richard II* is distinct from anything in the earlier histories. The *Henry VI – Richard III* series showed Shakespeare's precocious capacity for stylistic mimicry, for mastering and bettering the idiom of others. The ring of Marlowe is everywhere in the *Henry VI* plays, and enough echoes of Greene and Peele to arouse the suspicions of those who argue for collaborative authorship, not to mention the fury of the birds themselves whose feathers the upstart crow wore so effectively. In *Richard III* Marlowe gives way to Seneca as singing-master. It is in *Richard II* that, for the first time in the histories, the style is uniquely tuned to the subject: the grave ceremony without bombast, the controlled flights of lyricism, the disciplined high poetic mode. The writing in *Richard II* is its own thing, distinct from the style of the *Henry IV* plays or *Henry V*, as none of the earlier history plays is distinct from the others.

Shakespeare may have had a sequel to *Richard II* in mind but he did not definitely prepare for one. It is true that there is the Bishop of Carlisle's great augury of doom at the moment of the deposition/abdication when he prophesies that

> The blood of English shall manure the ground
> And future ages groan for this foul act.
>
> *(Richard II, 4.1.137–8)*

It is true, too, that King Henry ends the play full of remorse for the murder of his royal cousin and vowing to lead a crusade in atonement, a constantly frustrated vow which we shall see recur through the two parts of *Henry IV*. But these pointers forward do not need the completion of a sequel as Suffolk's embassy to France at the end of *1 Henry VI*, the battle of St Albans at the end of *2 Henry VI*, undoubtedly do. In *Richard II* also Shakespeare hardly takes care, as in the earlier sequence, to prepare his characters for later plays to come. Of the two figures who are to act as principal antagonists of *1 Henry IV*, Hotspur appears briefly in four scenes, Prince Hal is only once mentioned. Hotspur is first seen, as Harry Percy, in Act 2 scene 3 being introduced to Bullingbrook as a supporter of his cause, has a few lines as newsbearer in 3.3, joins in a melée of accusation and counter-accusation in the new Bullingbrook court of 4.1, and (significantly) recounts the doings of the Prince of Wales in 5.3. It is no doubt important that when Prince Henry is mentioned in Act 5 – 'Can no man tell of my unthrifty son?' asks the King (5.3.1) – it is Harry Percy who replies with a story of Hal preferring the stews to the tournament. With such allusions it looks very much as though Shakespeare was keeping his options open on a sequel with the two Henrys, Hotspur and Hal, as antagonists, without definitely committing himself to writing one. The legend of the wild Prince Hal was already well known, both from the chronicles and from the anonymous play *The Famous Victories of Henry the Fifth*. Maybe Shakespeare would write a play on this subject, maybe he would not.

It is this tentative progression, taking it one play at a time rather than planning a series as such, that continues through the second history play sequence. *1 Henry IV* takes up the action a year on from the events of *Richard II*: King Henry is still planning his crusade, though the year's gap has established the pattern of interruption by domestic troubles that will continue for the rest of his reign. The action from *Richard II* to *1 Henry IV* is nearly continuous, but the mode is very different. In *1 Henry IV* for the first time Shakespeare wrote in the form which was most popular with his contemporaries, that of the hybrid history. Spliced to the top line of the historical narrative, dramatised in blank verse from the chronicles, is a fictional prose comedy of low-life scenes contemporary with the audience. This is strikingly unlike the univocal historicity of the *Henry VI – Richard III* series or indeed of *Richard II*, a play with not a line of prose and no comedy. To move into *1 Henry IV*, therefore, with its rich underlife of Hal, Falstaff and Eastcheap, is to experience a complete theatrical change of scene.

There has been much debate as to whether Shakespeare planned two *Henry IV* plays or just one, with the second as an unpremeditated sequel. The argument has turned on such peculiarities as Hal's 'relapse': the fact that *1 Henry IV* ends with him redeemed to chivalry in his conquest of Hotspur, friends with his father, true heir to the throne, yet *2 Henry IV* starts with him as much at odds with his father as ever, regarded once again as hopeless ne'er-do-well. The second play reproduces the first very precisely (as might be expected of a mixture-as-before sequel): a long tavern-scene at 2.4 of each play in which there is a stratagem for the Prince to catch out the uncatchoutable Falstaff; the repeated alternation between tavern-scenes, court-scenes and scenes in the rebel camp; Falstaff in praise of sack instead of Falstaff in dispraise of honour. Though *2 Henry IV* has struck some critics as having the thinness of material associated with a cash-in sequel, it should be said that, as far as the chronicle is concerned, Shakespeare has saved up for a second part the whole of Henry IV's reign after the battle of Shrewsbury in 1403, ten more years and another crop of rebellions. Whatever the degree of planned relationship between the two parts, they each have a separate dramatic structure (even if it is the same structure repeated), and they each have a distinct stylistic signature, with the energy and verve of the first play giving way to a mortality-laden lassitude in the second.

The Epilogue to *2 Henry IV* provides the most striking evidence for Shakespeare's uncertain progress with his second history series. The Epilogue concludes with the possibility of a sequel:

if you be not too much cloyed with fat meat, our humble author will continue the story with Sir John in it, and make you merry with fair Katherine of France, where, for anything I know, Falstaff shall die of a sweat, unless already a be killed with your hard opinions. (*2 Henry IV*, Epilogue, 20–5)

Now it will not do to take this quite literally. Epilogues, like prologues, are highly conventionalised contraptions, and this may well have been a trailer for a Henry V play that Shakespeare already had in mind, if not in hand. Its peculiar positioning in the Folio text, on a separate page from the play itself that ends with a seemingly conclusive '*Finis*', makes it seem a detachable addition.[27] Still it is odd that, with the heroics of Agincourt in prospect, it is only the rather minor comedy of Princess Katherine that is offered as a highlight, and there seems to be a coy flirting with whether to bring back Falstaff or not. In the event, of course, Falstaff dies of his sweat in England rather than France between the action of *2 Henry IV* and *Henry V*. However, according to some scholars' reckoning, Shakespeare gave Falstaff an additional lease of life between the two plays in *The Merry Wives of Windsor*.[28] If this chronology is correct, it suggests that Shakespeare decided that the public was not yet too cloyed with fat meat to risk one more appearance of his popular clown, translated with several of his comic cronies out of history play into comedy, but that after that he decided, like Trollope with Mrs Proudie, that the time had come to kill him off.

With each of the plays in the *Richard II – Henry V* series Shakespeare seems to have been feeling his way as to whether to continue with another, not boldly planning ahead as with *Henry VI – Richard III*. Would the plays have been serially produced once they were composed, as I have argued the earlier history play sequence would have been? Possibly. The performance logic of playing sequels one after another, evident in Henslowe's *Diary*, might well have led the Chamberlain's Men to play *Richard II*, the two parts of *Henry IV* and *Henry V* in sequence. But the plays have none of the compelling coherence that invites, even demands, such serial production with *Henry VI – Richard III*. The continuity of action has to override substantial formal differences. The use of Rumour in the Induction to *2 Henry IV* is an interesting example for the analysis of this gapped seriality. Rumour is a theatrically inventive device to recapitulate, to remind the audience of where they are in the story, with the

Battle of Shrewsbury over, Hotspur dead, and the King's forces victorious. Though this is quite consistent with serial playing, it is noticeable that in the *Henry VI* plays Shakespeare did not feel the need for any such recapitulation, as though confident that the audience would remember their place in the narrative they had seen the afternoon before. Rumour, too, sets the distinctive tone for *2 Henry IV*, the leitmotif of decay and disease, in his evocation of the locale:

> this worm-eaten hold of raggèd stone
> Where Hotspur's father, old Northumberland,
> Lies crafty-sick.
> (*2 Henry IV*, Induction, 35–7)

The Induction thus provides a formal marker initiating the second part as another sort of play.

If this is true of the choric Rumour who introduces *2 Henry IV*, how much more significantly different is the apparatus of choruses in *Henry V*. In this last of the series of history plays, the Chorus acts as a mediator between audience and stage quite unlike anything else in the earlier histories. The willing suspension of disbelief, which enabled audiences to live through the events of the reigns of Henry VI, Richard III, Richard II, Henry IV dramatised live on stage, is replaced by a knowing commentator, orchestrating the action with a self-conscious mood-music, distancing spectators from the epic tableaux. Although there are references back to events from the earlier plays, most notably the King's contrite acknowledgement of his father's usurpation in his prayer on the eve of Agincourt, they are generalised rather than specific. An audience scarcely needs to have seen the run of action from *Richard II* through the two *Henry IV* plays to understand what goes on in *Henry V*. None of this necessarily means that the sequence would *not* have been played serially on the Elizabethan stage. It does strongly suggest, though, that *Henry V*, like its immediate predecessor plays, was created not as the concluding episode in an episodically conceived narrative but as a drama designed formally to stand alone.

Elaborate ideological explanations have been offered for the decline of the history play after 1600: the changed political atmosphere with the end of Elizabeth's reign, the beginning of James', with a concomitant shift in the politics of genre.[29] But at the simplest level it looks as though it was a theatrical fashion that had had its day. It is possible that Shakespeare through the later 1590s was watching cautiously for the end of the vogue that he had done so much to initiate with the *Henry VI* plays. That might help to explain why his second series of histories advanced more tentatively one play at a time, rather than being the single enterprise the earlier sequence was. Shakespeare's own position had also changed by the second half of the 1590s. As a regular member of the Chamberlain's Men from 1594, and a Globe Theatre shareholder in 1599, he had a security that would have allowed him to invest more time and effort in an individual play. For whatever company the *Henry VI* plays or *Richard III* were originally written, the attraction would have been a series of shows for quick delivery to feed the audience appetite for sequels, with the prospect of serial performance if they were successful. If this project of serialising the chronicles afforded a spectacular chance for a young and ambitious actor/playwright to make a name for himself, that name once made (as it already was by 1592), the project changed somewhat to a play-by-play sequence.

One last tail-piece to the story of the histories. The Essex conspirators in February 1601 famously commissioned a performance of *Richard II* on the eve of their rebellion. It is the most important example we have of the potential for contemporary political intepretation of a history play. But it is noticeable that Shakespeare's company did not object to producing the play because it might be thought treasonable; they objected because they did not think it would draw an audience. They 'were determyned to have played some other play, holdyng that play of Kyng Richard to be so old & so long out of use as that they should have small or no Company at yt', and it took a special subvention of 40 shillings to convince them to put it on.[30] Now this may well have been falsely naive evidence designed for political self-exculpation. But if taken literally, it could be an indication that already by 1601 the English history play was theatrically dead as a doornail. The conditions that had allowed Shakespeare to serialise the chronicles for the stage in two remarkable sequences of plays were over. It was to be 363 years before the serial production of those plays was again possible. But that is another story – for the next chapter.

CHAPTER TWO

Staging the national epic

Shakespeare's history plays did not disappear from the stage between the beginning of the seventeenth century and the middle of the nineteenth century, but they disappeared as series. Revivals of the individual plays often involved cannibalisation, as in Colley Cibber's (in)famous version of *Richard III* which held the stage from 1700 to the 1840s, an adaptation including borrowings not only from *3 Henry VI* but from *Richard II*, *Henry IV* and *Henry V* for good measure.[1] Particular political circumstances could inspire revival of generally neglected texts, like John Crowne's anti-Papist version of *Henry the Sixth* in 1681 or Nahum Tate's attempted disguise of *Richard II* as *The Sicilian Usurper* in the same year, down to a *2 Henry IV* staged in 1821 for its coronation scene to salute the accession of George IV.[2] On the whole the plays were produced in heavily cut and adapted forms to suit the need of the star actors of the day: the *Henry VI* plays virtually not at all, *Richard III* frequently but in Cibber's version, *Richard II* occasionally (edited to improve the King's part), *1 Henry IV* more than *2 Henry IV* because of its theatrically fatter Falstaff, *Henry V* surprisingly rarely down to the nineteenth century, and never with the Chorus. To make possible the conception and then the realisation of the histories played as series in the modern period it took several different historical changes: the new sense of the significance of a nation's history developed with romanticism; the institutionalisation of Shakespeare as cultural monument, and the concomitant drive to recover the complete canon in its full integrity; the growth of a non-commercial subsidised theatre with its altered forms of acting; the emergence of concepts of character from nineteenth-century fiction into twentieth-century theatre, film and television.

The romantic conception of the nation crucially involved the remembering, if necessary the invention, of the national past. It was by way of their shared memory of a shared history that a people could constitute themselves as a nation. A backward perspective upon the remotest time could supply a nation with a conceptual myth of origin; the inspiring figures and events of the past collectively formed the idea of national identity. This cultural nationalism was a product of a European romantic movement that in England could bring traditions of national sovereignty to a new consciousness; for Germany and other emergent European nations it represented a state of national integrity to which they aspired.[3] Within that context, paradoxically, it was not only Britain that was to treat Shakespeare as national icon. For the German romantics also, for Schiller, Goethe, Schlegel, as much as Coleridge, the Shakespearean drama could be claimed as cultural inheritance figuring national destiny. And it was to be in Germany, in the decade of national unification, that Shakespeare's history plays were first to be given serial production in the modern period.

In Germany as in England, centenaries were repeatedly the occasion for new levels of Bardolatry and the ever greater canonisation of Shakespeare as national poet. So 1864 was the year not only of Franz Dingelstedt's Weimar production of the history play cycle but of the establishment, also in Weimar, of the Shakespeare Gesellschaft and its *Shakespeare Jahrbuch*. In England the Tercentenary set going a movement that was to lead eventually to the opening of the Shakespeare Memorial Theatre in Stratford. It was in 1964 that the recently established Royal Shakespeare Company celebrated the Quatercentenary with its production of the history plays as *The Wars of the Roses*. In the century between 1864 and 1964, various forms of non-commercial theatres had developed around the canonical figure of Shakespeare, not only in Stratford with the Memorial Theatre but with North American festivals from Oregon to Stratford, Ontario. The plays through the late nineteenth and early twentieth century were clawed back from the actor-managers who had used them in mangled form as star acting vehicles. A new emphasis on the integrity of the plays, the restoration of complete texts, and fidelity to the spirit of their original creation, went with an impulse towards the theatrical recovery of the whole canon. Within such a context the massive monumentality of the cycle of history plays made their production seem specially attractive: hence such an event as the production of the histories by F. R. Benson in Stratford in 1906, or by the Pasadena Community Playhouse in 1935.

The subsidised theatres brought with them changed dramatic practices. Ensemble rather than star-centred playing became possible, and history plays which had been long rejected because of their large casts and lack of single dominant roles could be staged. What is more, serial productions of the histories made parts which seemed limited in just one of the plays into rich and rewarding acting opportunities: King Henry or Queen Margaret through the *Henry VI* plays, Bullingbrook/Henry IV from *Richard II* into the two parts of *Henry IV*. The changed perception of parts such as these was facilitated both by the increasingly psychological reading of character in the modern period, and by habits of reading/viewing from the nineteenth-century *Bildungsroman* to television serials and soap-operas. Modern audiences are conditioned to see human beings as the individual products of formative changes through time, and used to apprehending such changes by fictive instalment plan. However differently conceived character might have been in Shakespeare's rhetoric-based drama, in the serial histories modern directors and actors could perceive recognisably developing figures. A 'Medieval Soap Opera' was how Michael Bogdanov thought of his 1980s *Wars of the Roses*.[4] The purpose of this chapter is to chart the story of the serial productions of the histories from their first romantic conception in the nineteenth century through to the age of television and video.

ROMANTICISM AND THE NATIONAL EPIC

The idea of Shakespeare's histories as stageable series originated in the romantic period with Schiller. Already at work on the *Wallenstein* trilogy, he wrote to Goethe in November 1797 of the impact made on him by the *Henry VI* plays and *Richard III*:

I have latterly been reading those of Shakespeare's plays which treat of the Wars of the Roses, and upon finishing *Richard III* find myself filled with amazement. This last play is one of the sublimest tragedies I know, and at the present moment I could not name any other of Shakespeare's that could claim comparison with it. The grand destinies commenced in the preceding plays are here completed in a truly grand manner, and are connected by means of the sublimest of ideas . . . It would truly be worth the trouble to adapt this whole series of eight plays for the German stage, with all the means now in our power. It might introduce a new epoch.[5]

Writing back the next day from Weimar, Goethe enthusiastically agreed. Nothing further seems to have come of the project, but August Wilhelm Schlegel in his *Lectures on Dramatic Art and Literature*, originally delivered in 1808, had a comparable vision of the history plays as an integrated whole:

> The dramas derived from the English history, ten in number, form one of the
> most valuable of Shakespeare's works, and partly the fruit of his maturest age.
> I say advisedly *one* of his works, for the poet evidently intended them to form
> one great whole. It is, as it were, an historical heroic poem in the dramatic form,
> of which the separate plays constitute the rhapsodies.[6]

Coleridge, who saw history plays as a transitional form between the epic
and the drama, dreamed of a massive enterprise in which Shakespeare's
histories would be made a part of an even greater unity, a sequence on the
reigns of all the English monarchs from the Conqueror. This superseries
would then be played each Christmas as a way of representing to the
English the epic of England's past.[7]

It was, appropriately enough, in Weimar in 1864 that these notions
of the Shakespearean histories as integrated series were first realised
theatrically. Franz Dingelstedt, the director of the Weimar Theatre, had
had considerable experience of producing Shakespeare as manager of the
Bavarian Royal Theatre in Munich before moving to Weimar in 1857,
and it was he who conceived the idea of staging an adapted 'cyclus' of the
two English historical sequences as Weimar's tribute to Shakespeare in
his Tercentenary year.[8] Dingelstedt knew of Schiller's letter to Goethe,
and may also have been following up on his own very successful all-day
production of the complete *Wallenstein* trilogy in celebration of Schiller's
birthday on 9 November 1863.[9] Having already brought *Richard II* and
the two parts of *Henry IV* into the theatre's repertoire in 1863, Dingelstedt
added *Henry V* for a four-play sequence in the first week of January
1864, and brought his programme to a grand climax in the week of the
Tercentenary itself, April 1864, with successive performances of the full
history cycle from *Richard II* to *Richard III*.

Dingelstedt's cycle was heavily adapted and revised, reduced from
eight to seven plays by the extensive re-writing of *Henry VI* and the virtual
elimination of Part I. His object in the revision was to bring out what
he saw as the architectonic design of the whole, a five-act, neo-classical
structure:

> *Richard II*, in which the House of Lancaster succeeds to the throne by way of
> usurpation, is the exposition (Act I). The complication (Steigerung) of the plot
> occurs in *Henry IV*, which, presenting the usurper trembling from his own son,
> forms the antithesis to the thesis of the previous act. In *Henry V*, the action reaches
> its climax, Lancaster is at the peak of power and fame (Act III). In *Henry VI*, the
> turning point (Umschlag) follows: Lancaster loses the crown in consequence of

weakness and betrayal. Tyranny, the sole remedy against the impending civil war, results in catastrophe (Act IV). In *Richard III*, finally, the dissolution and self-destruction of the House of York is followed by the union of the houses in Henry Tudor, and the action is resolved (Act V).[10]

Later conceptions of the histories were also anticipated in dividing the cycle into two sequences, the first culminating in the hero Henry V, the second in the anti-hero Richard III.[11] As Germany moved towards unification, Dingelstedt pointed up in his prologue to the whole cycle the contemporary lessons to be drawn from England's struggles through the Wars of the Roses to the desired end of the reunited houses of York and Lancaster in the monarchy of Henry VII.[12] Though the cycle was designed as a special Tercentenary celebration, subsidised by the Grand Duke of Saxe-Weimar-Eisenach 'who provided the funds for the new costumes, decorations, and the new and brilliant *mise en scene*,'[13] it was successful enough for Dingelstedt to revive it in 1875 and 1876 as manager of the Hofburgtheater in Vienna.

Shakespeare's three-hundredth birthday in England was celebrated by nothing more momentous than a production of the previously unrevived *2 Henry VI*.[14] But 1864 did provide the impetus for the establishment of the Shakespeare Memorial Theatre in Stratford, founded in 1875, opening in 1879. The conception, the impetus and much of the money for the Stratford theatre came from the local brewer Charles Flower, whose aims had to be achieved in opposition to the normal practices of Shakespearean production of the time. Where nineteenth-century actor-managers raided Shakespeare for individual plays, parts and scenes that would make for successful Victorian theatre, Flower wanted the Memorial Theatre over successive yearly festivals – initially only week-long sets of productions centring on Shakespeare's birthday – to stage the entire Shakespearean canon. This was a source of contention between him and F. R. Benson, the actor-manager whose company provided the mainstay of the Stratford festivals between 1886 and 1919, as Sally Beauman, the historian of the Stratford Memorial Theatre, makes clear:

It was Flower's idea, for instance, to present a complete cycle of history plays, a project never before attempted [*sic*], and one which Benson resisted for years. He was happy to include in his repertoire those history plays which provided him with a superb leading role – *Richard II* for example, which became one of his most famous parts, and *Henry V* and *Richard III*. He was far less enthusiastic about the two *Henry IV* plays, and the *Henry VI* trilogy of which Flower was a passionate advocate. When *Henry VI, Part I*, was first produced at Stratford, in 1889, in a version reworked by Charles Flower, Osmond Tearle's company, not Benson's, performed it. Ten years later, in 1899, when Charles Flower was dead, his widow Sarah was still trying to persuade Benson to undertake a history cycle, but without success. It was a 'daring experiment' of a kind that did not appeal to him.[15]

Nonetheless Benson did eventually attempt this 'daring experiment' and, with his festival offerings at Stratford in 1901, and more fully again in 1906, is generally credited with being the first producer in the modern period to stage a cycle of Shakespeare's histories in English. The six plays of the 1901 'Week of Kings' (*King John, Richard II, 2 Henry IV, Henry V, 2 Henry VI, Richard III*) made their mark on Yeats who recorded his impressions of the experience in his essay 'At Stratford-upon-Avon', and was to recruit Benson's company for his own Irish Literary Theatre performances in the autumn of the same year.[16] In the 1906 festival, with the addition of *1* and *3 Henry VI*, and the removal of *King John*, Benson came close to staging the complete sequence of the two four-play series, though still oddly without *1 Henry IV*. In casting and production, however, Benson's history cycles still had many of the hallmarks of the nineteenth-century tradition. As actor-manager he took all the leading roles himself: Richard in *Richard II*, Hal in *2 Henry IV*, the King in *Henry V*, Talbot in *1 Henry VI*, the Cardinal (no doubt for his death-scene) in *2 Henry VI*, Richard of Gloucester in *3 Henry VI* and again in *Richard III*. (The less than definitively dominant parts for which he had to settle in the *Henry VI* plays suggest why he resisted producing the plays for so long.) He was praised for the 'historical and archaeological side' of his production of *2 Henry VI* in the traditional terms of praise for Victorian pictorial theatre: 'With an Irving-like minuteness of study of detail Mr F. R. Benson has gone into this deeply, and he has wisely secured the best of aid in transporting the atmosphere and colour of a brilliant period of history on to the stage.'[17] The *Athenaeum* reviewer, though polite about the well-studied 'dresses, armour, and pageantry' of the production, could have done with rather less of them: 'The whole series suffered so much from cutting, contraction, and transposition, in order to give intervals lengthy enough to permit the changing of scenes and costumes, that many might have wished to have less scenery and more Shakespeare, in his native town at least.'[18]

Benson's productions of the histories and their reception were very much of their time, the reviewer's criticism quoted above being repre-sentative of the growing movement for playing Shakespeare whole with-out the scenic embellishments and the consequent textual distortions which were the staple of the actor-manager's era. But this was still an

avant-garde position as far as actual theatre practice went, and not even
in the special circumstances of the Stratford festival could the histories
be produced without deferring to the accustomed tastes of the audiences. There was much in the plays that remained unacceptable, and
that Benson did not tone down enough for some reviewers: 'Although the
character of that vile and wretched being, Dol Tearsheet, cannot very
well be omitted, it might be stripped of some of its offensive features.'[19]
Joan in *1 Henry VI* continued to be a problem. Dingelstedt had left her
out altogether from his Weimar cycle; however much Schiller might
have admired the *Henry VI* plays, the author of *Die Jungfrau von Orleans*
could hardly have sanctioned Shakespeare's Pucelle. From reviewers' accounts it sounds as though, against the grain of the text, Joan was thoroughly romanticised in Benson's version. 'Miss Tita Brand looked the
inspired maid (Joan La Pucelle), and played well up to it. The intensity
of her emotions, the dignity of her pretensions, and the sublime confidence of her wild convictions were well maintained.'[20] At the time of the
Entente Cordiale, with Joan having become Venerable in 1894 and soon
to be beatified in 1909, the more virulently Francophobe prejudices of
1 Henry VI no doubt needed to be softened. The political colouring of the
production emerges interestingly in Benson's 'Note on the Production
of Henry VI' in which he argues that

the wanton aggression against France, was inevitably followed by civil disruption
at home. That the War of the Roses, were practically a punishment, for a War
of greed and spoliation, which reached its climax in the murder of Joan of Arc.
That in the process, the King-man degenerated from the type of Henry IV
and Henry V to that represented by Edward IV and Richard III. Finally how
during the death and the ruin of so many nobles and gentry, the commons of
England were growing in power and importance, and laying the foundation
of the English Empire; and how clearly Shakespeare rejects that machiavellian
theory of politics which proved the ruin of Florence and Italian Liberties.[21]

In this Edwardian reinterpretation, England repented the crime of its
enmity against France, its execution of Joan. And where Dingelstedt had
read the plays in the light of then current German aspirations towards
unity, Benson's is a Whiggish view of history, with the manifest destiny of
the British Empire already emerging from a dark age of fifteenth-century
civil war that had at least the long-term benefit of decimating the feudal
aristocracy.

While there was admiration for the piety of completing 'Mr Charles
Flower's scheme of presenting all the actable plays of Shakespeare' with
the 1906 history sequence, the plays did not succeed financially, and it

was concluded without too much regret that such a work as *3 Henry VI*
'probably will never again be seen on the Stratford stage'.[22] The
Stratford-upon-Avon Herald was wrong in that assumption, but it took almost
sixty years for it to be proved wrong. It needed special circumstances, special audiences, a subsidised theatre, to make possible an unexpurgated,
unadapted production of the histories as a cycle. This combination came
together in the summer of 1935 in Pasadena, California.

PASADENA, BIRMINGHAM, STRATFORD

The Pasadena Community Playhouse had been established in 1917 as
an initiative of Gilmor Brown, an actor-manager who had toured the
country with small companies of his own before settling in Pasadena.[23]
Associated with the little theatre movement, the Playhouse included in
its repertory avant-garde works and experimental productions of classic
plays. With a quite small company of professional actors, the Playhouse
was able to rely on the support of a large body of enthusiastic amateurs,
on students from its own drama school, and on the financial patron-
age of Pasadena's wealthy community which funded the building of the
Playhouse's own theatre in 1925. For such a theatre, the mounting of
a large-scale series of connected productions was both possible and de-
sirable. And so for its first Midsummer Festival in 1935, the Playhouse
offered 'The Ten Chronicle Plays of W. Shakespeare. Presented as a
group for the first time in the history of the English Speaking Stage.'
With two plays, eight performances a week, mounted in chronological
order, the Festival ran through July to mid-August and was advertised
nationally as an educational/tourist package. An academic dimension to
this package was the series of lectures given weekly through the season by
the Shakespearean scholar Oscar J. Campbell based in the Huntington
Library. The formula worked and, by the end of the first month of the
Festival, some 55,000 people had attended the performances in the
800-seat theatre.[24]

The emphasis of the productions was on fidelity to Shakespeare.
Full texts of the plays were acted, and as Campbell put it, 'the original manner of presentation, uninterrupted by acts and scenes has been
followed... you are "getting Shakespeare pure"; liberated from Belasco
smother of decoration, restored to its original sweep and flow'.[25] This
neo-Elizabethan minimalism of setting was compensated for by costumes, in the case of *Richard II* borrowed from Paramount Pictures'
latest Cecil B. DeMille epic. A number of the actors also were on loan

from Hollywood down the road, including Gyles Isham playing Henry V;
Isham had been cast as Prince Hal in the 1932 Stratford production of
the two *Henry IV* plays, and was currently working at MGM. For the
most part, though, the leads were played not by name actors but by
young novices just graduating from drama school, and the availability of
large numbers of willing amateur extras meant that crowd scenes were
genuinely crowded. It is probable that the quality of the productions,
by international professional standards, were not all that high, with
Gilmor Brown himself playing what sounds like a fairly hammed-up
comic Falstaff. The Festival's significance rather is for the precedent
it set: given the right situation, the histories were stageable as a series
and, once staged, the sense of their significance changed. The theatrical
possibilities of the history play sequence, and the interaction of theatrical and academic interpretation were only to be fully realised after the
war.

It was the Birmingham Repertory Theatre productions of the three
parts of *Henry VI* in 1951–3 that first definitively proved that those plays
were playable, and made a special impact when played in sequence.
There seems to have been no original intention of producing them as a
series when Douglas Seale's production of *2 Henry VI*, 'a very seldom performed play,'[26] opened in April 1951. Sir Barry Jackson's Birmingham
Rep was by that stage well established as one of the most adventurous
of the British repertory theatres. Jackson, having pioneered modern-
dress Shakespeare in the 1920s and undertaken massively ambitious
projects such as the staging of Shaw's *Back to Methuselah* cycle, had revi-
talised Stratford in his period as director of the Memorial Theatre there
(1945–8). The principles of the repertory movement, the lack of a star
system, the use of young and energetic actors playing as an ensemble, the
risk-taking made possible by enlightened financial backing (in the case of
the Birmingham Rep, Jackson's own money), all of these with imaginative direction and set design contributed to a revelation of the powerful
theatricality of the *Henry VI* plays.

2 Henry VI was so successful in 1951 that it was followed by *3 Henry VI*
in 1952, and the trilogy completed with *1 Henry VI* in 1953 when all
three were played as a sequence both in Birmingham and in the Old Vic
in London. What astonished the reviewers was simply how effective the
plays were. The *Manchester Guardian* reaction to *3 Henry VI* was typical:

The chief among many virtues in the Birmingham Repertory Theatre's production of the third part of 'King Henry VI' is not the company's courage in

giving us the play at all, so much as the fact that it does not seem specially coura-
geous. It is made to appear, on the contrary, the most natural thing in the world.
We get the play on its merits, as if these were all-sufficient... Though entirely
straightforward, it does not drag for ten seconds nor bore for ten minutes in the
entire three hours.[27]

A director no longer looking for the kind of starring part which Benson
failed to find in the individual *Henry VI* plays could bring out the range
of major roles which built cumulatively over the three plays, Gloucester,
Suffolk, York, Queen Margaret and King Henry. The boy-like Jack May
as the saintly fool/king made a special impact, anticipating the outstanding performance of David Warner in Stratford ten years later which was
to establish Henry as one of Shakespeare's great acting parts.

A single permanent set by Finlay James helped to enforce the unity of
the trilogy once the three plays were in place. The period and the atmosphere were suggested by a facade of three Gothic arches, one large central one with two smaller flanking it, and turreted walls at diagonal angles
to the facade enclosing the forestage. The military alternated with the
ecclesiastical, the omnipresence of the latter suggested by using monks
as recurrent extras and stage-hands. The text of the plays was frequently
cut to simplify the narrative or to reduce diffuseness, but there seems
to have been little interpretative re-shaping of the plays. Certainly their
violence and brutality were not disguised. Offstage screams underlined
the horror of the death of Joan in *1 Henry VI*, the burning of the witch
Margery Jourdain in *2 Henry VI*; the paper crown, used in the mock-
crowning of York in *3 Henry VI* 1.4, was taken from the dead body of a
jester, stabbed to death trying to save the young Rutland in the previous
scene.[28]

The production was apparently without overt ideological design, but
the impression made on reviewers was of a satiric exposé of the plays'
power politics. Kenneth Tynan, reviewing a compressed two-part revival
in London in 1957, commented:

Superficially, the three parts of *Henry VI* seem jingoistic and Churchillian: history
is made by martial patriots engaged in a series of martial brawls. It takes a
director as sharp as Douglas Seale to unearth the vein of savage irony that
runs through the plays... After the ranting has faded, the scene that stays most
tensely in the mind is one in which nobody's voice is raised above a regretful
plea: the despised king yearns for a shepherd's life...[29]

The uncompleted design of the trilogy of *Henry VI* plays was suggested
by what Tynan called 'a magnificent stroke of textual audacity' at the

final curtain:

Alone on stage after the pomp of Edward's coronation, Gloucester embarks
on the opening soliloquy of *Richard III*. Before long his voice is drowned by
an offstage clamour of loyalty to the new king: obliviously he goes on, and is
still, when the curtain falls, grimacing and gesturing, an inaudible power-driven
puppet, the authentic agent of death.[30]

This device was matched at the opening of *1 Henry VI* with the Epilogue
of *Henry V* before the funeral of the dead king. For audiences unfamiliar
with the *Henry VI* plays these quotations reminded them of their relationship to the much better-known *Henry V* and *Richard III*. But they acted
also as narrative ellipsis dots before and after the sequence represented,
to register its status as extracted section from the continuum of history.

The Birmingham Rep *Henry VI* series was not initially planned as a
series, and was without an explicit conceptual design. By contrast, the
Stratford production of the second tetralogy, produced as part of the 1951
Festival of Britain, set out to show the coherent integrity of the four plays
from *Richard II* to *Henry V* and their unified significance. The overarching
scheme of Anthony Quayle's direction (which he shared with John Kidd
and Michael Redgrave) was set out already in the programme notes for
the opening *Richard II*:

It is generally agreed that the four plays of this season's historical cycle form a
tetralogy and were planned by Shakespeare as one great play. They present not
only a living epic of England through the reigns of the three kings, but are also
a profound commentary on Kingship.

The true hero of the whole play is *Henry the Fifth*, who personified, to the
people of Shakespeare's England, the ideal King: brave, warlike, generous, just,
and – it must be added – loving humour.

To offset this hero, the tragic *Richard the Second*, who would seem to have all
the defects of Prince Hal's virtues, is not only historically, but dramatically, the
perfect counterpoise and prologue.[31]

That 'general agreement' on the integral unity of the tetralogy may have
been a slight exaggeration, but the influential work of two Shakespearean
scholars during the war had definitely shifted opinion in that direction.
There was not only Tillyard's *Shakespeare's History Plays* (1944) which had
popularised the idea of the two tetralogies as a single grand scheme
animated by the unifying conception of the so-called 'Tudor myth'. But,
simultaneously and independently, John Dover Wilson, in his book *The
Fortunes of Falstaff* (also 1944) and his Cambridge editions of *Richard II*
(1939) and *Henry IV* (1946), had promoted the reading of the second

tetralogy as a consistent sequence built around the concept of kingship and, in Hal/Henry V, the education of the perfect king. Wilson's influence on the Quayle Stratford productions is obvious, and he in fact contributed the historical background section to a book devoted to the productions.[32]

The reviewers were at first resistant to the reinterpretation of some of the major parts made necessary by the overriding design of the whole. So, for example, Michael Redgrave's very mannered Richard II disappointed those who brought expectations based on John Gielgud's or Alec Guinness's lyrical/poetic performances. The effete atmosphere of Richard's court was stressed with his attendants, in the shorthand of the prompt-book referred to as 'butterflies', arrayed in 'pastel pinks, light blues and golds'.[33] By contrast the opposition, the powerful barons led by Northumberland who would soon be supporting Bullingbrook's bid for the throne, were plain men with regional accents and costumes of russets, dull reds and greens. As Richard's frivolousness was played up to underline the political situation out of which the rest of the events were to flow, so in the *Henry IV* plays Anthony Quayle, himself acting Falstaff, reduced the attractiveness of the fat clown to promote sympathy for the Prince in his decision to reject him. Richard Burton was much admired as Hal – 'instead of a lighthearted rapscallion Mr Burton offers a young knight keeping a long vigil in the cathedral of his own mind'[34] – but again memories of the heroic Henry V of Olivier made it difficult for reviewers to accept Burton's (literally) smaller-scaled Henry.

It was Quayle's policy to bring in big names to head up his cast at Stratford. He made full use of the star status of Redgrave, who not only played Richard and a violently energetic Hotspur in *1 Henry IV*, but directed *2 Henry IV*, performed as the Chorus of *Henry V*, not to mention playing Prospero in *The Tempest*, the fifth play of that Stratford season. The young Burton, already a major draw, was lured back from New York by the prospect of the three-play part of Hal/Henry. Again though, as with the Birmingham Rep *Henry VI* series, what the Stratford histories allowed to emerge was the cumulative significance of parts previously thought to be secondary. Thus virtually every reviewer praised the performance of Harry Andrews as Bullingbrook/Henry IV and the way its strength altered the perspective on the plays. In *1 Henry IV*, *The Times* reviewer commented:

Mr Harry Andrews plays Henry IV with a concentrated vigour which brings tinglingly alive the man who is efficient enough to usurp a kingdom but lacks the imagination to rule it. While Mr Andrews is on stage there is no fear that the play will surrender its dynamic unity of royal history to the static unity of a pervading humorous personality.[35]

2 Henry IV gained even more from being played in sequence with continuity of narrative and personnel:

By itself it is little more than the comedy of Falstaff with a little tiresome historical stuff sticking in its edges. In the series, as we saw it tonight, it becomes a piece of significant history, with a fine climax in Henry IVth's death scene played with emotion and strength by Harry Andrews as the King and Richard Burton as the Prince.[36]

Tanya Moisewitch's permanent set all in wood, a central platform midstage with circular steps coming down from it on both sides, the throne with canopy above always on stage left, allowed for the establishment of a spatial structure for the sequence. The throne was always associated with the monarch, whoever that happened to be at the time,

Plate 2 Set for 1951 production of *Richard II*, Shakespeare Memorial Theatre, Stratford: designer Tanya Moisewitch

and the area around it was referred to in the prompt-books as Royalty Corner. In the encounters between the forces of the crown and the rebels in *2 Henry IV* Act 4, the staging was intended to encourage state partisanship: 'The Royal Commanders issue from Royalty Cor., and we are to suppose that their forces – the ones which stay the ground – are identified with the audience, who should feel themselves on the side of the King.'[37] The antithesis between Richard II's inadequacies and Henry V's qualities as king, upon which the whole sequence was built, was underscored visually. At the beginning of *Richard II* the King had a processional entrance ending with a ceremonial acceptance of the orb and sceptre. In *2 Henry IV* 5.2, the about-to-be Henry V 'makes an entrance identical with Richard's first entrance but his manner of acknowledging the courtiers is in marked contrast'.[38]

The production of the series as a whole thus worked to an interpretative design, with directorial decisions taken consistently to support this design. Hence Redgrave's 'affected mince' as Richard;[39] hence the playing of Falstaff as 'superbly funny but openly contemptible';[40] hence the deepening of the relationship between Hal and his father: 'This father is noble, generous, slow and above all direct. This son is deep, reserved, assured but essentially complex.'[41] These all represented choices on the basis of suggestions available within the texts. Though the plays were edited, they were not adapted to suit the production's conceptual strategy. Only at the very end of *Henry V* was text actually re-written to make manifest the significance of the series as dramatised. In place of the ironic coda of the Chorus's final reminder of the disastrous reign of Henry VI that was to follow historically, Patric Dickinson grafted in new lines:

> . . . by which the world's best garden he achieved
> And nourished there the red rose of his blood.
> Awakened from the self-despising dream
> Of tavern-victories hallowed by Sir John,
> He moves in his true measure: so our theme
> From Richard's winter builds this summer throne;
> Which oft our stage hath told, and for our sake
> In your fair minds let this acceptance take.[42]

This was to give the series as a whole a rising curve ending with the unequivocal triumph of the perfect King Henry, and to edit out an awareness of the approaching downturn which Shakespeare seems so deliberately to have included.

THE WARS OF THE ROSES: THE CONCEPT OF THE SERIES

The principle of adaptation in the interests of ideological objectives was taken much further in the famous John Barton – Peter Hall collaboration on *The Wars of the Roses*. The decision to compress the three *Henry VI* plays into two was in the first place apparently a purely practical one, as Barton explains: 'however much we want to explore and popularise the lesser-known plays of Shakespeare and his contemporaries, we cannot afford to present more than two of them in a single season. For this reason alone, to have performed the three *Henry VI* plays as they stand was out of the question.'[43] Hall and Barton had both seen the Birmingham Rep production of the *Henry VI* plays and thought them 'oddly incomplete. In order to interest audiences in the plays as a single entity, we not only decided to use the overall title of *The Wars of the Roses*, but on occasion to play the whole cycle on a single day' (*Wars*, xvi). This involved not only massive cutting, about half the original 12,350 lines removed, the creation of two new plays *Henry VI* and *Edward IV* out of the three parts of *Henry VI*, but most daringly and controversially the writing in by Barton of substantial amounts of new blank verse. The justification for this throroughgoing adaptation was the assumption that the Shakespearean texts 'were almost certainly not originally conceived as a cycle. It is more likely that the success of the first part compelled sequels, and Shakespeare's view of history clarified as he wrote' (*Wars*, xii). Barton's objective as he re-cast and re-wrote the play seems to have been to introduce consistently through the sequence as a whole that 'clarified' view of history attributed to Shakespeare.

Fundamental to this view was Tillyard's scheme of the 'Tudor myth'. England was cursed for the primal crime of the deposition and murder of Richard II, and for that crime the house of Lancaster was visited with the whole vicious circle of civil war, only finally exorcised with the union of York and Lancaster in the accession of Richmond as Henry VII. *The Wars of the Roses* represented, in many ways, the series of plays Shakespeare would have written if he had had the benefit of reading Tillyard's *Shakespeare's History Plays*. As Tillyard saw the history plays, they were the grandly consistent embodiment of the orthodox political and social morality of the Elizabethan period, preaching order and hierarchy, condemning factious power-seeking and the anarchy of civil war to which it led, commending the divinely sanctioned centralised monarchy of the Tudors. Barton and Hall worked to homogenise, to accentuate and underline the orthodoxy postulated by Tillyard.

The Wars of the Roses had thus an ideologically conservative infrastruc-
ture derived from the Tillyard school of criticism, hardly surprising seeing that Barton and Hall had read English in Cambridge in the 1950s
when Tillyard was Master of Jesus College. Much more surprising is
that this influence should have been combined with the influence of
Jan Kott. Hall recalled the excitement of reading Kott's *Shakespeare Our
Contemporary* in 1962 on the train going to Stratford to begin work on *The
Wars of the Roses* (*Wars*, xi), and a quotation from Kott was included in the
production's programme notes:

There are two fundamental types of historical tragedy. The first is based on
the conviction that history has a meaning, fulfils its objective tasks, and leads
in a definite direction. Tragedy here consists in the cost of history, the price
of progress that humanity must pay. The tragic figure then is the man out of
step. He who hinders or hurries the relentless steamroller of history must also
be crushed by it, simply because he comes too soon or too late... There is
another kind of historical tragedy, originating in the conviction that history has
no meaning but stands still, or constantly repeats its cruel cycle; that it is an
elemental force, like hail, storm, hurricane, birth, and death.[44]

The first conception of historical tragedy is like Tillyard's in so far as
it is posited on a teleologically purposeful vision of history. The second
is closer to Kott's own, the absurdist Kott who re-read Shakespeare
as the contemporary of Beckett. Barton and Hall's *Wars of the Roses* in
conception and production was an amalgam of the two.[45]

If the overall ideological perspective of the series was Tillyardian,
many of the production values were radically modernist. The verse
throughout was drastically cut to reduce rhetorical afflatus, and delivered
with a Brechtian alienated hard edge. The *realpolitik* of the power-game
in all its stark aggressiveness was reflected in the austere brutalism of
John Bury's set design, with its revolving constructivist shapes of metallic
panelling, matching the heavy armour and huge clanging broadswords
wielded by the contesting parties. As political faction-fighting degenerated into military conflict, the production played upon images resonant
with significance for a post-war generation culminating in the jack-
booted bodyguard of Richard III. Individual scenes such as the torture
of York were given a ferocity of treatment comparable to the theatre
of cruelty. In its awareness of the relentless dynamics of power, in its
detached and cold playing style, in its harsh and unyielding visual impact, *The Wars of the Roses* belonged to that generation of RSC productions – including Peter Brook's 1962 *King Lear* – which owed so much to
Jan Kott.

Barton and Hall's work was most of its time trying to articulate a vision that would reconcile the apparently conflicting ideologies of a Tillyard and a Kott. In this the idea of the Council, and its theatrical manifestation the council-table, were central. *The Wars of the Roses*, like the 1951 Stratford series, used the throne as a key property of the permanent set, but to it was added a large shield-shaped wooden table around which sat the Council of State. The table (in the television version embossed with the successive monograms of the monarchs, HVI, EIV, even briefly EV) marked the changing fortunes of the wars, as did the altering personnel of the Council as one faction after another took control. Humphrey of Gloucester was associated in the Barton–Hall production with the institution of just and responsible government by the council. A key moment then came when the council had been packed with Gloucester's enemies, and the King was too weak to defend him. It is this failure that precipitated the slide downward into the civil wars and tyranny that were to follow.

Peter Hall wrote in the Introduction to the published text of *The Wars of the Roses* that 'The tension between man the animal in action, murdering to protect or lying to save, and moral man trying to rule by a developed human ethic is what always makes history tragic' (*Wars*, xii). The later plays in the sequence, *Edward IV* and *Richard III*, again and again brought out the animal primitivism of the action. Barton gave Margaret lines mourning the death of her lover Suffolk at the hands of a lynch-mob:

> He had no sooner quit the palace
> But he was seized by their stinking hands,
> His beauty fang'd, his body torn asunder,
> As if a pack of wolves had savag'd him.

And Henry acknowledged that his abdication of responsibility brought this situation about:

> My wolves, my wolves! for I did make them so.
> (*Wars*, 78)

Later the three sons of York, Edward, George and Richard were played like half-grown hounds as they tore together at the dead body of their enemy Clifford. The tragic inevitability of this descent into animal violence and its concomitant political disorder were part of the post-war Kottian vision of the production. But in Hall's statement quoted above, the superiority of 'moral man trying to rule by a developed human ethic' is assumed, and in the overall conception of the sequence it is assumed also that moral man must ultimately triumph. And so the Elizabethan political orthodoxy, read into the history plays by Tillyard and others, was adapted by Barton and Hall into a 1960s liberal humanism. The hard truths of politics were not shirked; the dynamics of power and violence within society were exposed. Yet these hard truths were told as monitory illustrations of what remained as an optimistic belief in a better way, an underlying confidence in the movement of history towards a model of ordered and enlightened government.

The Wars of the Roses was an immense success in 1963 and, revived in 1964 together with productions of *Richard II*, both parts of *Henry IV*, and *Henry V*, the complete sequence became the RSC's Quatercentenary production at Stratford, a hundred years after Dingelstedt in Weimar similarly celebrated the Tercentenary. With the second tetralogy there was no adaptation and relatively full texts were used, the direction shared by Clifford Williams along with Peter Hall and John Barton. The continuity of the whole was maintained by using the same set – 'John Bury's . . . two huge *periaktoi* (revolving three-sided "houses" which keep their basic shape but acquire new faces for each play)'[46] – and the same actors. In the case of the character of Exeter, a number of supporting parts were coalesced through the several plays to provide a single observer/choric commentator, a part taken by Donald Burton through the whole sequence from *Richard II* to *Richard III*. The mounting of the series, though, made possible other forms of significant doubling. One of the extraordinary features of *The Wars of the Roses* had been the trust the directors placed in young and inexperienced actors. It was true that they had two major established figures in Donald Sinden as York and Peggy Ashcroft playing a superb Queen Margaret (with a French 'r' lisp throughout). But the production depended crucially on the performances of two actors not long out of drama school, David Warner as Henry VI and Ian Holm as Richard III. In both cases the results were remarkable, the characters growing and developing in psychological depth as the action went on, Warner's Henry from gauche and shambling adolescent to tortured saint taking upon himself the sins of his people, Holm's Richard from tough young tyke on the battlefield to credibly loveless, misogynistic psychopath. The two actors were cast again in the second tetralogy in complementary or antithetical starring roles: Warner played Richard II as another variety of weak king; Holm, the anti-hero of *The Wars of the Roses* as Gloucester/Richard III, became the hero Hal/Henry V. Though not all reviewers were as happy with these performances as with their previous parts, some thinking Warner's Richard too like his Henry, the casting represented a successful challenge to the old star system. Holm's playing in both parts especially was designed to contrast with the virtuoso achievements of Olivier. His Richard was deliberately low-key, naturalistic, ordinarily good-looking, against Olivier's fascinating monster. His Henry was saluted as a 'Henry for our Generation' and in this *Henry V* for the first time since Olivier the reviewer 'did not sigh for a little touch of Larry in the night'.[47]

With the 1964 RSC production the idea of the histories as series achieved complete theatrical credibility:

For all their uncertainties of authorship and random order of composition, the eight plays of Shakespeare's cycle of English histories amount to our nearest approach to a national epic; a dislocated masterpiece indeed, with some giant limbs and some only half-grown, but one which shows a strong element of internal unity when its separate parts are performed in sequence.[48]

the strip-cartoon pleasure of seeing the histories in sequence is such that it now seems inconceivable that we were content to have them otherwise.[49]

This acceptance of the cycle's unity was achieved by some fairly programmatic adaptation by Barton and Hall in *The Wars of the Roses*, and by the strength of the ensemble acting principles at the RSC which dispensed with centripetal star casting. There was also another dimension which may have contributed to the establishment of the history series, and that was television.

Already in 1960, the BBC had mounted a fifteen part televised series of the eight English history plays as *An Age of Kings* (though with a reduced *1 Henry VI*).[50] This series drew upon the theatrical experience of the Birmingham Rep *Henry VI* productions, using many of the same actors in its ensemble cast who played multiple parts throughout,[51] with some stars drafted in for major roles: Sean Connery as Hotspur, a very young Judi Dench as Katherine of France. It made use of what amounted to a permanent set. But it was throughly adapted to a television idiom in dividing the plays up into episodes, each with its separate title – *Richard II* was screened as 'Part 1: The Hollow Crown', 'Part 2: The Deposing of a King' – and with forward-pointing endings to each episode. So, for instance, the penultimate part of the whole series, 'Part 14: The Dangerous Brother', ended midway through *Richard III* with a tableau of Gloucester, candle in hand, looking down at his nephews, the sleeping princes. It has been argued that *An Age of Kings* represented a landmark event in television: it 'was highly influential in British television in the formation both of a kind of serious issue-based

Plate 3 Cover of *Radio Times*, April 1960, advertising BBC Television production of *An Age of Kings*, directed by Michael Hayes, produced by Peter Dews

"soap opera" and of serial adaptations of classics'.[52] Equally, however, in this interchange between theatre and television, *An Age of Kings*, together with the 1965 BBC screening of the Barton–Hall *Wars of the Roses*, had a crucial effect on the perception of Shakespeare's histories. These television productions were significant not only because they brought the history series to infinitely wider audiences than ever would have seen them in the theatre, and because they represented the growth of the cultural export market in Shakespeare to be most fully realised in the BBC Television Shakespeare project. The success of such productions, the willingness to accept the notion of the histories as a coherent series, must have been influenced by the more general milieu of television watching conditioned by multi-part historical docudramas and mini-series, not to mention soap-operas. Habituation to episodic narrative, to developing relationships with actors playing the same characters through a sequence, to the unfolding of meaning over a series of 'to be continued' parts, all of these supported a new belief in Shakespeare's history plays as an integrated cycle.

ROYAL SHAKESPEARE COMPANY, ENGLISH SHAKESPEARE COMPANY

Highly successful theatre productions, like other major cultural events, reduce the field of possibility for successors. The 1963–4 Stratford histories were unrepeatable and later directors at the RSC, if they wanted to stage the history plays as series, had to find other means of doing it. In the 1970s Terry Hands directed what amounted to two new and different 'tetralogies', though in both cases these came about adventitiously for practical, theatrical reasons. Having agreed on productions of the two parts of *Henry IV* and *Henry V* for their 1975 season, the RSC Board of Directors (in Hands' absence) decided to add in *The Merry Wives of Windsor* – which Hands had already directed in 1968 – to make up a Falstaff-dominated quartet.[53] Likewise the great success of Alan Howard's Henry V in the 1975 season must have been a key factor in the decision to revive that production in 1977 and play it ahead of the three parts of *Henry VI*, with Alan Howard cast also as Henry V's son Henry VI. In spite of the best efforts of the productions, neither new grouping succeeded in imposing itself upon the critics. The 1975 *Merry Wives* was drawn into alignment with the *Henry IV / Henry V* plays by having Falstaff similarly costumed and all the overlapping characters played by the same actors. A programme note by Ronald Bryden on

'The Education of a King' put best foot forward in making a case for the continuity of theme:

Falstaff *is* paganism, the natural force of unguided appetite. The threat he presents to Hal is the temptation to refuse a king's role and be his natural self; but in his own person he conveys the consequences of such temptation – his natural self is a shapeless bulk without identity, mindless and changeable as a child.[54]

But reviewers saw in the *Merry Wives* only an overplayed and derivative revival of Hands' earlier successful production. Hands justified his casting decision to double Alan Howard as the two King Henrys in 1977 in terms of a perceived affinity:

[the two parts] should be played by the same actor . . . The boy who develops has all his father's vision finally, and the perception of what should be done, but lacks his father's physicality and the ability to carry it out by war, by the system that exists.[55]

Howard's double performance as Henry V/VI was admired, but there were complaints of the artificiality of tacking *Henry V* on ahead of the *Henry VI* plays, and frustration at not having a *Richard III* following on. Once again, the notion of a revised tetralogy remained notional.

The keynote of Hands' direction of the histories was a theatrical return to essentials. On a largely bare stage he used token signs, visual synecdoches to suggest atmosphere and meaning. Thus, for example, the leitmotif of ageing and decay in *2 Henry IV* was conveyed by a leaf-strewn playing area overhung by gnarled withered branches. The English countryside setting of *2 Henry VI* was manifested in a grassed-over stage, contrasting with the battlefields of France of *1 Henry VI*. The inherent theatricality of public role-playing was brought out by having the initial scenes of *Henry V* acted in uncostumed rehearsal rig, bringing in costumes by degrees as the action moved towards the heroics of the French invasion. Hands' deliberate experiment with the *Henry VI* plays, in reaction against the interpretative adaptation of Barton and Hall, was to play them straight and play them whole: 'We decided to . . . just put it all very crudely, very naively down on the stage – everything that was there, warts and all, in the hope that one or two of them would be beauty spots.'[56] This proved to be the success of the production as far as the critics were concerned:

Terry Hands has no great thematic revelations to make; indeed, his strength is to have cast off the intellectual superstructure, returned to the original text, and followed his own temperamental bent for colour, tempestuous action, and variety of tone . . . the performance continually grips attention through its mobile command of narrative.[57]

The neo-Elizabethan production . . . proves its worth again and again. Scene melts into scene, each one contrived with a masterly simplicity that announces its content at once, so that there is as much continuous action as in a football match.[58]

And so, finally, in 1977 England saw its first ever professional production of the *Henry VI* plays, unadapted, unrevised, more or less as the First Folio left them to us.

There is, of course, by definition no such thing as a 'straight' production, no production that does not reflect interpretative decisions or ideological inflection. The issue for modern productions of the histories has been rather how overtly such interpretations should reflect contemporary ideological concerns, and how radically they should challenge traditional historical readings of the texts. Peter Hall in the 1964 *Wars of the Roses* had opted for what he called an 'almost neo-Brechtian approach to the plays', what Robert Shaughnessy, who quotes this remark, calls 'a circumspect revision of Brecht'.[59] There was no such temporising in Giorgio Strehler's 1965 *Il gioco dei potenti* (*Power Games*), a two-part adaptation of the three *Henry VI* plays at the Teatro Lirico in Milan. Indeed the *Times* reviewer, while respectful to Strehler's directorial reputation, accused him of over-egging the style of the master: 'Mr Strehler fails to out-Brecht Brecht' read the headline.[60] The production, which Strehler re-staged in revised versions in Salzburg in 1973 and in Vienna in 1975, borrowed from Brecht the device of an ironically narrating chorus, in the Milan version opening with the *Henry V* 'O for a muse of fire' speech, and continuing through the two parts with speeches drawn from ten different plays.[61] The political emphasis was on the ordinary people, 'by turn victims, puppets, or unconscious protagonists in the unfolding of their own history', as the critic of *Il giorno* put it.[62]

The central image of the play – concentrated in three contrasted battle scenes – was of a roundabout, a wild carousel of the struggle for power, which culminated in the final image of what Strehler describes as the 'dance of the youthful aspirants to the throne': a tableau of powerful gestic force with Richard of Gloucester spotlit, fists clenched, as richly-dressed couples whirl past.[63]

A comparably radical interpretation was Denis Llorca's 1978 French version of the *Henry VI – Richard III* plays presented as a single nine-hour spectacle with the title *Kings*, 'a symbolic feast in four seasons':

Kings is more a ritualistic enactment, a poetic recreation about fleeting time, than a historical spectacle. Through his terse narration of the desperate struggle fought by the mighty to assume power, Llorca tentatively suggests that the ultimate reality is not the crown or the *libido dominandi* but changing nature, life and death, and the Works and Days of the people. Indeed, in a remarkable feat of stagecraft, the most breathtaking scenes were the *tableaux vivants* displaying work in the fields, the grape- and corn-harvests, the fires of vigils, and the dirges and dances of the country folk. These scenes functioned in counterpoint to the ruthless contests between the feudal dynasts who entered the fray and bit the dust in the political arena . . . [64]

Such a production represented a re-reading of Shakespeare's histories in the light of modern historiography, reading back into the plays the lives of the unchronicled common people that Shakespeare, following his chronicle sources, had omitted.

The BBC Television Shakespeare productions of the two history plays series well illustrate the contrast between an ideologically interventionist direction and its opposite. The initial project, as devised by Cedric Messina, emphasised historical authenticity and a realistic playing style in what was conceived of in monumental terms: 'It was decided that the English histories, from *Richard II* through all the *Henry IVs*, *V* and *VIs* to *Richard III* would be presented in chronological order, so that some day in the not too distant future, the eight plays that form this sequence will be able to be seen in their historical order, a unique record of the chronicled history of that time.'[65] Given the mixture of studio production and outside broadcasts, it was decided 'Any form of extreme stylisation was just not on.'[66] Although there was some appreciation for the historicity of these early BBC Television histories, there were also loudly voiced complaints of their dullness.[67] Whether in response to such criticism or not, there was a marked change in style for the *Henry VI – Richard III* series, produced initially by Jonathan Miller and directed by Jane Howell. Although period costumes were preserved in this series (something insisted upon by the series' backers *Time-Life*), there was a radically counter-illusionist permanent set inspired by a Fulham adventure playground. The playing style guyed the militaristic rhetoric of the speeches; as an alienating device, characters frequently spoke asides direct to camera.[68] Nothing could have been less like the realising, historicising direction of the first history series.

A direct confrontation between more or less radical reinterpretations of the history plays came in the late 1980s with the simultaneous staging of a new *Wars of the Roses* by the English Shakespeare Company and *The Plantagenets* by the RSC. Adrian Noble's *Plantagenets* was identifiably in an RSC tradition established by the earlier productions of Barton–Hall and Hands. It was an adaptation along roughly the same lines as the Barton–Hall *Wars of the Roses*, compressing the first tetralogy into three plays, called *Henry VI, The Rise of Edward IV*, and *Richard III, His Death*. However, Noble's cutting and revisions were undertaken almost entirely in the interests of narrative economy, without the sort of explicit ideological design of Barton and Hall. He seemed rather to be following Hands in allowing meanings to emerge from the scenic juxtapositions of the narrative instead of imposing a directorial scheme of significance upon the whole. He developed from Hands, for example, a technique of overlapping scenes and simultaneous staging. So the battle of Bordeaux in *Henry VI*, in which the heroic Talbot goes down to death with his son, was played as part of a continuous sequence with the capture and burning of Joan, marriage plans for King Henry, court intrigues over peace with France, and the wooing of Margaret by Suffolk. The dead bodies, left lying on the stage after Bordeaux, were briefly animated to act as the spirits who refuse to answer Joan's desperate invocations, but were back in place as the dark detritus of the battlefield when Henry and Gloucester discussed marriage spotlit downstage, or when Winchester dispatched to the Pope the promised bribe for his Cardinal's hat. The anguished body of Joan held at the stake at the point of death was a figure in a continuing tableau behind Suffolk's sexual negotiations with Margaret. These were potent theatrical ironies but not organised according to an overt interpretative agenda.

Where *The Plantagenets* was different from its RSC predecessors was in its use of visual display. In place of the single, austerely modernist permanent set of *The Wars of the Roses* or the empty-space emblematic staging of Hands' *Henry VI*, Noble used a highly pictorial, at times positively operatic, mise en scène. There was lavish costuming, with the first appearance of the French leaders all in gold, on cloth-of-gold-covered hobby-horses; the wars themselves were often rendered as a pageantry of swirling pennants and standards. For set-piece scenes, the stage groupings had a strong formal symmetry. At a key moment after the French coronation of Henry, for example, (*Henry VI*, Act 1 scene 13[69]), the King was centrally enthroned with Humphrey of Gloucester in black robe, carrying his long staff of civil authority as Lord Protector, to his right just forward of the throne, Winchester in ecclesiastical gold gown to the left just behind the throne. Downstage, left and right, knelt Vernon and

Basset, the quarrelling contenders of the red and white rose factions seeking leave to combat, while their principals, York and Somerset, stood one on each side between them and the King. With such picturesque clarity Noble's direction figured the politics of the situation: the weak King, the older generation of conflict between church and secular power, the newly emerging faction-fighting of York and Lancaster which would escalate into the Wars of the Roses. Noble worked in *The Plantagenets* as an ideologically unself-conscious director, providing audiences with a flexible and gripping narrative enforced by the spectacle of the stage.

It was in a sense in reaction against this sort of RSC direction that the English Shakespeare Company *Wars of the Roses* was conceived, though the enterprise was under way well before *The Plantagenets* was staged.[70] The partnership of Michael Bogdanov and Michael Pennington began with both parties frustrated and disillusioned by the major state-subsidised theatres, the National Theatre and the RSC, in which they had frequently worked as director and leading actor respectively. The institutionalisation of these theatres, their lack of urgent commitment, the subordination of artistic initiative to administration, all provided the background to what became the dissident ESC, just one initial away from the RSC it challenged.[71] In the case of Bogdanov, in particular, there was in addition a strong political incentive to produce the history plays. Burning with anger at the electoral system which had returned Margaret Thatcher to power on a minority of the popular vote, he saw *Henry IV/Henry V*, with which the company started, as 'plays for today, the lessons of history unlearnt':

The Grand Mechanism of the Polish critic, Jan Kott, in full sway, the escalator shuttling mice and men up to the top, where the golden crock of Imperialism shone brightly, waiting for the next attempt to snatch it from its podium. We were in the era of New Brutalism where a supposed return to Victorian values under the guise of initiative and incentive masked the true goal of greed, avarice, exploitation and self.[72]

So one of the drives behind the ESC production of what was to become *The Wars of the Roses*, the complete cycle of the eight history plays reduced to seven, was to take out on tour to audiences away from the cultural centres of Stratford and London, stripped-down, newly relevant versions of the plays, to bring Shakespeare to them and to bring him home to them.

In order to have the historical sweep of the plays end up in the present, *Richard II* was given Regency costuming, the transition from the reign of

Richard to that of Henry IV marked by the change from the decadent dressiness of Richard's court to the sober frock-coated Victorianism of his successor Bullingbrook. But Bogdanov as director did not feel bound by this historical design scheme and, as a long-term exponent of modern-dress Shakespeare, used contemporary styles and images eclectically as needed. The Regency Richard II was attacked by hoods with flick-knives, shot with a pistol from behind by Exton. Immediately after the hand-to-hand combat in full medieval armour of Richard III and Richmond at Bosworth, the scene shifted to a television studio where the victorious Richmond was being made up to give his final speech as a television address to the nation. The directorial aim was to find instant reference points for audiences of the 1980s. So, for example, the burning of Joan was seen in silhouette as a necklace-burning, an image made familiar by the horrifying deaths in the South African townships. Pistol and his mates, as the English invaders of France in *Henry V*, were football hooligans who unfurled a banner reading FUCK THE FROGS.

With such a polemic adversarial political stance, there could be no authorised authority figures within the Bogdanov–Pennington *Wars of the Roses* or, in the aftermath of the Falklands, any unironised military heroism. Sir Walter Blunt, the incarnation of honour in *1 Henry IV* ('I like not such grinning honour as Sir Walter hath', says Falstaff at Shrewsbury contemplating his dead body), was reduced to a conventional stiff-upper-lip officer type, while the sympathetically treated Hotspur had his set-piece paean –

> By heaven, methinks it were an easy leap
> To pluck bright honour from the pale-fac'd moon

– excised. There was no room in Bogdanov's production for any positive idea of authority, nothing equivalent to the ideal of kingship expounded in the 1951 Stratford history series, or the implicit concept of responsible government informing the Barton–Hall *Wars of the Roses*. In the ESC *Wars of the Roses* of the Thatcher era, anyone in power became suspect Establishment whether in the red uniforms of the officers, the purple of the episcopate, or the dark suits of the businessmen/politicians.

The ESC *Wars of the Roses* offered a Shakespearean history cycle for the 1980s, politically engaged, dissenting from the culturally cushioned atmosphere of the RSC, taking to audiences round Britain and eventually round the world 'a medieval soap opera of murder and intrigue in the Coronation boardroom'.[73] It was not that the plays were radically adapted to an *agitprop* agenda; rather the contemporary reference points

of costuming, character and idiom continually gave political coloration
to the action. There are, however, some paradoxes here. The fascinat-
ingly detailed account of the production of *The Wars of the Roses* given by
Bogdanov and Pennington in *The English Shakespeare Company* shows what
an enormous operation it was, and how it worked within the cultural
market-place of the 1980s. In many ways, for all its political dissidence,
the ESC was a model product of the Thatcherite period: Bogdanov and
Pennington as its originators showed the initiative, the entrepreneurial
skills, the capacity for taking hard management decisions (they had a
long-running dispute with the company over rates of pay which only
just stopped short of legal action), the business and marketing abilities
which were the featured values of the time. They succeeded in combining funding from the private sector (Allied Irish Banks among others) as
well as public bodies (Arts Council) according to the recommended practice of what Pennington refers to ironically as the 'Age of Feasibility'.[74]
Although they were in reaction against the cultural establishment represented by the major state theatres, and their touring policy was populist and anti-metropolitan, their participation in international festivals
abroad in Tokyo, Melbourne and Chicago was crucial to the finances
of the *Wars of the Roses* and made them a part of the high-prestige, high-
culture export market.

2000: TWO HISTORY CYCLES

In the year 2000, it was again possible to watch two very different serial stagings of the history plays. The Hamburg Schauspielhaus revived
Schlachten!, a condensed adaptation of all eight histories capable of being
played in a single day. This had had its first production in German at the
Salzburg Festival in 1999, but was originally created in Flemish by the
adaptor/translator Tom Lanoye and the director Luk Perceval.[75] As its
title of *Slaughter* suggests, it concentrated on the violence and brutality of
the series, and the extreme degeneration of the operation of power over
the period dramatised. In *Richard II*, adapted as *Richard Deuxième*, primitive oriental-style court rituals were observed, with an anvil as the symbol
of authority, a sledge-hammer struck upon it to signal the presence of
the king. By the latter stages of the *Henry VI* plays, the sons of York
were Mafioso-style thugs speaking a mongrel mixture of German and
gangster-American English. The reign of Richard III, *Dirty Rich Modder-
fokker der Dritte*, climaxed in a cannibal banquet in which he appeared to
eat the bodies of the young princes.

Very different was *This England: the Histories*, the Royal Shakespeare Company's millennium project of producing the two sequences of the history plays over two seasons. The *Richard II – Henry V* series was mounted over the spring and summer with separate directors and different playing spaces for the four plays. So, Steven Pimlott directed *Richard II* in stylish modern dress in the small auditorium of The Other Place, stripped down to a white box. The lyricism and the pageantry were reduced to a minimum to concentrate on the play's political issues. Michael Attenborough directed the two parts of *Henry IV* in the Swan, the RSC's Jacobean-style playhouse, in period costume and more traditional playing style. Although there was through-casting of the parts, David Troughton playing King Henry as he had Bullingbrook in *Richard II*, the characterisation was in some cases markedly different. Adam Levy, for instance, who had played Harry Percy in the earlier play as what one reviewer called 'a ridiculous Action Man',[76] was markedly more sympathetic in *1 Henry IV*. *Henry V*, directed by Edward Hall in the large Royal Shakespeare Theatre, was different again, anti-heroic, emphasising the costs of the war, distributing the speeches of the Chorus among the cast of soldiers, by way of democratising and subverting the univocal authority of the choric voice. For the second series of the plays, a single director, Michael Boyd, was responsible, with a high degree of narrative connections between the three parts of *Henry VI* and *Richard III*, all staged in a specially re-fitted version of the Swan, over the winter season 2000–1.

Coleridge maintained that 'in order that a drama may be properly historical, it is necessary that it should be the history of the people to whom it is addressed'.[77] Whatever it may be to be 'properly historical', certainly Shakespeare's history plays are different when addressed to a people other than that of Britain. *Schlachten!* resembles, in some sort, those earlier European adaptations of the history series, Llorca's *Kings*, Strehler's *Il gioco dei potenti*, Dingelstedt's founding serial production in Weimar in 1864. Each offers a model or paradigm of the movement of a nation through time, abstracted more or less from the specificity of the particular history as history. Where Dingelstedt re-shaped the cycle into a classical five-act structure, ending positively with the establishment of the Tudors as emblem for a new nation-state, *Schlachten!* imagined the plays as a latter-day Hobbesian war of all against all, a staged degeneration from archaic to modern barbarism.

There was a degree of irony in picking out the phrase, 'This England' from John of Gaunt's patriotic paean for the RSC history series. An

Plate 4 Poster for Royal Shakespeare Company production, *This England: the Histories*,
Stratford 2000

audience entering The Other Place – a theatre that in its very name bespeaks its minority status – before the beginning of *Richard II*, first in the *This England* series, heard a medley of language and music, Blake's 'Jerusalem', Gilbert and Sullivan, Churchillian-style oratory, that represented a tongue-in-cheek collage of Englishness. The very fact that the *Richard II – Henry V* sequence broke the narrative continuum by the use of different directors and designers was a deconstruction of the RSC's own history of staging the histories: the grand designs of Barton and Hall's *Wars of the Roses* in the 1960s, Noble's *Plantagenets* in the 1980s. This, appropriately for the year 2000, was a disparate, multiple rather than monolithic imagination of England's history. By casting black actors in key parts, notably David Oyelowo as Henry VI, the multi-ethnic Britain of the new century was made visible on stage in the representation of the monocultural England of the past. And yet the series was presented, packaged, as *This England: the Histories*, to climax in a week in May 2001 when all eight plays could be seen in sequence in London, the nation's capital. The canonical cultural status of Shakespeare for the British is reflected in this production by the Royal Shakespeare Company, playing quite full and faithful texts, very unlike the free arrangement of *Schlachten!* At the same time, the staging of the histories is made to suggest a modern 'Condition of England' representation: an article on the series in the *RSC Magazine* was entitled 'This Island Now'.[78] The programmes for the *Henry IV* and *Henry V* productions with quotations defining the nature of the nation across time, including statements from contemporary politicians and pundits, alerted audiences to the continuing relevance of the plays' issues of national identity.

Schlachten! and *This England*, as very different serial versions of the histories, are alike in their dependence on theatrical conditions that, over the last century and a half, have come to make such productions possible. These massive theatrical enterprises could not be undertaken without the resources available to a major municipal theatre such as the Hamburg Schauspielhaus, or the state-subsidised RSC. They depend equally on the audience culture of arts festivals and the monumental event. So, for instance, *Schlachten!* was originally staged as a co-production with the Salzburg Festival of 1999 and shown again at the Zurich Festival of 2000. Similarly Llorca's *Kings* was the centrepiece of the festival at Carcassonne in 1978. Only at festivals can a specialist audience be found to attend all-day, nine- or even twelve-hour marathon performances. At festivals, or at other special anniversaries to be marked with spectacular outsize performative monuments: the Shakespeare Tercentenary of 1864, the

Quatercentenary in 1964, the millennial project of the RSC in 2000. Response to serial productions of the plays has been conditioned by television viewing habits and by important screenings of the histories such as *An Age of Kings* or the BBC Shakespeare. But the theatrical productions are a defiant manifestation by modern theatre of what only modern theatre can do, to engage an audience with the live and continuous presence of a group of actors who show their virtuosity by doubling and trebling parts across play after play. Theatre may not be able to compete with the technological wizardry of the virtual media; still, it claims its own special immediacy as the one acting ensemble represents the succession of whole historical generations. It is a long way no doubt from whatever form of serial production took place in successive afternoons at the Rose or the Globe, yet something of the impulse to stage the nation on an epic scale remains the same.

PART II

Henry VI – Richard III

CHAPTER THREE

War imagined

Think when we talk of horses that you see them
Printing their proud hoofs i'th'receiving earth
(*Henry V*, Prologue, 26–7)

For Shakespeare, and for most of the audiences of Shakespeare's time, the representation of war could only be the imagination of war. Although the age of the soldier 'Seeking the bubble reputation / Even in the cannon's mouth' might have been one of the statutory seven ages of man, relatively few Elizabethans would themselves have seen active combat.[1] With the resources available to the theatre of the late sixteenth century, battle scenes were always going to be heavily dependent on an audience's suspension of disbelief, as the Chorus of *Henry V* so repeatedly underlines. Where 'four or five most vile and ragged foils' did duty for the armaments of Agincourt, there was necessarily developed a code of conventional and stylised representation of war. Whatever might be the limitations in the visual display of fighting – and we have to allow for the conventional modesty topos in the Chorus of *Henry V* – they could be supplemented by the rich pageants of language which were the staple of the Elizabethan drama. If the opera isn't over till the fat lady sings, in Shakespeare the battle is not finished until the victor or the vanquished has declaimed his long set speech of triumph or resignation.

In writing a series of four plays dramatising the reigns of Henry VI and Richard III, Shakespeare set himself the task of representing a period of almost continuous war: the last thirty years of the Hundred Years War, the Wars of the Roses, the confused conflicts over the English monarchy which ended (more or less) with the Battle of Bosworth. How was this stretch of time to be made into something other than just one damned battle after another? It was part of Shakespeare's design in serialising the chronicles, as I argued in Chapter 1, to concentrate the war with the French into *1 Henry VI* instead of allowing it to continue, as it did historically, well into the period dramatised in *2 Henry VI*. In the sequence as a whole, different forms of war provide variety and narrative progression according to a pattern of changing dynamics. Four distinct types of conflict can be distinguished by their orientation within a field of force. The war between England and France (dramatised for an English audience) turns on difference, a partisanship of us and them. The two sides are constructed to illustrate the oppositions of national character by which the English can congratulate themselves on being staunch, upright, strong and masculine, over against the shifting, effeminate and double-dealing French. This sort of conflict of self and other is to be contrasted with civil war, the war of self on self. If the war between England and France is organised around difference, then the essential structural characteristic in the Wars of the Roses is the sameness of the opposing factions. Where the English are imagined as inherently unlike the French, there is an interchangeable symmetry in the battles between the red rose and the white. A central antithesis of the *Henry VI – Richard III* series is between the 'naturalness', so to speak, of the divisions of England and France and the unnaturalness of civil war which pits like against like, brother against brother, father against son.

Yet even before the Wars of the Roses have actually begun in Shakespeare's plays, there is a third distinct if related sort of conflict that erupts temporarily. The vectors of force in both the English–French war and the dynastic disputes can be conceived as lateral in so far as they oppose powers of equivalent status, national army against national army, Yorkists against Lancastrians. But the Cade revolt introduces a vertical class dimension to conflict, with the assault of peasants upon the nobility, the attack of the Kentishmen up from the country on London. Jack Cade is of course suborned by the Duke of York, and his quickly quelled rebellion acts as overture to the outbreak of civil war when York returns from Ireland and openly claims the crown. Still the uprising, while it lasts, disrupts class stratification as the fission of rival titles to the throne breaks apart the unity of the monarchy. In the three *Henry VI* plays the action moves from the partisan war of difference between English and French through to the ever more bloody internal divisions of England's civil wars, including a glimpse of the potential for revolution in the Cade revolt. In *Richard III* a fourth and final kind of battle is fought out between good and evil. Although there are spiritual and moral differentiations in the *Henry VI* plays, the sinister enchantments of Pucelle used to overthrow honest English Talbot, the 'good Duke Humphrey' against the wicked Cardinal of Winchester, right and wrong become increasingly impossible to identify clearly in the snarled cycle of revenge. In *Richard III* the concentration of monstrous evil in the one figure of the king makes for a polarised holy war in which, at the Battle of Bosworth, the forces of righteousness definitively overcome the power of darkness.

Through the *Henry VI – Richard III* series Shakespeare thus imagines war as a succession of different types of war with equivalently varying emotions: glory, horror, pity, triumph. It is one of the aims of this chapter to show the way in which those successive forms of war are represented, their sources in the chronicles, and the extent to which they are shaped into a developing pattern over the sequence. But the imagination of war that Shakespeare and his audiences constructed in the 1590s has had to be repeatedly re-imagined in the modern period, and I am as much concerned here with such re-imaginings as with the original constructions. Twentieth-century theatrical conditions have changed the means of representation, and with them audience expectations: more graphic violence and less declamatory rhetoric are likely to be demanded. The shifting political attitudes brought about by mass world war and the increasingly immediate visibility of real-life conflict, wherever it happens, necessarily alter how war is imagined and represented. The history play series, as a series, allows for changing representations of war through time; successive modern productions equally allow us to see changing views of those changing representations; and it is this double set of changes that the chapter sets out to explore.

FORCE AGAINST FRAUD: ENGLAND V. FRANCE

> The fraud of England, not the force of France,
> Hath now entrapped the noble-minded Talbot
> *(1 Henry VI, 4.4.36–7)*

This comment of Sir William Lucy, as Talbot faces death at Bordeaux because of the quarrels of Somerset and York, is an indignant expression of normality inverted. Fraud is the proper attribute of France, force of England. Throughout *1 Henry VI* the English typically, characteristically, win all the pitched battles fought on fair terms. They only lose when the French use underhand or supernatural powers against them, or when they are betrayed by quite exceptional cowardice (Fastolf) or dissension on their own side. For a popular English playwright dramatising the events of the reign of Henry VI there was a problem with the representation of the war with France. Here was no Crécy, Poitiers or

Agincourt to boost national pride; this was the period in which England yielded up all that Edward III, the Black Prince, Henry V, had gained. Shakespeare's successful sleight of hand in *1 Henry VI* was to show the English managing to win all the battles and yet lose the war. Joan the Pucelle uses her devilish powers to relieve the siege of Orléans, it is true; but the English (quite unhistorically) scale the walls and retake it. The French slyly disguise themselves to capture Rouen, only to have it recaptured from them again within the day. The play tactfully elides the circumstances by which both Orléans and Rouen ended up finally in the hands of the French.

In the scheme of things by which the English are inevitable victors who yet meet defeat, the French born losers who somehow contrive to win, Talbot is the embodiment of English force, Joan of French fraud. Even before we meet him, we hear of Talbot in the first scene of the play in characteristic mode, embattled, surrounded, fighting against terrible odds –

> valiant Talbot, above human thought,
> Enacted wonders with his sword and lance.
> (1.1.121–2)

– and only taken prisoner because deserted by the cowardly Fastolf and stabbed in the back by a 'base Walloon'. His heroic strength is constructed around his Englishness, his masculinity, and his veteran soldiership. At the death of Salisbury (treacherously ambushed from above), he vows revenge:

> Frenchmen, I'll be a Salisbury to you.
> Puzel or pucelle, dolphin or dogfish . . .
> (1.4.105–6)

The historical Talbot, as a fifteenth-century nobleman, would no doubt have spoken French quite as fluently as English, but it suits Shakespeare to make his character a monoglot Englishman whose perplexed ignorance of the words 'pucelle' or 'dauphin' is the mark of his plainspeaking superiority. His masculinity is defined not only against Joan but in the curious little episode with the Countess of Auvergne. The Countess lures Talbot to her castle in the hope of taking prisoner this archenemy of her country. She is amazed at how little he resembles his reputation physically, not the Hercules, the 'second Hector' she expected to see, but 'a child, a silly dwarf', a 'weak and writhled shrimp' (2.3.19–21). Yet Talbot can demonstrate to her that what is visible is only a 'shadow of myself'. The substance is made manifest when he winds his horn and his soldiers appear: these are Talbot's 'sinews, arms, and strength' (2.3.62). Encoded in this little lesson in military might is an image of English masculinity as more than it looks, a hidden power rather than a showy outside.

Talbot is the representative of old England, the soldierly generation of Henry V that goes down to defeat one by one in *1 Henry VI*. In Strehler's *Il gioco dei potenti*, when Henry VI ascended the throne, the ruling class suddenly aged and succumbed to the new generation'.[2] This was no doubt intended by Strehler to correspond to the workings of the Kottian Grand Mechanism, but *1 Henry VI* supplies a cue for it in the characterisation of all of Henry V's contemporaries as ageing figures from the last reign. The tragedy of the victorious King Henry was that he died so young – 'too famous to live long' (1.1.6). Yet his *younger* brother Bedford, who speaks this funeral elegy, is addressed contemptuously by Pucelle as 'good greybeard' (3.2.50), and is to die shortly afterwards as 'old Bedford', speaking lines modelled on the 'Nunc dimittis' of the aged Eli (3.2.110–11). The historical Bedford was forty-six when he died in 1435. 'Old' Salisbury who 'first trained' Henry V 'to the wars' (1.4.78), dies in the first act, 'old' Bedford dies in the third; it is Talbot, last of this old guard, who must die in the fourth act. The popular function of this figure in the theatre, as we can see from the Nashe *Pierce Pennilesse* passage, was not only to live again 'the terror of the French' but to bleed afresh, and to 'have his bones newe embalmed with the tears' of the audience. The old England commemorated in Talbot is at its most heroic in defeat, its heroism indeed defined by defeat.

Pucelle is everything that Talbot is not, French to his English: his massively unambiguous masculinity is met by her dubious gender; his bull-like forward force in war is countered by her shifting stratagems; his unwavering integrity shows up her protean lack of principle. 'Puzel or pucelle' Talbot snorts derisively, it does not matter to him which she is. The phrase is generally glossed to mean 'virgin or whore', matching the following antithesis 'dolphin or dogfish', highest and lowest in the categories of fish (1.4.106n.); but it may contain a hint also of 'puzzle'.[3] It is Joan's puzzling indefiniteness over which Talbot typically refuses to puzzle his head. She claims to have miraculous powers from heaven, but she may well be a witch. She is known as Pucelle, the Maid, and tells the Dauphin 'I must not yield to any rites of love / For my profession's sacred from above' (1.2.113–14), yet in the rout after the recapture of Orléans she appears to have been disturbed out of the Dauphin's bed. In no way is the contrast between Talbot and Pucelle made stronger than in the scenes where they face death. The extended pathos of Talbot's end in the company of his son John, their contest in honour, the identity of the two in death as a figure for the principles of continuity and true inheritance, all of this enshrines an ideal of English male aristocratic valour. The captured Pucelle by contrast twists and turns before her accusers: denies her own honest peasant father, pretends to high birth, proclaims her innocence and virginity, but then pleads pregnancy in an attempt to escape burning, alleging one lover after another as the father, ending (when she sees she is doomed) with a witch's curse on her English executioners.

Such a version of the war between England, led by the forceful Talbot, against France, typified by the fraudulent Pucelle, may have suited the 1590s, but at least in relation to the treatment of Joan of Arc it proved a profound embarrassment for later generations. The distasteful version of Pucelle was one of the reasons why *1 Henry VI* was for so long judged to be unShakespearean, and even when returned to the stage (in Benson's 1906 Stratford version) she was played heroically against the lines. Richard Dickins, eyewitness of the 1906 production, in arguing that such a performance misrepresented the spirit of Shakespeare's time, felt the need to preface his criticisms with a fervent profession of admiration:

There is probably no educated Englishman living to-day who does not venerate the name of Joan of Arc as that of one of the purest and noblest women of all time, and who would not give a year of his life to wipe away the stain of her cruel murder, but, I think quite inevitably, that was not the English point of view three hundred years ago.[4]

The discrepancies between the modern reputation of Joan and the Shakespearean character has continued to demand directorial intervention in productions of *1 Henry VI*, most obviously in Llorca's *Kings* where 'Shakespeare's biased, nationalistic attitude was exposed in heavy asides to the audience'.[5] Even without such thoroughgoing subversion of the text, some degree of counter-reading of Joan and the war in France has been thought necessary.

There are, in fact, openings for counter-readings within the Shakespearean text, deriving from his sources. Hall, Shakespeare's main narrative copytext for the *Henry VI* plays, gives short shrift to Joan of Arc. Not only extremely nationalistic but militantly anti-Catholic, Hall is indignantly dismissive of Joan's 'visions, traunses, and fables, full of blasphemy, supersticion and hypocrisy, that I marvell muche that wise men did beleve her, and lerned clarkes would write such phantasies' (Bullough, III, 57). Hall had so very little time for Joan that he gave hardly any details of her story; he summarises her trial, for example, in a single good riddance to bad rubbish sentence: on her capture at Compiègne she 'was sent to the duke of Bedford to Roan, wher, (after long examinacion) she was brent to ashes' (Bullough, III, 61). It may have been for this very reason that Shakespeare turned to Holinshed's fuller account. If he had decided to build Pucelle into the major French antagonist to English Talbot, he would have needed more material than Hall could afford him. Holinshed had read the accounts of Joan by those gullible 'lerned clarkes' Hall so condemned and, though he distanced himself from them by phrases such as 'French stories saie', or 'as their bookes make hir', he was prepared to include a positive description of the Maid at her first appearance:

Of favour was she counted likesome, of person stronglie made and manlie, of courage great, hardie, and stout withall, an understander of counsels though she were not at them, great semblance of chastitie both of bodie and behaviour, the name of Jesus in hir mouth about all her businesses, humble, obedient, and fasting diverse daies in the weeke. (Bullough, III, 75)

This is in striking contrast to Hall who uncharitably suggests that Joan remained a virgin 'because of her foule face, that no man would desire it' (Bullough, III, 56). Shakespeare ingeniously combines Hall's foul-faced with Holinshed's 'likesome' Joan, by having his character explain that due to a miracle of Our Lady she was transformed:

> And whereas I was black and swart before
> With those clear rays which she infused on me,
> That beauty am I blest with, which you may see.
> (1.2.84–6)

The shape-changing of Shakespeare's Joan thus partly derives from the mixed nature of his sources, combining the uncompromisingly propagandist Hall with Holinshed who, while retaining the prejudices of an English chronicler, introduced enough of the sympathetic French accounts to complicate the picture. The resulting discontinuities of the text could be exploited in modern production, most notably perhaps in Janet Suzman's brilliant performance in the Barton–Hall *Wars of the Roses*. With a galvanising energy, she erupted into the French court scene where an overcivilised and overcalculating Dauphin sat playing at chess: on the line 'Poor France now festers through thy dalliance' – one of John Barton's

textual grafts (*Wars*, 7) – she kicked over the chess-board, and proceeded
to defeat the Dauphin in a convincingly strenuous single combat conducted with heavy longswords.[6] Yet, with her spiky butch haircut and
tough dark face, she remained an antiheroic outsider within the power
play of the wars. The alienated playing style of the production allowed
her to step outside her role for moments of cynical commentary. So,
for instance, when she had succeeded in winning Burgundy by patriotic
persuasion, she could turn aside to the audience/camera and remark
drily, 'Done like a Frenchman, turn and turn again' (*Wars*, 23), underlin-
ing the charade-like nature of the whole performance. By contrast, the
scene where Joan's spirits desert her was played with passionate desper-
ation: Suzman actually cut her hand to offer up her blood, tore open the
throat of her armour to allow the spirits in to her breasts. There was very
human terror in her pleading for her life with her English captors; but
once she saw that her case was hopeless, she was allowed a return to a
calm dignity in her final curse upon England. This performance made a
strength out of the inconsistencies of the text. Instead of trying to establish
a single through-line for the part, Suzman's Joan fulfilled a number of
roles, as tomboy rough diamond and female victim, as enigmatic leader
(perhaps inspired, perhaps only shrewd actor/manipulator), as icono-
clastic onlooker and farseeing prophet of doom. Each of these worked
potently within the individual stage moment without being subordinated
to any one controlling reading of the character.

Other later productions sought to naturalise or to sanitise Shakespeare's Joan. Charlotte Cornwell in the 1977 RSC staging appeared
at first as 'a giggling half-wit',[7] Brenda Blethyn in the BBC Television
version played a robust northern wench, and Francesca Ryan (for the
ESC) was a land-girl figure in breeches and tweed coat. Bogdanov as
director of the ESC version made significant cuts to dispense with the
less sympathetic aspects of the part. So the satiric aside on Burgundy's
change of allegiance – 'Done like a Frenchman: turn and turn again' –
was shorn of its derisive second half and became a half-line of joyful
congratulation: 'Done like a Frenchman!'[8] The Fiends who appear so
bodily in Shakespeare's 5.3 with such telling stage directions – '*They walk,
and speak not*', '*They hang their heads*' – were removed altogether and Joan's
prayers were addressed devoutly to the Virgin, 'Holy mother', rather
than to the original Satanic spirits.[9] A more enterprising and visually
effective modern way of rendering Joan's summoning of the demons
was adopted in *An Age of Kings*, where a dancer in miniature was seen
dancing before a close-up of Eileen Atkins' eyes.

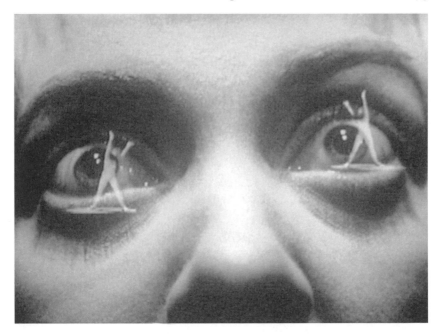

Plate 5 Still from *1 Henry VI* in *An Age of Kings*

Joan has had to be thus re-written, counter-read, in modern productions because the war in which she figures has had to be re-imagined for modern audiences. Talbot could not be wholly deheroised, though the BBC Television Trevor Peacock, got up in armour with heavy leather shoulderpads, was made to look like a bad-tempered American football-player, and the General Gordon-like performance of Michael Fenner for the ESC, complete with Victorian moustache and whiskers, was associated damagingly with blimpish imperialism.[10] But the capture and killing of Joan were reconceived to illustrate the brutality of war in general and the English in particular. Shakespeare's text affords no clear indication on how Joan is actually taken. She is given an exit after the Fiends have deserted her; this is followed by the stage direction '*Excursions. Burgundie and Yorke fight hand to hand. French flye*', after which York addresses Pucelle, 'Damsell of France, I thinke I have you fast' (F, *The first Part of Henry the Sixt*, TLN 2460–2). In the Barton–Hall *Wars* Joan is fighting hand to hand with York when '*Enter [Warwick] and soldiers to York's aid and disarm her*' (*Wars*, 36); she is then carried off tied on a spear like a big-game trophy. The idea that Joan is not taken in fair fight was carried through in both

Plate 6 The capture of Joan of Arc (Janet Suzman), *Wars of the Roses*, RSC production
directed by Peter Hall and John Barton, Stratford 1963

the ESC production, and in the RSC *Plantagenets* where she was captured
in a net, no doubt picking up on the suggestion of York's 'I have you fast'.
What modern directors have done is exactly to reverse the associations
in the original text of France with fraud, England with honourable force.

But it is not in a spirit merely of changing the partisanship that such alterations are undertaken. The sadistic brutality of the English, emphasised repeatedly in the scenes of the killing of Joan, point up the cruelty of war itself. Emrys James, as York in the Hands production of 1977, sniffed his white rose as Joan was dragged off to the burning; Michael Cronin, the ESC Warwick, sat savouring a glass of wine as he watched her burn. The fact of the death at the stake, kept off the stage by Shakespeare, has been brought mercilessly home to modern audiences. The 1953 Birmingham Rep *1 Henry VI* had screams and smoke, but still offstage; the ESC sought the immediacy of contemporary horror with the silhouette of Joan necklace-burned behind a screen; the *Plantagenets* had her crucified body hanging behind the action of the succeeding scenes. Directors since the Second World War, with the stridency of such theatrical statements, have sought to offset and distance themselves from the crudely patriotic partisanship of the wars between England and France in *1 Henry VI*, to complicate at least the national stereotypings with which those wars are constructed. The problem then is how to differentiate between this type of war and those others which follow in the continuing sequence of the histories.

THE COMMONS BELOW: THE CADE UPRISING

In *1 Henry VI* England is its court. With the exception of a few messengers, servants, dependents, and one appearance by the Lord Mayor of London, we never see anyone English in the play below the rank of nobleman. In *2 Henry VI* the situation changes, a change which the scenic design for the 1977 RSC production caught well. The raked stage was covered entirely with grass to remind an audience that this play, unlike the previous one, was on the home turf of England, and some of it at least in the countryside. This greensward was 'divided by a rope barrier':

On one side King, Queen and courtiers perambulate; on the other the lower classes gawp. As the evening proceeds they make their presence felt first as comic relief, then as the threatening embodiment of riot. After half time they swarm on to the field, uniting both roles in a fierce and bloody enactment of Jack Cade's rebellion.[11]

This enacts theatrically the pattern in the text of a progressively more prominent role for the underclass of ordinary people. It begins with the petitioners in 1.3 who have the bad luck to present their petitions to the corrupt Duke of Suffolk instead of the good Duke Humphrey, bad luck indeed as one of their petitions is 'Against the Duke of Suffolk, for enclosing the commons of Melford' (1.3.19–20). It continues with the semi-comic incident of the armourer and his apprentice (1.3, 2.3), and the exposure of the fake miracle of Saunder Simpcox (2.1). By the middle of 3.2 after the murder of Gloucester, 'many Commons' invade the royal presence at Warwick's back and constitute a threatening force amplifying his demand for Suffolk's banishment. So it is the expected culmination of a growing momentum when Cade and his men appear on the scene in 4.2. What is the relation between this progressive movement in the first four acts of *2 Henry VI*, and the various representations of conflict in the four-play series? Are we to see the Cade revolt, when it comes, as a top-down result of the court faction-fighting, prefiguring the Wars of the Roses to come, or is it a bottom-up surge of proletarian revolt against a weakened authority above?

The unfortunate petitioners of 1.3 may be assumed to betoken real grievances of the rule of the favourite Suffolk, grievances that the petitioners might expect the just Lord Protector Gloucester to put right. The enclosure of common land was a generic complaint, symptomatic of aristocratic oppression of the poor, in the text apparently designed to elicit sympathy. Certainly Queen Margaret's action in tearing the petitions is typical of her arbitrary contempt for law and due process. The 'good' Duke Humphrey's exposure of the fake blind man Simpcox and his wife, with his final order to have them whipped, may strike modern audiences as less than compelling evidence of his goodness; sympathetic emphasis often now falls on the Wife's exit-line 'Alas, sir, we did it for pure need' (2.1.156). In an Elizabethan context it may have been otherwise. For this incident of the detection of a bogus saint's miracle, Shakespeare turned aside from his main sources to Foxe's *Actes and Monuments of Martyrs*, where it is given as an instance of Gloucester's capacity to 'reforme that which was amisse' (Bullough, III, 128). This may suggest that the episode was included to give further positive Protestant colouring to the Lord Protector whose arch-rival is the Romish Cardinal.

The incident of the armourer and his apprentice is an intriguing instance of the representation of the commons and its relation to national conflict. The episode in Hall is one of those occasional events drawn in by the omnivorousness of the annalist: 'This yere [1446], an Armerars servaunt of London, appeled his master of treason, whiche offered to bee tried by battail' (Bullough, III, 105). The outcome, as in Shakespeare, was the overconfident master drinking too much and being defeated by his servant. In the chronicles this story has nothing whatever to do with the main political narrative, but Shakespeare, finding it on the very next page of his source to the wrangling between the Yorkists and Lancastrians over the Regency of Normandy, contrived ingeniously to tie it in. The accusation of treason made by Peter the apprentice against his master Thomas Horner was 'for saying that the Duke of York was rightful heir to the crown' (1.3.23–4). It is this accusation, eagerly brought to the attention of the court by Suffolk against his rival York, which is made the deciding factor against York being given the French Regency (1.3.200–1). With the dispute between Horner and Peter, Shakespeare sketches in a hint of the dynastic rivalries penetrating into the life of the ordinary people. When questioned by the King Horner vehemently denies that he ever said that York was rightful heir to the throne:

> KING HENRY Say, man, were these thy words?
> HORNER And't shall please your majesty, I never said nor thought any
> such matter. God is my witness, I am falsely accused by the villain.
> PETER (*holding up his hands*) By these ten bones, my lords, he did speak them
> to me in the garret one night, as we were scouring my Lord of York's
> armour. (1.3.181–7)

The need to connect an armourer with the Duke of York, and to provide a plausible occasion for the alleged treasonous speech, produce this tiny cameo of a working evening in the life of master and servant.

The incident of the accusation, and the mock trial by combat following from it, can be read in different ways. It may be construed as evidence of the disruptive effects of York's (as yet concealed) ambitions trickling down the social system to the level of armourer and apprentice. But it also suggests an independent life of those lower orders that mimics and parodies that of their superiors. The grotesquerie of master and servant bound to trial by combat derives not only from its apparent inequity: the master can 'accept the combat willingly' (1.3.207) while the servant, completely untrained in arms, takes it to be a virtual sentence of death. Trial by combat (dramatised in all its ceremony in *Richard II*) was essentially a chivalric mode travestied in the fight between the drunken Horner, supported by his carousing neighbours, and the fearful Peter urged on by his fellow prentices. Given that this is so, it is difficult to know what is the intended effect of the fight and its result. A marginal note to Holinshed's account points up a properly orthodox moral: 'Drunkennesse the overthrow of right and manhood'. What is more, to offset the bad example of servant defeating master, Holinshed adds a punitive endpiece absent from Hall:

'The false servant, he lived not long unpunished; for being convict of felonie in court of assise, he was iudged to be hanged, and so was, at Tiburne' (Holinshed, 626). Shakespeare by contrast allows Peter to end in a triumphant vindication of innocence and a promise of reward from the King (2.3.91–8). Was the audience intended to cheer on this unexpected victory of the underdog, to take it as evidence of the guilt of York (who in the immediately previous scene laid out formally to Warwick and Salisbury his genealogical claim to the crown) or merely to laugh at the absurdity of it all?

This incident of the armourer and his apprentice, in its reversal of hierarchical categories and its guying of aristocratic modes of conflict, prefigures the Cade revolt. The Cade uprising has attracted a great deal of critical attention in recent times. It has proved a talking-point in the debate on the nature of subversiveness in Shakespearean drama: whether marginal, dissident and oppressed elements within the playworld are represented in order to be contained by the society's political orthodoxy, as the new historicists have it, or can be construed (if only retroactively) as a radical challenge to such orthodoxy, according to the cultural materialist theory.[12] In the case of Cade, it depends on the extent to which he is taken to be a creature of York. It is from York that we first hear of Jack Cade, associated with the untamed disorder of Ireland where York himself is headed at the time:

> In Ireland have I seen this stubborn Cade
> Oppose himself against a troop of kerns
> And fought so long till that his thighs with darts
> Were almost like a sharp-quilled porpentine;
> And in the end, being rescued, I have seen
> Him caper upright, like a wild Morisco,
> Shaking the bloody darts as he his bells.
>
> (3.1.360–5)

This speech brings into play an extraordinarily rich mix of ideas. Cade is 'a headstrong Kentishman', yet can disguise himself 'like a shag-haired crafty kern' so as to spy unnoticed among the Irish – in Holinshed, but not in Hall, he is himself an Irishman (3.1.360n). The monster of hardihood, stuck about with spears like a porcupine, yet resembles the Morris-dancer of traditional popular sport. 'This devil' is to be York's 'substitute' (3.1.371) during York's absence in Ireland, testing the chances of the Yorkist claim by his trumped-up pretence of being the pretender John Mortimer. But is Cade, so vividly conjured up here in York's speech, only a York-substitute to hold the stage for Act 4 and act as advance skirmisher for the full-scale dynastic war that breaks out in Act 5? Or is the Cade revolt its own different thing?

In dramatising the rebellion Shakespeare chose to give it less political credibility than it might have had. Holinshed, for instance, includes a formal set of grievances of the rebels, detailed local complaints of wrongful oppression contrary to law by agents of the King, as well as demands that the King should take back into his council 'the true lords of his roiall blood' (Holinshed, 633), notably the Duke of York, that the heirs of the Duke of Suffolk should be disinherited, and the murderers of Gloucester punished. Printed thus in the chronicle, such claims of the rebels have at least the serious authority of the written document couched in the forms of law. By contrast, it is the specifically populist mark of the Cade rebels, as Shakespeare represents them, that they are opposed to all law, all writing. 'The first thing we do', says Dick the Butcher, 'let's kill all the lawyers' (4.2.63). The luckless Clerk of Chartham dies simply because he is a clerk who can read and write, paying the price for generations of the illiterate, hanged because they could not avail themselves of the benefit of clergy. The ultimate proposal for the triumph of oracy also comes from Dick, who suggests to Cade that in the new dispensation 'the laws of England may come out of your mouth'. Cade agrees, delivering an oral edict that inaugurates the new revolutionary era:

I have thought upon it, it shall be so. Away, burn all the records of the realm; my mouth shall be the parliament of England. (4.7.10–12)

Michael Hattaway believes that for the original audience 'this surge of dispensation of justice by the people may well have been seen from a double perspective, with a degree of horror but also with a degree of glee as the privileged get their comeuppance' (2 *Henry VI*, Introduction, 31). This is a telling insight, as it corresponds to a more general doubleness in the representation of the Cade rebellion. The initial introduction of Cade has him mouthing his absurd pedigree, with the comic absurdity of it underscored by asides from henchman Dick:

    CADE My father was a Mortimer –
    DICK (*aside*) He was an honest man, and a good bricklayer.
    CADE My mother a Plantagenet –
    DICK (*aside*) I knew her well; she was a midwife.   (4.2.31–4)

The truth-telling Dick confirms to an audience that Cade's claims as royal pretender are completely false. Yet Cade here acts as a very specific parody of the Duke of York whose claim to the throne rests on just such parentage: his mother was a Mortimer, his father a Plantagenet, as he has explained earlier, at length, to his allies Warwick and Salisbury. The proletarian mimicry of that genealogical claim affirms class hierarchy by the laughter it arouses at the son of a bricklayer and midwife pretending to noble birth; but it may also undermine the position of those such as York who seriously make such pretensions.

The eruption of the commons up into a dramatic world, so far entirely peopled by the court and the aristocracy, is in one sense precontained by the very theatrical forms in which it is cast: Cade and his men speak a comic prose which confirms the normative reality of the high verse-speaking nobility. York will begin Act 5 with a majestic threat –

> From Ireland thus comes York to claim his right
> And pluck the crown from feeble Henry's head.
>
> (5.1.1–2)

– that makes the Cade revolt seem an impotent charade in retrospect. In the immediately preceding scene, an audience has watched the bogeyman rebel leader easily dispatched by a humble country squire. Yet the energy and violent destructiveness that Cade and his men bring into the play add a dimension to the action going well beyond mere comic relief. The effect of the Cade scenes is of a carnival combination of comedy and violence, mockery and menace, and modern productions illustrate the varying theatrical potential of such a combination.

Some of the inherent conservatism of the Barton–Hall *Wars* came out in the treatment of Cade. Roy Dotrice, playing the part, was made up with a bald head disfigured with a skin disease.[13] The horror of the revolt was increased by writing in an onstage murder of Sir Humphrey Stafford executed by Cade with a graphically castrating sickle movement, a sickle that was then brandished aloft as the fitting sign of the peasants' revolt. On the line 'men's wives be as *free* as heart can wish' (*Wars*, p. 92, emphasis added), Cade ripped open the dress of a bystanding woman: no Utopian sexual liberation this, but a licence to rape. When Old Clifford was sent to persuade the people to abandon their rebellion, his costume of armour and cloak, his neat beard and styled hair, added to the authority of his verse by contrast with the grotesque stocky figure of the counter-orator Cade. Barton and Hall's version of the revolt showed, if not a Renaissance horror of mob violence, at least a modern liberal democrat's terror of terror.

There were mixed views of the effect of the Cade rebels in the 1977 RSC version. 'Jack Cade's rebellion', thought one critic, 'is built up beautifully from small beginnings to general uproar; Cade is played with such understanding by James Lawrenson that it is hard not to fall in on his side.'[14] Another took a very different view: 'James Lawrenson, looking like Geronimo, is a bloodcurdling Cade, but not very funny; the horror of his scenes is there, but not the music-hall.'[15] The carnival element, even in the midst of the violence, was brought out in the 1988 *Plantagenets*. The rebels, at the highpoint of their success, cut off the heads of Lord Say and his son-in-law Sir James Cromer, and have them brought on stage on the end of two poles. The stage prop of the severed head, which first appears three scenes earlier with Margaret nursing the remains of her beloved Suffolk (4.4), is thus reduplicated. Adrian Noble took this proliferation one stage further, when he had the Cades appear in a subsequent scene with a whole harvest of heads on poles. The anarchic disorder figured by the severed head was there turned into a gruesome comic ritual.

The ESC version of the Cade rebellion was in some ways the most illuminating of all. Michael Pennington, last seen playing a silky Suffolk, reappeared as Cade with orange-dyed hair in a Union Jack singlet with a white rose at the centre. His followers waved flags and sported caps with England emblazoned on them; the banner above Cade's head wittily read FROM A JACK TO A KING. It was a National Front-style rally that Cade addressed and into which the unfortunate Clerk of Chartham accidentally wandered. This was a 1980s British way of identifying Cade's revolt as a reactionary rather than a progressive populism, bringing out the nationalist strain in Cade's rhetoric. The rebels vow 'to have the Lord Say's head, for selling the Dukedom of Maine' (4.2.137–8); when Say is captured Cade demands 'What canst thou answer to my majesty for giving up of Normandy unto Mounsieur Basimecu, the Dauphin of France?' (4.7.21–3). The motivation here is coloured by ignorant xenophobia – one of Say's offences is that he can *speak* French – but it also reminds an audience of the impact on England of defeat in the French wars. The ESC National Front version placed this as characteristic of a modern Britain that had lost an Empire but failed to find a role, working-class fascism diagnosed as a symptom of post-Imperial backlash. In the terms of Shakespeare's time, it might have been viewed as the consequence of having no foreign wars to divert and eliminate potential trouble-makers like the Cades: 'if they have no service abroad, they will make mutinies at home', as Nashe has it.[16] Either way an audience is reminded that the Cade rebellion comes after, and in the wake of, the war against France.

In some sense it is an interlude, almost a diversion, time out from the wars between England and France that precede it, and the Wars of the Roses that follow. Yet it also has its own place and significance within that dramatic continuum of conflict. The kingdom divided by faction at the top produces anarchy down below, from the armourer and his apprentice falling out over the royal claims of York and Lancaster to the countrymen of Kent all but overrunning London. The quarrels of the commons reflect the disunity of the should-be governors in the distorting mirror of comic travesty. At times proletarian insurgence is no more than an instrument of power in the hands of the already powerful, as in the rent-a-crowd violence that Warwick and Salisbury manipulate when they demand Suffolk's banishment, or in York's plans for Cade as Yorkist stand-in pretender. Yet Shakespeare, by taking additional material from the much earlier rebellions of Wat Tyler and John Ball, made of the Cade uprising a sort of generic peasants' revolt complete with Utopian egalitarianism: 'it was never merry world in England since gentlemen came up' (4.2.6–7). Cade's violently levelling topsyturvydom thus has a carnivalesque force which differentiates it alike from the grand national standoff of England against France that occupied so much of the first part of *Henry VI*, and the internecine dynastic battles which begin in Act 5 of the second part and climax in the third.

FROM ST ALBANS TO TOWTON

Three battles, across two plays, mark the outbreak of the Wars of the Roses and their escalating, degenerating violence. The action of *2 Henry VI* illustrates the proposition that politics is only war by other means, war no more than politics out in the open. The first three acts brilliantly dramatise the power play by which the one just man remaining, the 'shepherd of the flock' Duke Humphrey, is removed by the joint operation of the several factions who only want him out of the way to be at one another's throats. With Suffolk and Winchester meeting swift retribution for their complicity in Gloucester's murder, the one by the human agency of Walter Whitmore and the pirates, the other by the apparently divine nemesis of sudden illness and raving death, the board is cleared for a straight conflict of York with Lancaster. And once the smokescreen of the Cade rising has been removed that is what emerges, with York's return from Ireland in open rebellion and the elaborate formal stand-off of the Yorkist and Lancastrian leaders in 5.1, the first Battle of St Albans in 5.2.

The sequence, St Albans, Wakefield, Towton constitutes a single action, which together demonstrate the unbroken conception of the plays as a series. The V-shaped up and down of Yorkist and Lancastrian fortunes in these three battles represents in little the broader movement of the Wars of the Roses. At St Albans (*2 Henry VI*, 5.2–3) the Yorkists are victorious, an advantage they press home immediately with the invasion of the Parliament house and the effective abdication of Henry they enforce there (*3 Henry VI*, 1.1). A Lancastrian countermovement headed by Margaret and the 'northern lords' leads on to their bloody victory at Wakefield and the death of York (*3 Henry VI*, 1.2–4). This is then followed by a Yorkist recovery culminating in the decisive battle of Towton (*3 Henry VI*, 2.1–6). The pattern established by these three battles is repeated in broader terms in the rhythm of action following in the rest of *3 Henry VI*. With the accession of Edward IV to the throne and the capture of the deposed King Henry, the house of York seems to be completely dominant. But this situation is reversed by Edward's unwise marriage, the desertion of Warwick and Clarence, and the nominal reinstallation of Henry. The return to power of Lancaster does not last long, however, and with their defeat at Tewkesbury and the murder of Henry that follows, the play ends with the winter of discontent made glorious summer by the sun of York. Although *3 Henry VI*, with its constant to-and-froing of the balance of power, has some longueurs for modern audiences, and most directors have felt the need to cut it, anyone who reads right through the messy eleven years' chronicle that it dramatises, from 1460 to 1471, will be struck by the extraordinary piece of dramatic architectonics it actually is.

What is striking about the representation of the Wars of the Roses from St Albans on is the complete lack of partisanship available to an audience. England against France for Shakespeare's original audiences was us against them, and modern productions have had to struggle to try to resist such now unfashionable patriotic polarities. The Cade rising associated an audience with the upper classes in the anarchic menace of peasants' revolt, while simultaneously allowing them a kind of carnival pleasure in its popular disorder. But the Wars of the Roses, the conflict of York and Lancaster, are designed to be regarded with a purely disinterested spectatorship. An audience is engaged, is moved to excitement, to pity, to horror; yet in a conflict where there is no right to be discerned, only wrong piled upon angry wrong, stable support of one side against the other is impossible. Although we hear repeated again and again the dynastic issue over which the war is fought, whether or not York has a better claim to the throne, descended as he is through the female line from an older son of Edward III than Henry of Lancaster, the issue seems incapable of decisive resolution. York may have a stronger title but he is a rebel; Henry may have inherited a crown usurped two generations back, he may be personally weak and inadequate, but he is the reigning King.

This dynamic of force against force, with right undecidable, is first dramatised in the preliminaries to the Battle of St Albans as the allies and supporters line up on the two sides. The two sons of York appear to act as their father's 'bail' when his inveterate rival Somerset tries to arrest him; Old and Young Clifford enter to 'deny their bail' (*2 Henry VI*, 5.1.123). Salisbury and Warwick come on as heavyweight Yorkist champions, justifying their renunciation of their former allegiance to Henry on grounds of conscience. But the trading of insults back and forth between the two factions, the longstanding personal enmities between such as York and Somerset, make it apparent that conscience has very little to do with the battle which is to follow. Within the Renaissance stage convention of representing war, where the elaborate verbal build-up *is* much of the battle, the parting exchange between the young Richard of York and Young Clifford is symptomatic:

> RICHARD Fie! Charity, for shame! Speak not in spite,
>   For you shall sup with Jesu Christ tonight.
> Y. CLIFFORD Foul stigmatic, that's more than thou canst tell.
> RICHARD If not in heaven, you'll surely sup in hell.   (5.1.13–16)

Matching young contender with young contender in this last rhymed defiance is significant, as it prepares the way for a changeover of generations that takes place between the end of *2 Henry VI* and the beginning of *3 Henry VI*. In the first part of the series, York himself, then still untitled Plantagenet, was a student hothead rowing with Somerset in the Temple Garden. Although the double-time scheme of the *Henry VI* plays has each scene following on from the previous one without any lapse of time marked, York by the end of the second play is the patriarch father of sons old enough to take his part in battle. This pattern of two generations on the battlefield together is reduplicated in Salisbury and Warwick, Old and Young Clifford. The device is not only a way of representing the onward movement of history, as sons succeed to fathers in the inherited quarrel of York and Lancaster, but of dramatising the degenerative nature of the war as it spirals down into a vicious cycle of revenge.

The fight between York and Clifford, as the climactic encounter of the battle, is representative of an earlier chivalric mode of combat. Having killed one another's horses, they must grapple on foot, hand to hand and man to man. Both York and Warwick have been looking for Clifford, but York warns his ally off:

> Hold, Warwick, seek thee out some other chase,
> For I myself must hunt this deer to death.
>
> (5.2.14–15)

There can be no question of their fighting two against one. The duel begins with a proper exchange of courtesies; it ends with Clifford's resigned death-line, '*La fin couronne les oeuvres*' and York's pious envoi:

> Thus war hath given thee peace, for thou art still;
> Peace with his soul, heaven, if it be thy will.
>
> (5.2.29–30)

This is in marked contrast with the sardonic play upon mortal eschatology in the exchange of abuse between Richard and Young Clifford, quoted above, which ended the previous scene. And even more striking is Young Clifford's reaction to finding his father's body immediately after this. There has been no suggestion in the combat between York and Old Clifford that it is an unequal fight of a younger with an older man; quite the contrary, the symmetry of their contest makes them equal champions. Historically, in fact, York was four years Clifford's senior. Yet for Young Clifford it is the old age of his father which makes his death the barbarous outrage that he is determined to revenge. 'York not our old men spares; / Nor more will I their babes' (5.2.51–2). Young Clifford here prepares himself psychologically to be the merciless killer whom the audience of *3 Henry VI* will see murder the child Rutland:

> Henceforth I will not have to do with pity:
> Meet I an infant of the house of York,
> Into as many gobbets will I cut it
> As wild Medea young Absyrtis did;
> In cruelty will I seek out my fame.
>
> (5.2.56–60)

As the war goes into its second phase, the war-hardened sons of murdered fathers will abandon whatever Geneva conventions previously obtained to indulge themselves in a violence without limits.

This pattern of escalating violence and degenerating principles has been marked in all modern productions of the plays as series, though at different stages and by different means. In Jane Howell's BBC Television version it was reflected in the costuming, as the designer John Peacock explained: 'when York comes back from Ireland with his army they're all in leather, and that will get much more prominent in *Part 3*'.[17] The Barton–Hall *Wars* made the entry of the Yorkists into the Parliament house, the first scene of *3 Henry VI*, an equally important moment in the breakdown of social order. The scene opened (in the television production) with a shot of a battering-ram forcing down the door of the palace. York is in full armour as he ascends the throne. Donald Sinden in the part filled the throne with a kind of authority that David Warner as King Henry never had, but in the parley between the two which followed, the armour was always there as a reminder of the force used to occupy the royal seat. War may be politics by other means, but those other means alter the nature of the politics. The murderous impulses of the ambitious nobles involved in the conspiracy against Duke Humphrey in the early part of *2 Henry VI* had at least to be managed within the forms and rhetoric of law and due process. The forces that have been released by the beginning of *3 Henry VI* can be contained by no due forms, no principles of order, either in the court or on the battlefield.

This comes to a climactic illustration in the Battle of Wakefield with Clifford's killing of Rutland, and the Lancastrians' savage torture of York. Shakespeare had to go to both Hall and Holinshed to find the materials from which he created this horrific sequence. It is Hall who gives the fullest account of the murder of the twelve-year-old Earl of Rutland, captured by Clifford as his chaplain/tutor tried to get him away from the battlefield:

> The yong gentelman dismaied, had not a word to speake, but kneled on his knees imploryng mercy, and desiryng grace, both with holding up his handes and making dolorous countinance, for his speache was gone for feare. Save him sayde his Chappelein, for he is a princes sonne, and peradventure may do you good hereafter. With that word, the lord Clifford marked him and sayde: by Gods blode, thy father slew myne, and so wil I do the and all thy kyn, and with that woord, stacke the erle to the hart with his dagger . . . (Bullough, III, 177–8)

This was the source not only for Shakespeare's *3 Henry VI* 1.3, with the full pathos of Rutland's pleading for his life, but also for the fight between York and Clifford at St Albans, and the motivation it provides for Young Clifford's vengeance. Although the chronicle of the battle notes that Clifford died in it, there is no indication that it was York who killed him. Shakespeare, acting on the hint of Clifford's justification of his murder of the son at this later point in the narrative, created the duel between the two fathers at St Albans motivating Clifford's vengeance, which in its turn stands type of the new deadliness of the conflict.

In Hall Clifford follows up the killing of the son with insult to the (already dead) body of the father:

> Yet this cruell Clifforde, & deadly bloudsupper not content with this homicyde, or chyldkillyng, came to the place wher the dead corps of the duke of Yorke lay, and caused his head to be stryken of, and set on it a croune of paper, & so fixed it on a pole, & presented it to the Quene, not lyeng farre from the felde, in great despite, and much derision, saiyng: Madame, your warre is done, here is your kinges raunsome . . . (Bullough, III, 178)

Shakespeare found in Holinshed an alternative account that offered even better dramatic possibilities:

> Some write that the duke was taken alive, and in derision caused to stand upon a molehill, on whose head they put a garland in steed of a crowne, which they had fashioned and made of sedges or bulrushes; and having so crowned him with that garland, they kneeled downe afore him (as the Jewes did unto Christ) in scorne, saieng to him; Haile king without rule, haile king without heritage, haile duke and prince without people or possessions. (Bullough, III, 210)

From these separate materials the extraordinary *3 Henry VI*, 1.4 was created.

Shakespeare evidently wanted the Queen actually present, the leader of York's torturers; this was part of his development of her role as one of the major protagonists of the whole series, something to which I will be returning in the next chapter. The Holinshed comparison of the treatment of York with the mock crowning of Christ may have suggested, by way of Veronica's napkin, the napkin dipped in the blood of Rutland that Margaret gives to York to wipe his face. The Senecan horror of this, the sheer ingenuity of the torture, move the associations of the scene away from the Christian Passion that was its original model. It becomes a culminating moment in a revenge-cycle without real moral or spiritual significance. York is an object of pathos under the extremity of Margaret's taunting of him: even her ally Northumberland, one of the second generation sons of a father killed in the wars, is moved to pity:

> Beshrew me, but his passion moves me so
> That hardly can I check my eyes from tears.
> (1.4.150–1)

But as Margaret's tirades of deadly hatred are met with York's equally venomous rhetoric of tormented defiance, it is apparent that there is little or nothing to choose between the antagonists. It is only the contingent fortunes of battle that have left Margaret at York's mercy, rather than the other way round. This is war as it has become, with the accumulated burden of past injuries bearing down on the personal vindictiveness of those involved. Causes, principles, right, honour are all equally obsolete.

Elizabethan audiences probably had a greater appetite for staged battle-scenes than those of the twentieth century, at least to judge by the ten acts of the extremely popular *Tamburlaine*. Still, Shakespeare seems to have been conscious of the danger of monotony in an unending sequence of one bloody battle after another, and introduced into the Battle of Towton, the next after Wakefield, the contrastive scene of the King's meditation on war. A bare couple of sentences in Hall were elaborated into the opening of Henry's soliloquy: 'This deadly battayle and bloudy conflicte, continued .x. houres in doubtfull victorie. The one parte some time flowyng, and sometime ebbyng' (Bullough, III, 182).

> This battle fares like to the morning's war
> When dying clouds contend with growing light,
> What time the shepherd, blowing of his nails,
> Can neither call it perfect day nor night.
> Now sways it this way, like a mighty sea
> Forced by the tide to combat with the wind;
> Now sways it that way, like the selfsame sea
> Forced to retire by fury of the wind.
>
> (2.5.1–8)

Henry, 'chid' from the battle by his Queen and Clifford, sees it from outside as if it were a mere natural force of waves and wind completely beyond anyone's control. So far from willing on his troops to win, he can only neutrally and piously pray, 'To whom God will, there be the victory!' (2.5.15). It was on a molehill that York was placed at Wakefield in mockery of his kingly ambitions; it is on a molehill – in production always the same one however realised – that King Henry sits to contemplate his miserable failure as a ruler. Back before St Albans York had contemptuously told Henry he was not fit to be a king:

> That head of thine doth not become a crown;
> Thy hand is made to grasp a palmer's staff
> And not to grace an awful princely sceptre.
>
> (*2 Henry VI*, 5.1.96–8)

Here Henry contemplates with envy the humble life he has been denied. Between two alarum sounds of battle that frame the King's 54-line soliloquy is a still suspension of action in which the futility of power and the longing for another order of being is poignantly enacted.

It is specifically a pageant of civil war, not just any war. The passage from Hall that inspired it makes this clear: 'This conflict was in maner unnaturall, for in it the sonne fought against the father, the brother against the brother, the nephew against the uncle, and the tenaunt against his lord' (Bullough, III, 183). In that sequence of the 'unnatural' oppositions of civil war, Shakespeare focussed on son against father because of the way it meshed with other thematic configurations running through the series. In *1 Henry VI*, the heroic death of Talbot, father and son, stood as ideal of an English staunchness in war and of the truly transmitted inheritance of honour. The chivalric ideals of such as the Talbots have come to an end in *2 Henry VI* where, in the opening phase of civil war, the killing of fathers affords sons a justification for newly murderous battle-fury. The slaughter of the child Rutland, the torture of the father York, betoken a sort of personal intimacy of violence; the scene of the father-killer and son-killer acts as a summation of this process. These two are ignorant of what they do; they are merely caught up in the quarrels of their lords:

> From London by the king was I pressed forth;
> My father, being the Earl of Warwick's man,
> Came on the part of York, pressed by his master.
> (2.5.64–6)

They are human flotsam and jetsam, driven by the sea of the war imaged in Henry's speech; here, as nowhere else in the series, Shakespeare imagines ordinary men innocently entangled in the wars. The momentum that has built up from St Albans to Towton is of an ever-growing inwardness of violence beyond the control of the helpless and hopeless people involved. It will continue on for the rest of *3 Henry VI* and will only finally be altered by the refigured scheme of conflict that ends *Richard III*.

BOSWORTH: THE LAST BATTLE

In Richard Loncraine's 1996 film of *Richard III*, set in an imagined 1930s Britain, a pre-credits sequence shows us a grey-haired and trim-bearded Henry VI and his khaki-uniformed son Prince Edward in a wood-panelled country house serving as royal headquarters before the Battle of Tewkesbury. As the Prince busies himself with paperwork in the stillness of the night, a tank suddenly crashes through the wall behind him, and he is shot through the back of the head. The leading commando in the assault checks that the Prince is dead, before going in to the next room to blast the kneeling King with his machine-gun. Then, removing a gas-mask, he reveals the Hitlerian features of Richard of Gloucester/Ian McKellen. What we know as *Richard III* begins in the film proper at a York victory party, with the first half of Richard's 'soliloquy', 'Now is the winter of our discontent', a public speech of political self-congratulations delivered through a microphone to the assembled Yorkists; only the lines from 'But I that am not shap'd for sportive tricks' are spoken solus, addressed to the urinal by Richard alone in the Gents. Even as the court celebrates, dancing to a cabaret-singer's vamped-up version of 'Come live with me and be my love', the reminders of the war that has just finished are there in the hospital full of the mutilated and wounded, which Richard visits to find Lady Anne in the basement morgue mourning her dead husband Prince Edward.[18] The film *Richard III*, with its introductory lead-in gesturing back to the concluding events of *3 Henry VI*, brings home to its audience that this is to be a play set in peace-time, but also that it is a post-war play. *Richard III* is the one play of the series in which there is *no* civil war, *no* prospect of a foreign conflict, yet it is also the aftermath of those earlier wars that only Bosworth can resolve.

By the time of *Richard III* the Wars of the Roses are subject for memory, and subject for guilty memory: the guilt is something new. In *3 Henry VI* a number of major figures of the conflict – York, Clifford, Warwick – die on the battlefield, and are given the final operatic arias befitting such principal players. York dies in tortured anguish, defying his torturers; Clifford, Lancastrian loyalist to the end, regrets only the downfall of his faction that his death will bring:

> O Lancaster, I fear thy overthrow
> More than my body's parting with my soul!
> (*3 Henry VI*, 2.6.3–4)

Warwick mourns his own lost greatness in a setpiece meditation on human mortality (*3 Henry VI*, 5.2.5–28). But it is striking that none of these men, responsible for so many brutal deaths as they have been, acknowledge that responsibility with anything like contrition. By contrast, in the 'peace-time' deaths of Clarence, Rivers, Grey, Hastings, Buckingham, there is a newly insistent theme of crime and punishment as they go to execution. In that retributive pattern, spelled out formally in Queen Margaret's curses, the killing of young Prince Edward stands out as one of the outstanding crimes to be expiated, coming particularly vividly before Clarence in his nightmare vision of hell. Enacted in *3 Henry VI*, the murder of Edward might appear one more callous killing in a play where such matters have become all but routine. In *Richard III* it is re-membered as the last battlefield atrocity, summing up the whole series of such crimes going back to the savage death of Rutland. Where earlier warring characters lived by a jungle law, with might the only acknowl-edged right, in retrospective memory conscience begins to operate in those capable of conscience.

Richard himself, of course, is not of that number. His stabbing of Edward at Tewkesbury was a minor incident, natural outcome of his 'angry mood'. With as little compunction and without even the stimulus of an angry mood, he will send to their deaths all his subsequent victims – enemies, allies, brothers, nephews, wife all alike. Margaret watches with a fierce gloating glee as those responsible for the death of her son go to retribution, leaving only their killer extant:

> Richard yet lives, hell's black intelligencer,
> Only reserved their factor to buy souls
> And send them thither.
>
> (4.4.71–3)

The agent of hell, as Margaret calls him, can with more theological correctness be seen as the scourge of God, the impious implement of divine justice, visiting the sins of the guilty upon their heads before being himself destroyed. The effect of Richard, the conscienceless nemesis for others' crimes, is to make the cumulative guilt/responsibility of the civil wars to settle on himself and to allow a newly polarised conflict to emerge.

There are no battles in *Richard III* before the last battle of Bosworth. Richard kills under cover of peace: that is the essence of his part as Machiavel – 'Why, I can smile, and murder whiles I smile' (*3 Henry VI*, 3.2.182). The forms of legal due process are, ever more nominally, used for his several power purges. Clarence is executed, apparently by the King's due authority; a Scrivener is given eleven hours' employment writing out an indictment of Hastings, well in advance of Hastings' actual arrest (3.6). The way is prepared for the elimination of Lady Anne by leaking news of her illness: 'Rumour it abroad / That Anne my wife is very grievous sick' (4.2.51–2). In the next scene we hear that 'Anne my wife hath bid this world good night' (4.3.39). Only in the murder of the Princes in the Tower does Richard not even try to cover his murders with some show of law or pretext of plausibility. His peacetime reign of terror is increasingly evident as such to everyone. And the momentum is built up to ensure that, when an armed counterforce appears under the command of Richmond, it is to be welcomed as the just war to end the cycle of violence that in its final phase has gone underground, been given its last vicious twist. To ensure the maximum contrast between Richard's tyranny and the open war that will end it, Buckingham's revolt is elided. We no sooner hear of it as one more of the gathering forces mustering against Richard than it is over: 'Buckingham's army is dispersed and scattered' (4.4.519). In the chronicles considerable space is given to Buckingham's rising and the manner of his betrayal (Hall, fols. xxxix–xl; Holinshed, 744–5). But Shakespeare wanted no battle-scenes before the one big battle, and gives Buckingham one last appearance only as the final figure facing execution acknowledging the justice of his death.

Bosworth is prepared for with quite exceptional elaborateness. The gathering of the two forces under the rival leaders, the erection of the two tents, the succession of ghosts with their speeches now to Richard, now to Richmond, and finally the paired orations to the troops, deploy a massive system of theatrical symmetries to drive home all that the coming battle will mean. In the Wars of the Roses the equivalence between the two sides was a measure of their equal lack of moral justification. The appropriate metaphors voiced by the observer Henry at Towton were images of natural forces, a sea of physical power driven this way and that by wind and tide. Before Bosworth the opposing parties are those of political right against wrong, good against evil, the weight of accumulated guilt, heaped upon Richard by the ghosts of his victims, making of Richmond an avenging angel, if only by contrast. It is the measure of how altered a scene this is that Richard in his rallying cry to his troops tries so blatantly and unsuccessfully to sound the anti-French chauvinist note which worked so well back in *1 Henry VI*:

> Let's whip these stragglers o'er the seas again;
> Lash hence these overweening rags of France
>
> (5.3.329–30)

Richard's ploy here is seen as the empty rabble-rousing device it is, recalling the stigmatised prejudice of a Jack Cade rather than the heroic English staunchness of a Talbot. In spite of the fact that Richmond comes from Brittany, is an invader, and (on any impartial consideration of the evidence) had a very dubious claim to the throne, he is cast for the part of saviour against the demonised Richard.

Three scenes, some 400 lines of text, prepare for an encounter that is summarised in the briefest of stage directions:

Alarum. Enter RICHARD and RICHMOND. They fight. RICHARD is slain. Retreat and flourish. (5.5.0 SD)

Although no doubt the Elizabethan actors playing Richard and Richmond could have been relied on for a convincing piece of sword-play, and the distinguishable musical sounds of alarum and retreat would have given this its own dramatics,[19] the representation of the Battle of Bosworth is characteristic of the Shakespearean dramaturgy of war in the disproportionate amount of time and space devoted to speech and spectacle rather than fighting. Most modern productions have felt bound to make more of the last duel to the death of Richard and Richmond. The Barton–Hall *Wars* played it as a deliberately stylised conflict with a reprise of dream music used for the appearance of the ghosts. Richard was no longer visibly a human being at all but a horror-movie robot in steel with ball and chain attached to one arm, a huge sword he could hardly lift in the other hand, the crown precariously and absurdly perched on the top of his high helmet towering above the distorted armed hump of the left shoulder. Richmond, clothed in the armour of righteousness no doubt, needed to wear very little: a chain-mail throat-piece and a body covering that seemed little more than a cloak. By contrast with this, the ESC staged a battle of the titans which had both figures clad in complete medieval armour, black against gold, the more striking for the modern dress which had been used in the production up to that point.

Bosworth is climax and closure not only for *Richard III* but for the whole history play series and the wars it has dramatised. Barton and Hall, bent on enforcing an overarching ideological pattern to the sequence as a whole, made an unequivocal triumph of good over evil out of Richmond's defeat of Richard, enacted as the happy ending of the Tillyardian 'Tudor myth'. Richmond was solemnly crowned on the battlefield by the Bishop of Ely, with in the background the aged Exeter, a choric figure throughout the *Wars*, survivor of all the previous conflicts. The crowned Richmond, strongly played by Eric Porter as a mature, sincere and earnest states-man/warrior, delivered his final speech with crossed banners behind him, his head at the dead centre of the cross they made, signifying the now joined flags of the white and red roses. Again the ESC version of the same scene offers an instructive contrast. From the gladiatorial clangour of the Richmond-versus-Richard fight, there was a quick cut to the tele-vision studio where the newly installed Henry VII prepared to deliver his final speech as nation-wide address. The studio people applying the final touches to his make-up, the television monitors multiplying images of his face as he spoke, were all designed to make an audience extremely sceptical of the political rhetoric being transmitted:

> England hath long been mad, and scarred herself;
> The brother blindly shed the brother's blood;
> The father rashly slaughtered his own son;
> The son, compelled, been butcher to the sire.
> All this divided York and Lancaster,
> Divided, in their dire division.
> Oh, now let Richmond and Elizabeth,
> The true succeeders of each royal house,
> By God's fair ordinance conjoin together.
>
> (5.5.23–31)

These lines that encapsulate the images of past civil wars and inaugurate peace, in Bodganov's version became the PR commonplaces of any new political dispensation.

The play series as a whole shows an organic interrelationship between the several forms of war that follow in sequence: the contrast between the us-and-them battles with the French and the us-versus-us division of civil war; the disturbing potential disruptiveness of popular revolt; and the internecine rivalries of dynastic conflict. There is a degenerating spiral of violence through increasingly bitter hatreds over the generations, finally played out with the upturn towards a new political order. This, however, need not correspond to a single tendentious progression illustrating the providential political pattern postulated by Tillyard, and enacted in the Barton–Hall *Wars of the Roses*. Some sort of degenerative dynamic is rep-resented in virtually all productions of the plays as a series, but it does not have to correspond to one grand narrative. The ambiguous figure of Pucelle, the carnival energies of the Cade revolt, the passion of the tortured York, the King's meditation at Towton, all admit of different sorts of representation, in part because of the heterogeneous source materials from which they were derived. It is the very variousness of war, the changing emotions it evokes, and the way in which from play to play and battle to battle it is reconceived, that makes of the *Henry VI – Richard III* series the extraordinary theatrical epic rediscovered in the modern period.

CHAPTER FOUR

The emergence of character

For Harold Bloom there is little to be said for or about Shakespeare's first series of history plays. Of the 745 pages of *Shakespeare: the Invention of the Human*, the three *Henry VI* plays together only get 7, *Richard III* a further 9.[1] It is hardly surprising that this should be so. Given the thesis of Bloom's book that it was Shakespeare who invented the type of human individuality forming the modern conception of character, given that Bloom's argument leads to the summit of Shakespeare's achievement in the supremely characterised characters Hamlet and Falstaff, it is understandable that the *Henry VI – Richard III* plays should not detain him longer. For Bloom, character must be manifest in the uniqueness of a dramatic personality's speech; the inimitable utterances of a stage Hamlet or Falstaff resonate with the limitless possibilities of a suggested interiority. In these terms the figures of the early history series have nothing to offer – at best an offhand appreciation of the 'rancid charm' of Joan of Arc who is nonetheless only 'a smudgy cartoon compared with the human magnificence of . . . Falstaff'.[2] Bloom's defiantly romantic vision of character demands that it should be a freestanding subjectivity suggested in speech and action. Such a reading necessarily denies what represents a double source of interest in the observation of character in the early history series. One is Shakespeare's development out of latency of the chroniclers' protocharacters; the other is the evolution over the series of plays of roles whose potential depends on duration through time, rather than the immediacy of Bloom's declared characterisation.

What might 'character' be in Shakespeare, if it is not Bloom's instantly recognizable individuation, the very model of our modern sense of the human? Alan Sinfield offers one definition of the phenomenon as the appearance of a 'continuous or developing interiority or consciousness'.[3] Sinfield acknowledges the existence of such a phenomenon, but analyses the breaking points or 'faultlines' in major Shakespearean characters, Desdemona or Lady Macbeth, where the illusion of a coherent subjectivity founders. My concern in this chapter rather is to explore how, in the figures of the early history plays, the principle of 'characterisation' emerged in the first place out of the chronicle narrative. Character was not the business of the chronicler. An individual action might provoke a strong response, as when the previously uncharacterised Clifford is referred to as a 'deadly bloudsupper' by Hall following on his merciless killing of Rutland (Bullough, III, 178). But by and large moral judgements, analysis of individual conduct or temperament, are opportunistic and ad hoc, frequently inconsistent from one passage to another. The nature of events in action demands commentary that is never addressed towards the uniqueness of the individual and his/her actions, always towards the principles informing such actions, the exemplars that they represent.

In dramatising, Shakespeare was bound to shift the focus in so far as what an audience would see were the agents of history, not the chroniclers' serial narration of events. That does not by any means demand what Harold Bloom would call character. The ambitious nobles of the weak King Henry's court need hardly be differentiated from one another except as the action requires. So, for instance, Suffolk would be just one more wheel-of-fortune example of rise and fall, were it not for Shakespeare's decision to write in for him a love-affair with Queen Margaret. (The only chronicle suggestion for this is his crucial involvement in arranging the Henry–Margaret marriage, and some sexually neutral references to him as the 'Quenes dearlynge', a man the Queen 'entierly loved' (Hall, fol. clviii).) In many cases the history series made for a serially expendable cast of characters. Hence, for instance, the lack of reference to Talbot in *2 Henry VI* that has figured so largely in scholarly debates on the plays' order of composition. Talbot's life and death are structurally vital to *1 Henry VI*, but history moves on and by the second play the drama needs him no more. Shakespeare peoples his scenes casually, and as casually unpeoples them. In Hall two bystanders are recorded as having been killed in the incident where Salisbury received his mortal wound (Bullough, III, 55); a Sir William Glansdale and Sir Thomas Gargrave appear accordingly in *1 Henry VI*, 1.4, deep in conversation with their commander about the fortifications of Orléans. They are there only to be shot minutes later, as Odysseus' companions in the Cyclops' cave were there only to be eaten.

From such merely animated names to the major players in the series – Somerset, Suffolk, Warwick – Shakespeare characterises more than the chroniclers do, but only so far as he needs to characterise for the purposes of his narrative, or as the legendary afterlives of his historical figures demand. In some cases it was the business of Shakespeare to render on stage the historical reputations that his audience already knew. So, for example, Warwick the Kingmaker might not have been widely known by that specific soubriquet in Shakespeare's time,[4] but his kingmaking capacity was well established as the measure of his greatness. In *The Mirror for Magistrates* he is made to exclaim:

> Hast thou ever heard of subject under sonne
> That plaaste and baaste his soveraynes so oft,
> By enterchaunge, now low, and than aloft?[5]

So already in *2 Henry* VI, 2.2 Warwick is made to foresee his own future as kingmaker –

> My heart assures me that the Earl of Warwick
> Shall one day make the Duke of York a king

– and York can reciprocate:

> Richard shall live to make the Earl of Warwick
> The greatest man in England but the king.
> (2.2.78–9, 81–2)

The audience is there to watch Warwick become the figure history has pre-assigned him to be. This is the implication also for the character of Talbot in Nashe's famous accolade: 'How would it have ioyed brave *Talbot* (the terror of the French) to thinke that after he had lyne two hundred yeares in his Tombe, hee should triumphe againe on the Stage.' 'The terror of the French' is like a Homeric fixed epithet in the collective memory of Talbot; the pleasure of *1 Henry VI* is to see him in action, doing his terrorising once again.

In dramatising the chronicles, Shakespeare moves towards characterisation in so far as the agents of historical action are shown defined in and by that action, action that is seen to be specifically their doing. Yet he is still working within the idiom of stylised, rhetorically based conceptions of character. And inconsistency is not necessarily a concern. Character remains subordinate to the needs of narrative; Shakespeare remains loyal to his chronicle sources, sometimes stubbornly so. This means that individual figures might be in some sense discontinuous from play to play. G. K. Hunter, speaking of the Queen who appears in all four parts of the series, puts the case that 'Each Margaret (*Henry VI*I, II, III and *Richard III*) is in fact a different Margaret, accommodated to a different structure and operating in terms of a different range of relationships and effects.'[6] Yet even if this is true, in creating dramatic figures who appear over a whole series of plays, Shakespeare affords a tempting opportunity for modern actors, directors and audiences to watch a process of development, of the emergence of character. As Peter Saccio points out, the Elizabethan audience's 'fundamental model for character change was religious conversion, the sudden descent of grace. A modern audience expects a slower process: our models for character change derive from the theories of Freud or Piaget or Erikson about childhood and maturation.'[7] Added to this there is the inheritance of ideas of the individual formed by experience derived from the nineteenth-century *Bildungsroman*, and the theatrical influence of Stanislavskian 'building a character'; the result is a multiply conditioned modern expectation that there should be 'through-lines' of growth and change in dramatic personae. What Shakespeare's text provides may be a series of successive stills, images of the 'characters' embedded within the specific scenes and situations in which they appear. What modern directors have done is movie-making: creating continuity and development, smoothing into an aetiology of character the discontinuously characterised figures of the text.

The object of this chapter is to trace the effect of the double emergence of character in the *Henry VI– Richard III* plays: character as it emerged out of the set reputations and stray suggestions of the chronicle material, and character as it emerges from the extended dramatic existence afforded by the series as series. Five of the central figures may stand to illustrate the process and its implications: the Lord Protector, Humphrey Duke of Gloucester, who is so important throughout *1 Henry VI* and whose death provides the climax of *2 Henry VI*; Richard Plantagenet, Duke of York, the secret or declared pretender to the throne for so much of the three *Henry VI* plays; King Henry and Queen Margaret, the only characters to appear in all four of the plays, although in the case of Henry only as a corpse and a ghost in *Richard III*; and Richard III himself, as he works his way up to that title.

HUMPHREY OF GLOUCESTER, RICHARD OF YORK

The Duke of Gloucester became in his posthumous afterlife almost statutorily the 'noble duke', 'Good Duke Humphrey'. In the preamble to his tragedy in *The Mirror for Magistrates* (where he is one of the very few victims of fortune treated as wholly blameless for his death) he is identified as 'commonlye called the good Duke'.[8] Shakespeare casts him as the last surviving one of the high-minded and public-spirited brothers of the heroic Henry V, the antagonist of the late king's illegitimate uncle, the Bishop of Winchester. In *2 Henry VI* he alone withstands the country's descent into the chaos of faction fighting, and it is to eliminate this pillar of public order that the factions conspire to have him murdered. However, Gloucester does not consistently bear this character from the beginning, either in the sources or in Shakespeare's drama. The chronicles, for instance, bring out at some length how unlucky or unwise Gloucester was in his choice of wives. His first wife Jacquet he persisted in claiming, even at the cost of an international war, though she was married to the Duke of Brabant. When a papal judgement went against him in this dispute, his second choice was just as bad from Hall's point of view:

Wherfore he, by wanton affeccion blinded, toke to his wife Elianor Cobham doughter to the lord Cobham, of Sterberow, whiche before (as the fame went) was his soveraigne lady and paramour, to his great slaunder and reproche. And if he wer unquieted with his other pretensed wife, truly he was tenne tymes more vexed, by occasion of this woman . . . (Hall, fols. xciii–xciii v)

Shakespeare suppresses the first wife altogether, and makes his Gloucester blameless in the misconduct of Eleanor; her dealings in witchcraft, which bring her into disgrace and make him vulnerable to his enemies, are completely without his sanction. But at the start of *1 Henry VI* Gloucester is not unequivocally the exemplary good Duke that he is to become.

It is after all Gloucester who is the first to break the ceremonious decorum of King Henry's funeral, the scene with which the play (and the series) starts. The chief mourners, Bedford, Gloucester, Exeter, each contribute their set speech of lamentation to the choric threnody. But when Winchester joins in with a pious paean of praise, the mere mention of the Church is enough to provoke Gloucester to a snort of rage:

> WINCHESTER . . . The church's prayers made him so prosperous.
> GLOUCESTER The church! Where is it? Had not churchmen prayed,
>   His thread of life had not so soon decayed.   (1.1.32–4)

And they are off, snarling at one another in a startlingly unseemly way, provoking Bedford to remonstrate: 'Cease, cease these jars and rest your minds in peace.' The disrupted funeral of Henry V, the first of many such aborted ceremonies in the series, stands in for the inability of the King's kinsmen to get along, the fatal propensity for royal infighting which will be the downfall of England. And it is the good Duke Humphrey in this scene who begins the squabble.

The scales of audience approval would have been tipped towards Gloucester, in so far as his opponent here and throughout is the Bishop of Winchester. The Bishop is to become a cardinal – by 1.4 in the First Folio he already is a cardinal, even though in a later scene confusingly we see him acquire his cardinal's hat – and cardinals had an almost uniformly bad reputation on the English Protestant stage of the time as the very types of corrupt Catholic temporal power. In a state-versus-church confrontation, with Gloucester opposed to the unmistakably wicked Winchester, there could be no doubt as to where audience sympathies were intended to lie. Yet it takes two to quarrel, and in the formulation of the chronicle the Gloucester–Winchester feud is seen as an almost impersonal force for destruction:

In this season fell a greate division in the realme of England, which, of a sparcle was like to growe to a greate flame: For whether the bishop of Winchester . . . envied the authoritee of Humfrey duke of Gloucester Protector of the realme, or whether the duke had taken disdain at the riches and pompous estate of the bishop, sure it is that the whole realme was troubled with them and their partakers . . . (Bullough, III, 48)

Shakespeare finds a theatrical equivalent for this even-handed rendering of the nobles' divisiveness in the blue coats and the tawny coats, the liveries of the followers of the Duke and Bishop who slug it out in *1 Henry VI*, 1.3. The anarchic faction fighting marked by these opposing colours has a Tweedledum-Tweedledee-like interchangeability that anticipates the Wars of the Roses themselves. As there is to be no clear right and wrong, only a disastrous fission, in the opposition of the red rose to the white, so, in the dynamics of the stage, Gloucester's blue coats are as culpable as Winchester's tawny coats in the spectacle of their riot.

As *1 Henry VI* proceeds, this sense of Gloucester's quarrelsome feuding diminishes and he becomes increasingly the upright public servant seeking the good of his country, unlike the corrupt prelate Winchester, whom we see paying off the papal legate for his cardinalate (5.1). By *2 Henry VI*, the situation has been re-figured and all of the court is opposed to Gloucester, each for his/her own self-interested ends. To Winchester's longstanding enmity is added the power-hungry ambitions of the Queen and Suffolk, Somerset and Buckingham, and the long-term aims of Richard of York. It is in the interest of all of them to snare 'the shepherd of the flock, / That virtuous prince, the good Duke Humprey' (2.3.73–4). Yet even here there are oddities in the characterisation of Gloucester, such as the St Albans scene (2.1). In this scene there resurfaces once again the personal feud between Gloucester and Winchester at its most undignified. Their traded insults in asides end in a challenge to a duel. Gloucester's muttered threats, which have to be disguised from the would-be peacemaking king, are hardly very edifying coming from the statesmanlike Lord Protector:

> Now by God's mother, priest, I'll shave your crown for this,
> Or all my fence shall fail.
>
> (2.1.51–2)

This may have gone down well with the anti-papist element in the original audience, but for Gloucester the good governor it seems distinctly indecorous.

There are ways to play the part that can make sense of the apparent discontinuities in the character of Gloucester. 'There goes our Protector in a rage', the Cardinal observes slyly, when Gloucester exits in the first scene of *2 Henry VI*, exits specifically in order not to get involved in a further quarrel: 'If I longer stay / We shall begin our ancient bickerings' (1.1.140–1). This can be read as a sort of keynote to the character. Gloucester has a temper he cannot always control but, to his credit, he tries. As the (palpably false) accusations against him mount in a later scene, he simply leaves, returning fifteen lines later:

> Now, lords, my choler being overblown
> With walking once about the quadrangle,
> I come to talk of commonwealth affairs.
>
> (1.3.147–9)

A Lord Protector accustomed to command, moved at times by uncontrollable gusts of anger, especially when his honest and direct nature is provoked by the deceits of the corrupt: such a characterisation can make sense of Gloucester at loggerheads with the Cardinal while maintaining his position as the 'good Duke'.

So it seemed to work as played by David Burke in Jane Howell's BBC Television production. Gloucester's tender love for his wife in their one scene alone together was made convincing by a flare of his temper at her overreaching ambition –

> Nay, Eleanor, then must I chide outright:
> Presumptuous dame, ill-nurtured Eleanor

– only to die back immediately into a tired gentleness when she bridled at his reproof: 'Nay, be not angry; I am pleased again' (*2 Henry VI*,

1.2.41–2, 55). In Burke's version of the Lord Protector, the habit of command bordered on a sort of overconfidence in his powers of control. In *1 Henry VI* when the proposition that Henry should marry Margaret was first mooted by Suffolk, Gloucester practically laughed off the idea:

> You know, my lord, your highness is betrothed
> Unto another lady of esteem:
> How shall we then dispense with that contract
> And not deface your honour with reproach?
>
> (5.5.26–9)

He is completely taken aback to discover that Henry, weak and malleable as he seems to be, is capable of going his own way and making his own decision.

That is one naturalising way of making the character of Gloucester look convincingly consistent. Barton and Hall's *Wars of the Roses*, however, demanded a much more radical recasting of the part. In Barton's compression of much of the first two parts of *Henry VI* into a single play, he wanted to show that 'The central action concerns Henry's relationship with Gloucester and their ultimate failure to help one another. Gloucester himself is the principal character' (*Wars*, xviii). In order to supply a political and psychological masterplan for the play – and the series – Gloucester was re-written into the wise father-figure whom Henry in his weakness and ignorance betrays. This was to compensate for what Barton saw as the worrying 'lack of depth, development or interplay of character among the principals'. So, in an invented sequence, Gloucester proposes a principle of majority verdict in council debate, with the King retaining an overriding veto when necessary (*Wars, Henry VI*, Scene 6), as a means of avoiding political feuds while training the young ruler up for the power of kingship. In due course this is seen to misfire, when the council vote is packed against Gloucester himself, and the King is too weak to use his royal authority to protect him. Henry's guilt at having been responsible for Gloucester's fall and death, his awareness that he has failed his true protector and adviser, then provided a dynamic for the future development of Henry's character (which in the Shakespearean text was judged by Barton to be not 'complex, merely wet' (*Wars*, xviii)). But in order to provide this dramatically productive characterisation of Gloucester as father-tutor to the King, it was necessary to 'lose most of the bickering between Gloucester and Winchester' (*Wars*, xix) including the late challenge to a duel in the St Albans scene. Humphrey of Gloucester in the Barton–Hall version is the 'good Duke' 1960s style.

Gloucester, inherited by Shakespeare from the chronicles with a largely consistent reputation, appearing in the first two of the four-play series, presents relatively simple problems for modern directors or actors; it is not hard to find a clear character line for him, even if in the case of Barton and Hall, for strategic reasons, it took a fairly major overhaul. Richard of York, the main contender for the throne and a principal protagonist across three plays, is another matter. Again a contrast between the Barton–Hall and the Howell BBC Television conceptions of the figure may supply a starting-point for the issues. We first meet York in the Temple Garden scene followed immediately by his encounter with the dying Mortimer, adding the sense of dynastic deprivation to the injury sustained in the confrontation with Somerset. In the *Wars of the Roses* version, the enfeebled Mortimer (Charles Thomas) was made up with warts and boils on his face; feverish and desperate, he panted out his legacy of vengeance and ambition to York. At the moment of his death, a towering Donald Sinden playing York looked down at him from the foot of the bed, and spoke a half-contemptuous epitaph:

> Here dies the dusky torch of Mortimer,
> Chok'd with ambition of the meaner sort.
> *(Wars, 12)*

The choking gasps of the dying pretender associated Mortimer himself with the 'ambition of the meaner sort' now quenched. An audience was left in no doubt that, with York, that meaner ambition was now to be translated into a grand major key.

By contrast, Bernard Hill, in the equivalent scene of Howell's *1 Henry VI*, was a very youthful York deeply moved by his dying uncle's speech. A long-held close-up, while the dynastic claims of the Yorkists were enunciated, juxtaposed the white-haired, blind head of the aged Mortimer (Tenniel Evans) with the anguished young face of York. At the moment of death, Hill turned to the camera with an expression of genuine grief and anger, unequivocally directed out towards those responsible for Mortimer's death:

> Here dies the dusky torch of Mortimer,
> Choked with ambition of the meaner sort.
> (2.5.123–4)

The ambitions of the house of Lancaster were those of the 'meaner sort' extinguishing the light of the noble and true cause of the Mortimers, the cause descending to York as its heir. York's youth in this scene was in line with Howell's overall strategy for the series, progressing from an adolescent atmosphere of war as play here in *1 Henry VI*, to the deadly grown-up seriousness of the civil wars to follow. But its local effect was to render humanly sympathetic, at this its point of origin, York's ambition for the throne.

The attitude towards the Yorkist claim in the chronicles is necessarily ambiguous. The very structure of Hall's chronicle, in particular, celebrating as it did in its title 'the union of the two noble and illustre famelies of Lancastre and Yorke', meant that the struggle between the contending families could not be represented as having clear right on one side or the other. The dynastic case of the Yorkists based on their descent (albeit through the female line) from Lionel Duke of Clarence, an older son of Edward III than John of Gaunt, ancestor of the Lancastrians, was itself a strong one. On the other hand, due succession of the crown through two generations from the usurping Henry IV gave Henry VI a secure right of possession. In Hall's chronicle, Richard is represented as only beginning to move towards establishing his right to the throne in 1448 after the death of Gloucester, and only because of the political situation of the time:

Rychard duke of Yorke, beyng greatly alied by his wyfe, to the chief peres and potentates of the Realme, over and besyde his awne progenye and greate consanguinitie, perceivyng the Kyng to be a ruler not Ruling, & the whole burden of the Realme, to depend in the ordinaunces of the Quene & the Duke of Suffolke, began secretly to allure to his frendes of the nobilitie, and privatly declared to them, hys title and right to the Crowne. (Bullough, III, 108)

There is no attempt here – or elsewhere in the chronicles – to adjudicate on that 'title and right' itself. Rather, the power vacuum created by the King's weakness and the downfall of Gloucester, the ascendancy of the Queen and Suffolk, create a situation where it is possible, even necessary, for York to make a bid for the crown. Whatever the rights and wrongs of the dynastic issue, the rivalry between York and Lancaster is a disaster for the country, a disaster brought about as much by the failure of Henry's government as by the political ambitions of York.

Now Shakespeare, in electing for dramatic purposes to 'seed' York in the first play of the series, and show the origins of the Wars of the Roses unhistorically early in the 1420s, creates the potential for reading the character in the two different ways of Barton and Hall, on the one hand, and Howell on the other. Donald Sinden was the great pretender from the beginning, his motives muffled from public view for a time but always apparent to the audience. Bernard Hill was a callow youth who, at a moment of vulnerability following his humiliation by Somerset, is given what feels like a just cause for seeking revenge on behalf of himself and his mistreated uncle. It is only by degrees that he will grow into the feud-hardened political contender. There are cues for both character trajectories in the text. York, following the chronicle, is shown fighting long and hard as Regent in France, so that when the corrupt Cardinal announces negotiations for a peace treaty, there may be a genuine note of patriotic outrage in his response: 'Is all our travail turned to this effect?' (*1 Henry VI*, 5.4.102). York's bitter sense of injury at the disadvantageous match between Henry and Margaret involves resentment at the loss to the kingdom – *his* kingdom. The warrior who meets Old Clifford on the battlefield at St Albans is a man of heroic chivalry, even if from the loyalist Clifford's point of view a rebel. As suggested in the last chapter, York may be seen to represent a standard of honour in contrast to the generation coming after him: at least he *wants* to keep his oath to Henry allowing him life tenure of the crown – it is his wholly power-hungry sons who persuade him to break it. There is thus material in the text for a reading of York as a man of some principle, understandably driven to claim the crown by a sense both of personal injury and of public wrong.

Yet, particularly in *2 Henry VI*, there is also a portrait of York as that most feared of Elizabethan stage bogeymen, the underhand, scheming usurper. The very first scene exposes the power politics lying behind the court assembled to celebrate the marriage of Henry to Margaret: Gloucester against Winchester, Buckingham and Somerset against both Gloucester and Winchester, Salisbury and Warwick for Gloucester, and in the end of it all – York for himself. The structure of the scene, with the successive peel-off of the several factions leaving the stage, gives theatrical dominance to the character who remains to soliloquise at length. This speech represents a dramatisation of the chronicle's account, quoted earlier, of how York came first to pursue his claim to the throne in 1448 after the death of Gloucester. But what is deployed here is a language of covert ambition and conspiratorial energy that is the standard Elizabethan idiom of the power-driven hero-villain. His choice of faction is purely strategic, his object is his own:

> And therefore I will take the Nevilles' part
> And make a show of love to proud Duke Humphrey,
> And, when I spy advantage, claim the crown –
> For that's the golden mark I seek to hit.
>
>   (1.1.237–40)

In point of fact, he will take part in the conspiracy against 'proud Duke Humphrey' and assent to his death, leaving the Nevilles to take revenge on the other conspirators. And in his second major soliloquy, coming at a pivotal point of the play after Gloucester's murder has been plotted with his connivance, his voice and tone are those of the Macbeths to come:

> Now, York, or never, steel thy fearful thoughts
> And change misdoubt to resolution:
> Be that thou hop'st to be, or what thou art
> Resign to death – it is not worth th'enjoying.
>
> (3.1.331–4)

The ambivalence of the part of York is in some sense structural. The chroniclers left the issue of the Yorkist right to the throne an open question; they were almost bound to do that, given that a part of the legitimacy of the Tudor dynasty under which they lived derived from that claim – it was Henry Tudor's marriage to Elizabeth of York that gave substance to his otherwise distinctly shaky genealogical pretensions. Yet a conservative tilt to the chronicle narration leaves the account of York's open challenge for the kingship shocked and uneasy. After the defeat of the Lancastrians in 1460, York entered London

> with a sword borne naked before him, and toke his lodgynge in the kynges awne palayce, wherupon the common people babbeled, that he should be Kyng, & that kyng Henry should no longer reigne. Durynge the tyme of this Parliamente, the duke of Yorke with a bolde countenaunce, entered into the chamber of the peres, and sat downe in the trone royall, under the clothe of estate (which is the kynges peculiar seate) . . . (Bullough, III, 173)

Hall here may not be denying York's dynastic entitlement; what follows is York's speech making his claim in fullest and clearest form. But there is anxiety about the naked sword as token of conquest, about the idea that popular opinion – 'the common people babbeled' – should have a part in the transfer of power, and at the lèse-majesté of York's occupation of the sacred spaces reserved for the King. The dramatic version of this in Shakespeare is the armed invasion of the Parliament-house, the modern production image the battering-ram splintering the locked doors of that Parliament. The history plays may not constitute a Tillyardian monolith of conservative ideology, but Shakespeare carries through from the chronicles a strain of fear at the disruption of the established state that makes York, the pretender to the throne, a darkened figure.

The ambiguous standing of York derived in part from the chronicles, but Shakespeare made of it something different by his dramatisation of a human career across three plays from young manhood to death on the battlefield. However it may be construed in individual performances, we are shown in succession the young hothead quarrelling in the Temple Garden, the Regent at war in France, the patriarch father of the three fierce sons who back him in his claim to the throne, the captured soldier in defeat facing torture and execution. To follow through these vicissitudes of a stage figure is to engage with a human life in action, to see it change and take shape. In production this necessarily involves a gradual ageing, the visible alterations in form and bearing that come with the transition from one time of life to another. The degree of sympathy accorded York in his evolution into the declared challenger for the crown, the balance between principled self-belief and unprincipled self-seeking, will vary from production to production. But York's continued presence is a continued animation of the action, so that an audience watching him can feel what it is to live in time through history. This need not have a sharp specificity of individual 'character', the specificity that we associate with later Shakespearean characterisation. Yet it makes for a complex, weighted sense of York's life as it comes to its end in the final confrontation with Margaret, whether that scene is played as grandly heroic in suffering or stoically enduring. More of that presently, when we look at the significance of this scene in the depiction of his antagonist.

KING HENRY AND QUEEN MARGARET

Two modern adaptations, the 1960s *Wars of the Roses* of Barton and Hall, and the 1980s *Wars of the Roses* of the English Shakespeare Company, compressed the three *Henry VI* plays into two, and both chose to end their first play at the same point, drawing upon material from the fourth act of *1 Henry VI*. Both RSC and ESC concluded with Queen Margaret mourning over the severed head of Suffolk, and with Henry's lines:

> Come, wife, let's in and learn to govern better;
> For yet may England curse my wretched reign.
> (4.9.48–9)

In the original text, this comes in the thick of ongoing action – the Cade revolt is just coming to an end, York has menacingly returned from Ireland. The adaptations make of it instead a point of rest, reserving the Cade revolt and the York rebellion for the next play. It represents in this rearrangement a gloomy reflection on the story of the reign of Henry

VI so far, and a doleful prognostication of what is to come. It also stands as a breakpoint in the marriage of Henry and Margaret. Suffolk is dead, who made that marriage and was third party to it throughout; Margaret mourns openly for his death, barely reproved by Henry. Gloucester, Henry's protector and wise counsellor, is dead, a death Margaret helped to bring about. Henry's lines are a gesture towards a new start with Margaret, a gesture that (in the case of the ESC version) she signally ignored: June Watson playing Margaret simply walked past Henry who, left alone, put on his glasses and turned to his book. For Barton and Hall, for Bogdanov, for most modern productions of the plays, the unhappy reign of Henry VI is integrally bound up with the dysfunctional marriage of the King and Queen.[9]

For much of the forty years of what Hall calls 'the Troubleous Season of Kyng Henry the Sixt' the King himself is not really there. It is not just that, with his accession at nine months old, there is the long period of his minority when the realm was bound to be ruled by protectors and regents. Even after Henry was grown up, his incapacity for government meant that much of the chronicle is taken up with the doings of his ministers and generals, the rival contenders for power around him, rather than with his actions or reflections on his character. Late on, commenting on the brevity of his restoration by Warwick in 1470–1, Hall speculates on why Henry should have been so consistently unfortunate:

> This yll chaunce & misfortune, by many mens opinons happened to hym, because he was a man of no great wit, suche as men comonly call an Innocent man, neither a foole, neither very wyse, whose study always was more to exell, other in Godly livynge & vertuous example, then in worldly regiment, or temporall dominion, in so much, that in comparison to the study & delectacion that he had to vertue and godliness, he little regarded, but in manner despised al worldly power & temporal authoritie . . . But hys enemies ascribed all this to hys coward stommack, affirming that he was a man apt to no purpose, nor mete for any enterprise, were it never so small . . . Other there be that ascribe his infortunitie, onely to the stroke & punishment of God, affirming that the kyngdome, which Henry the .iiii. hys grandfather wrongfully gat, and uniustly possessed agaynst kyng Richard the .ii. & his heyres could not by very divyne iustice, longe contynew in that iniurious stocke: And that therfore God by his divine providence, punished the offence of the grandfather, in the sonnes sonne. (Hall, fols. ccx–ccx v)

This, typically for the chronicles, gave Shakespeare a menu of options for characterising the king whose reign he was to dramatise over three plays. He was a holy fool, too pious for politics; he was a feeble and inadequate man; he was being punished for the sins of his grandfather, the illegitimate usurper Henry IV.

The keynote for Henry is struck with his very first speech in Act 3 of *1 Henry VI*, after he has been allowed two acts as a decent amount of stage time in which to grow up. He addresses his two outstandingly quarrelsome relations:

> Uncles of Gloucester and of Winchester,
> The special watchmen of our English weal,
> I would prevail, if prayers might prevail,
> To join your hearts in love and amity.
>
> (3.1.65–8)

'I would prevail, if prayers might prevail': Henry begins as he is going to go on, in hypothetical conditional mood, caught between an earnest belief in prayer and the pre-consciousness of its practical inefficacy. The effect is, if anything, worse when he makes an effort to speak with authority as, for instance, in his peace-making efforts in the quarrel between Vernon and Bassett, footmen in Somerset and York's battle of the roses:

> Let me be umpire in this doubtful strife.
> I see no reason, if I wear this rose, [*Putting on a red rose*]
> That any one should therefore be suspicious
> I more incline to Somerset than York:
> Both are my kinsmen, and I love them both.
>
> (4.1.151–5)

It is a fine moment in the theatre, as the King, bent on illustrating the absurd arbitrariness of the emblems, genuinely hesitates between red and white. The private exchange between York and Warwick after the King's exit marks the point:

> WARWICK My Lord of York, I promise you the king
>   Prettily, methought, did play the orator.
> YORK And so he did, but yet I like it not
>   In that he wears the badge of Somerset.
> WARWICK Tush, that was but his fancy; blame him not:
>   I dare presume, sweet prince, he thought no harm.　　(4.1.174–9)

No doubt Warwick is right, Henry 'thought no harm', but he has no conception of the political significance of his action immediately detected by York. The King's 'fancy' in choosing the red rose is written into the historical script of the York-versus-Lancaster wars to come.

It is the inadequacy of Henry rather than the illegitimacy of his title that is most prominent in the first two *Henry VI* plays. It is not until the Parliament scene of *3 Henry VI* that the King, under the force of York's dynastic arguments supported by the hitherto loyal Exeter, admits in an aside 'I know not what to say, my title's weak' (1.1.134). Shakespeare never unequivocally endorses the third of Hall's possible explanations for Henry's misfortunes, divine providence revenging the wrongs of his grandfather. The justice of the King's right to the throne must be left as undecidable as that of York. However, between the two other readings of Henry, holy fool or just fool, a balance is struck allowing different performance possibilities.

It was the piety of Peter Benson, playing Henry in Jane Howell's BBC Television version, that was stressed from the start, enhanced by having Benson, as an unnamed hooded monk, sing a dirge for Henry V in the opening funeral ceremony. Ralph Fiennes in Adrian Noble's *Plantagenets*, Paul Brennen in the ESC *Wars*, David Oyelowo in Michael Boyd's *This England* production, came over rather as idealists with a misplaced belief in the power of principle in politics, gradually ground down by circumstances. In the 1960s *Wars of the Roses*, the development of David Warner, gauche and awkward in the opening scenes, his graceless movements suggesting his unkingliness, was suggested by changes in bearing and costume. With the addition of a cloak to the plain robe that he wore from the beginning, he was made to look positively friar-like, and he grew into a saintly authority making of his death a full Christian martyrdom. He sat in meditation before a cross, as if in intimate companionship with the almost equally contemplative Judas-like Richard (Ian Holm) who was about to kill him. What Shakespeare most distinctively added to the figure of Henry, besides the two notes of weakness and holiness variously emphasised in modern performance, was the inadequate sexuality that makes his relationship to Margaret so central.

There is one suggestion of Henry's impotence in the chronicles. Hall records in 1453 the birth of an heir to Henry and Margaret, 'whose mother susteyned not a little slaunder and obloquye of the common people, saying that the kyng was not able to get a chyld, and that this was not his sonne' (Hall, fol. clxxvi v). The parentage of Prince Edward is never really questioned in Shakespeare, but this passage may have prompted his introduction of Margaret's infidelity. Elsewhere, in Holinshed, testimony is offered of Henry's sexual modesty:

Plate 7   Richard of Gloucester (Ian Holm) and Henry VI (David Warner),
Wars of the Roses

having in Christmasse a shew of yoong women with their bare breasts laid out
presented before him, he immediatlie departed with these words: Fie, fie, for
shame; forsooth you be too blame. (Holinshed, 691)

Girlie-shows, fifteenth-century style, were not to the taste of Henry VI.
A lack of manliness associated with political weakness, a suggestion of
impotence, a pious abhorrence of unchastity, all may have contributed
to suggest Henry's sexual deficiency. And Suffolk's role in arranging the
marriage of Henry and Margaret, his position as the King's proxy in
marrying the Queen in France, the chronicle reference to him as her
'dearlynge', may have produced the lover to supply the needs that the
King could not.

The first description of Margaret in Hall is apparently not unflattering:

This woman excelled all other, as well in beautie and favor, as in wit and policie,
and was of stomack and corage, more like to a man, then a woman. (Bullough,
III, 102)

But that ominous – from a patriarchal point of view – note of gender reversal is taken up and extended in the fuller sketch of her character that accompanies her antithetical marriage partner. King Henry, we are told,

was a man of meke spirite, and of a simple witte, preferryng peace before warre, reste before business, honestie before profite, and quietnesse before laboure.

All these characteristics of an unmanly man can be construed in his favour: 'He gaped not for honor, nor thristed for riches, but studied onely for the health of his soule; the savynge wherof, he estemed to bee the greatest wisedome, and the losse thereof, the extremest folie that could bee.' This has scriptural authority to recommend it as Christian truth, however unkinglike that truth might be: 'For what shall it profit a man, if he shall gain the whole world, and lose his own soul?' (Mark 8: 36). But the complementary matching portrait of the Queen that follows has no such divine sanction:

But on the other parte, the Quene his wife, was a woman of a greate witte, and yet of no greater witte, then of haute stomacke, desirous of glory, and covetous of honor, and of reason, pollicye, counsaill, and other giftes and talentes of nature belongyng to a man, full and flowyng: of witte and wilinesse she lacked nothyng, nor of diligence, studies, and businesse, she was not unexperte . . . (Bullough, III, 105–6)

Strong virtues all, and if applied to a man phrases like 'haute stomacke', or 'covetous of honor' would have nothing pejorative about them. In this context, however, the indecorum of such qualities in a woman gives them the flavour of sins, pride and covetousness. It is no surprise when this setpiece rhetorical study of Margaret by Hall turns into standard misogyny: 'but yet she had one poynt of a very woman: for often tyme, when she was vehement and fully bente in a matter, she was sodainly like a wethercocke, mutable and turnyng' (Bullough, III, 106). And we are off into her jealous conspiracy against the Duke of Gloucester.

The marriage between Henry and Margaret is a disaster for England because her unwomanly spirit of ambition supplies all too well the gap left by his lack of the manly virtues. But, as Hall puts it, 'This mariage semed to many, bothe infortunate, and unprofitable to the realme of England, and that for many causes' (Bullough, III, 103), not just because of incompatibility of temperament. It was literally unprofitable. Margaret not only brought no dowry; the marriage involved the ceding of the French provinces of Maine and Anjou to her father. And her father, though he was styled King of Jerusalem, was a nobody in the major league of European power politics. Shakespeare draws upon this sense of the disgracefulness of the misalliance in the opening scene of *2 Henry VI*, where Gloucester is so appalled by what he reads in the articles of marriage settlement that he drops the paper and can read no further. Indeed, the evident disparity of the match was no doubt a further hint for the sexual motivation of Suffolk: what could have induced Suffolk as peace negotatiator to agree to such a thing? Why was he 'to[o] muche affectionate to this unprofitable mariage' (Bullough, III, 71)? It could only be because he himself was overly affectionate to the woman.

Shakespeare, however, adds another dimension to Margaret's ill reputation in the chronicles; she is foreign, she is French. Most of England's queens must have been foreign: international alliance was the norm in dynastic matches. In the chauvinist spirit of Elizabethan drama, however, Shakespeare highlights the alien orgins of Margaret of Anjou. Many critics have pointed out that Margaret makes her first appearance in *1 Henry VI*, captured by Suffolk immediately after the exit of Joan, captured by York. No sooner is England rid of one troublesome Frenchwoman than another is there to take her place. In Boyd's *This England* production, the two parts were doubled. Within minutes of Fiona Bell, tied to the stake as Joan of Arc, having disappeared through the trap into the space below suggestive of the fire, she reappeared on the battlefield as Suffolk's captive. What is more, the dark red costume she wore was identical with that of the attendant spirits who had accompanied Joan throughout the earlier action, and forsook her finally before her defeat. Margaret, in this production, was literally demonized from the start. Again and again throughout the plays, Margaret's unwomanliness, her upstart origins, her foreignness, are compounded in the abuse hurled at her by her enemies, nowhere more fully and more eloquently than in York's final denunciation of her in *3 Henry VI*, 1.4. In this great tirade she is the 'She-wolf of France, but worse than wolves of France'; in her jumped-up position as queen she verifies the proverb 'That beggars mounted run their horse to death'; she is, most famously of all, a 'tiger's heart wrapped in a woman's hide'.

For feminist interpreters, Margaret becomes 'the first tetralogy's most sustained example of the danger which ambitious and sexual women pose to English manhood and to English monarchy'. Jean Howard and Phyllis Rackin argue that 'in demonizing Margaret', the plays 'also invested her with astonishing sensuality and power'.[10] From the point of view of modern directors and actors, Margaret's dominant presence over most of four plays makes possible a sustained character development in which the sexual dynamics of her marriage are crucially related to her political role. Suffolk in their first battlefield encounter improvises the idea of the Margaret–Henry marriage in an extended aside:

> I'll win this Lady Margaret. For whom?
> Why for my king – tush that's a wooden thing!
> . . . Yet so my fancy may be satisfied,
> And peace established between these realms.
>
> (*1 Henry VI*, 5.3.88–92)

Two birds with one stone. The 'wooden thing' Henry will do as a stooge for Suffolk's own designs on Margaret – the international peace treaty is an afterthought. Margaret seems from early on to speak Suffolk's language. When he cheekily takes a kiss from her as a token of love to the king, she answers him back in kind:

> That for thyself: I will not so presume
> To send such peevish tokens to a king.
>
> (5.3.185–6)

For Shakespeare's original audiences this might have been a sign of Margaret's pre-adulterous inclinations from the beginning. For modern audiences, by contrast, there is likely to be at least some sympathy with the situation the Queen finds herself in when married to her 'wooden thing' husband. She complains to Suffolk of the poorness of the principal in comparison to the substitute who married her on behalf of the King:

> I tell thee, Pole, when in the city Tours
> Thou ran'st a-tilt in honour of my love
> And stol'st away the ladies' hearts of France,
> I thought King Henry had resembled thee
> In courage, courtship, and proportion.
> But all his mind is bent to holiness,
> To number Ave-Maries on his beads . . .
> I would the College of the Cardinals
> Would choose him Pope and carry him to Rome
> And set the triple crown upon his head:
> That were a state fit for his holiness.
>
> (*2 Henry VI*, 1.3.45–59)

The convention of a noble ambassador entering into a proxy marriage on behalf of his monarch here turns into the very real frustration of a woman with a husband whose sexual inadequacy fits him only for the celibate life of the clergy. Her affections remain with the potent man who impersonated the King.

The intensity of Margaret's feelings for Suffolk makes of the murder of Gloucester a climax not only in the play's political struggle, but in the triangular relationship of wife, lover, husband. In the chronicle narrative, Suffolk was as much Henry's favourite as Margaret. They both equally tried to shield him from the consequences of his complicity in Gloucester's downfall and death. The King decreed his banishment only 'to appease the furious rage of the outragious people, and that pacified, to revocate him into his olde estate' (Bullough, III, 112). In Shakespeare, however, the announcement of Gloucester's murder is for Henry a moment of revelation marked by his collapse into a swoon. When he comes to, it is to the complete conviction of Suffolk's treachery:

> Thou baleful messenger, out of my sight!
> Upon thy eye-balls murderous tyranny
> Sits in grim majesty, to fright the world.
> *(2 Henry VI, 3.2.48–50)*

In this instance for the first – and only – time, he completely and unequivocally overrules Margaret.

MARGARET O Henry, let me plead for gentle Suffolk.
KING HENRY Ungentle queen to call him gentle Suffolk.
No more I say: if thou dost plead for him,
Thou wilt but add increase unto my wrath. (3.2.289–92)

Where else in the three plays that bear his name does the King speak of his 'wrath'?

This sudden banishment of Suffolk does not seem in any way motivated on Henry's side by sexual jealousy. Certainly it has not been played that way: with David Warner, for instance, it appeared more like possession. It as though the holy fool has had, in his lapse out of consciousness, an instinctive intuition of the nature of Suffolk's evil in the murder of Gloucester. But for Margaret the banishment of Suffolk is a terrible emotional loss, not just a political defeat. Their extended parting (3.2.300–412), in the most fully elaborated rhetoric of Shakespeare's early style, is likely to be something of an embarrassment in the modern theatre where it is often heavily cut back. The scene, however, in which the Queen nurses the severed head of her lover in the presence of the King makes a powerful impact. Peggy Ashcroft as Margaret in the Barton and Hall *Wars of the Roses* had up to this point always appeared regally poised and controlled. There was a grotesque contrast here with the figure of anguish, cheek and hands blood-bedabbled, her white wimple spattered from the gory head of Suffolk that she nursed in her arms. Mourning black similarly changed the face of Julia Foster, the Queen in Howell's BBC version. The Margaret who loses Suffolk in such a spectacularly bloody way, who is beyond concealing her grief, is to be fundamentally changed thereafter. The gentle King may accept her mourning over Suffolk with no more reproach than the sad reflection:

> I fear me, love, if that I had been dead,
> Thou wouldest not have mourned so much for me.
>
> (4.4.23–4)

But there is no way that she will be able to accept his offer of a new start to their marriage and partnership in power: 'Come, wife, let's in and learn to govern better.' The fierce and implacable Margaret of *3 Henry VI* and *Richard III* is already in place.

Even if we accept G. K. Hunter's proposition of the discontinuity of the character of the Queen – 'Each Margaret (*Henry VI* I, II, III and *Richard III*) is in fact a different Margaret' – the effect of one actor playing those different Margarets is likely to supply an illusion of continuity, of change and development. In Ashcroft's version there was a deep psychological modelling of the part. Her mocking of the captured York, for example, showed a masochistic underside to the sadism. Her assault on York, especially the description of Rutland's death and the smearing of his father's face with blood, was accompanied by hysterical laughter in which sobbing could be heard as well. Her torture of her enemy was partly a torture to her too, an anguish of hatred that she had to drive herself to sustain. When the previously silent York began his denunciation of her, 'She-wolf of France', this was her pay-off, to be greeted by peals of triumphalist laughter. But as he moved into the pathos of what she has done to the young Rutland, 'How could'st thou drain the life-blood of the child', the laughter died. In the television broadcast the camera held the focus on Ashcroft's face, as she fought to subdue grief. Eventually a tear was seen to force itself from the Queen's eye and move slowly down her still face. There was no such emotion in June Watson's playing of the part for the ESC. She was stony-faced as she circled the almost equally stoical York (played by Barry Stanton). There was no hint of triumph when York did finally break down in sobs for Rutland, and it was with a mere hint of a nod in an unflinching face that she gave the signal for his execution. This hard-boiled style, though, made all the more effective the single piercing scream she gave later at Tewkesbury when her son Edward was stabbed to death.

The Margaret of *Richard III* most strikingly illustrates Hunter's point about the breaks between the character in the several different texts. She is no mere continuation of the monstrous queen of the *Henry VI* plays: she is given a quite new function as Senecan Ate figure, the cursing personification of nemesis. And yet acting continuities are still possible. A costuming design feature skilfully naturalised the transition from one part to another in the case of June Watson. Her Margaret had moved into military uniform from the outbreak of the wars, a khaki only distinguishable from the other Lancastrian officers by skirt in place of trousers. This militarisation went with the hardening of the persona after the death of Suffolk. In *Richard III*, she reappeared in the shabby remnants of uniform, her cap crazily askew, looking convincingly like a deranged streetwoman kitted out in Army and Navy surplus. And that is one way of playing the vengeful prophetess lurking about the court of the Yorkist kings. At a different level, Ashcroft's distinctive 'r' lisp, initially suggestive of her foreignness (adopted also by Penny Downie in Adrian Noble's *Plantagenets*), bespoke the individuality of the person who continued on into the political afterlife of *Richard III*. With the aid of such visual and oral prompts, it is possible to see in the latter-day Fury of the final play, stylised as her language is, the Margaret of the earlier series: as energetic in hatred as ever, finding it as hard as ever to muster pity or forgiveness, nursing her grievances accumulated over a lifetime of bitter trauma and loss.

Henry and Margaret in the history play series make sense together, make sense of one another. His weakness as man and king brings out her strength as a predatory need for power. The sexual counterpart of this is the adulterous affair with Suffolk to which Margaret gives herself the more passionately because of the monk-like temperament of Henry. With this love brutally killed, an answering brutality grows in her. As a substitute for the dead man she fully loved, given the wraith of a man who is her husband, she transfers whatever capacity she has left for love to her son Edward, only to have him killed too. And it is the relict of all these desires, horrors and hatreds who appears in *Richard III*. An equivalent character-track is supplied to take Henry from the young and naive boy-king, palpably unfit for his office, to the saintly martyr who missed canonisation only because the frugally minded Henry VII discovered that the Vatican rate for making a king a saint was prohibitively dear (Bullough, III, 208). Apparently infatuated with Margaret from the first time he is told about her by Suffolk, he is overcome by her beauty and natural dignity at her first appearance. It is the strength he lacks that he admires in her. He thanks God for the marriage which is to give him

Plate 8 Queen Margaret (June Watson) in English Shakespeare Company
production of *Richard III*, directed by Michael Bogdanov, 1988

'A world of earthly blessings to my / soul If sympathy of love unite our thoughts' (*2 Henry VI*, 1.1.22–3). Alas for the 'if'. Henry, unable to satisfy his wife, unable to control her, increasingly unhappy with her aggressive pursuit of power, grows in isolation into the miserable embodiment of an unworldly faith. Shakespeare may not create the sort of character-driven drama of a royal marriage this sort of summary suggests. But he does make possible the plausible playing of his parts so that, over the stretch of action from *1 Henry VI* to *Richard III*, we can feel that we are seeing and understanding two key lives growing in action and history.

RICHARD III

Richard III is Shakespeare's first stand-alone history play and Richard III his first finished theatrical character, a gift of a part for actors from Colley Cibber to Ian McKellen, even if for two centuries played in Cibber's notorious actor's cut version. The character of Richard is so unlike the others in the first history play series, however, in part because it came to Shakespeare pre-characterised, indeed pre-dramatised. For the pathetically brief reign of Edward V and the beginning of the reign of his usurping uncle, Hall spliced in Thomas More's *History of King Richard III*, unusually for Hall even acknowledging that was what he was doing.[11] More's *History* was centred round the character of its protagonist, introduced in classic fashion in contrast to his two older brothers:

Richard duke of Gloucester the third sonne (of whiche I must moste entreate) was in witte and courage egall with the other Edward and George, but in beautee and liniamentes of nature far underneth bothe, for he was litle of stature, evill featured of limnes, croke backed, the left shulder muche higher than the righte, harde favoured of visage, such as in estates is called a warlike visage, and emonge commen persons a crabbed face. He was malicious, wrothfull and envious ... (Bullough, III, 253)

And we are off into the great portrait of the monstrous Richard Crookback that forms the basis for Shakespeare's king. More's history, formed on the model of classical life-writing, stands apart from the chronicle mode into which it is set, by the way the personality of its protagonist is dramatised in elaborately described situations complete with invented speeches. It is from More directly, for instance, that Shakespeare takes the brilliantly vivid council scene in which Richard asks for the dish of strawberries from the Bishop of Ely's garden, before his tyrant's tantrum leading to the summary execution of Hastings. (More, of course, may have had an eye-witness report of such a scene from his master John Morton, the same Bishop of Ely, in whose household he was a page.) It is notable that the bulk of Shakespeare's play *Richard III* is given over to that stretch of action covered by More up to the point where his *History* broke off just before the rebellion of Buckingham.

Where Hall does not have More's narrative to transcribe, he relies on Polydore Vergil (whose *Anglica Historia* was written at about the same time as More's *History*, and may have been known to him[12]) to provide an account of Richard's life before the death of Edward IV. Shakespeare, however, imaginatively extends this prehistory of the villain-king by having Richard appear already at the Battle of St Albans in *2 Henry VI*. Richard's early reputation as a soldier, referred to by More, documented in Hall with accounts of his victories in Scotland in the 1470s, might have justified this precocious battlefield appearance, even though the historical Richard would have been only three years old at the time. But to give to the deformed tyrant of More's *History* an adolescence or young manhood, and have him appear in two plays in which he was not central before his own tragedy, was to complicate the 'character' of Richard that emerges.

One further extension back of this process may help to illustrate the point. In the BBC Television production of *2 Henry VI*, 2.2, the scene of York's exposition to Warwick and Salisbury of his genealogical claim to the throne, was given a domestic setting. York, first seen as a very young man in the Temple Garden scene of *1 Henry VI*, was here somewhat older, hoping to persuade the venerable grey-haired Salisbury on to his side with the help of his long-term friend and contemporary Warwick. As a visual marker for the stage of life York had reached (and an emblematic token for the political situation) the scene opened with three small boys playing skittles with figures painted to look like the principal Lancastrians, King, Queen, Cardinal, Gloucester. At the conclusion to the scene, the very tall Mark Wing-Davey playing Warwick, triumphing at York's success in converting his father to their cause, swung one of the boys up on to his shoulders with the lines:

> My heart assures me that the Earl of Warwick
> Shall one day make the Duke of York a king.
> (2.2.78–9)

Framing his face were the legs of the child, with the left one in callipers. This was the third son of York, the future Richard of Gloucester. Thus to flag Richard's disability in terms that, for a 1980s television audience, would still have had associations of childhood polio, created a pathos colouring in advance a reading of the character to come. But even without such an added glimpse back to Richard's childhood, the texts of *2* and *3 Henry VI*, by creating a history for the character before he stands revealed as the hunchback usurper, suggest a graph of development explaining, if not justifying the person he becomes.

For More, Richard's outward deformity could plausibly be construed as the mark of his inherent evil. He tells the stories of Richard's ominous birth, feet first and already with teeth, and admits they could be prejudiced exaggeration – perhaps, but then again perhaps not:

> whether that menne of hatred reported above the truthe, or that nature chaunged his course in his beginnynge, whiche in his life many thynges unnaturally committed, this I leve to God his judgemente. (Bullough, III, 253)

Charitably spoken, but there is no doubt that More right through his *History* shows Richard's deformation of physique as the outward manifestation of his wickedness. He is the person he is from the unnatural moment of birth. In Shakespeare this is at least complicated by the appearances of Richard before the death of his father. He is the youngest, the fiercest, and the most intransigently loyal of the three sons of York. In the opening scene of *3 Henry VI*, as the several achievements of St Albans are displayed before York, Richard comes out as youngest = best when he throws down the head of the Duke of Somerset: 'Richard hath best deserved of all my sons' (1.1.17). (The company's stage-property head must have had a fair bit of rattling round in this series.) Richard, it is true, is the one who convinces his father to break his oath to Henry with the Tamburlainian incentive of monarchy justifying all:

> And, father, do but think
> How sweet a thing it is to wear a crown,
> Within whose circuit is Elysium
>   (1.2.28–30)

But such overreaching ambition is not at this stage the specific attribute of Richard: the scene begins with Edward, Richard and Montague (whom Shakespeare seems to have thought of as York's brother-in-law) arguing about who should take on the task of convincing York to claim the crown immediately. Though it is not until the Battle of Towton in 2.2 that George replaces Montague in the Yorkist threesome, the identity of the three scions of York is enforced in the image of the three suns coming together that appears to Edward and Richard in 2.1, just before they receive the news of the death of their father, and is interpreted as an omen of the joint strength of the 'sons of brave Plantagenet' (2.1.35). It is not until the very middle of the play, 3.2, that Richard is given his first major soliloquy and steps out from his role as one of the sons of York into the solo intriguer Gloucester.

This great speech (raided by actors playing Richard III in the later play down to Olivier) occupies exactly the same position in the text as that of Richard's father in *2 Henry VI* (3.1.331–83). It is an equivalent aria of power, with the menacing would-be pretender to the throne emerging fully from the shadows and speaking out in full-throated theatricality the grandeur of his ambition. But in the case of York there has been the build-up of motivation, the tangle of right and wrong in his dynastic claim and the political struggle in which he is emmeshed. Richard's speech comes from nowhere, is entirely self-generated, without any vestige of justification. He has no possible claim to the crown, he does not pretend he has; he is driven by the will alone. Here for the first time is More's villain with his long-nurtured ambitions: 'he longe in kynge Edwarde his tyme thought to obtaine the crowne in case that the kynge his brother, whose life he loked that evill diet would sone shorten shoulde happen to diseace' (Bullough, III, 253). This is Shakespeare's cue for the opening of Richard's speech, which comes immediately after Edward's controversial decision to marry Lady Elizabeth Grey ending with his exit-line, 'Lords, use her honourably'.

> Ay, Edward will use women honourably –
> Would he were wasted, marrow, bones, and all,
> That from his loins no hopeful branch may spring
> To cross me from the golden time I look for!
> (3.1.124–7)

Yet in pointing the contrast between Edward's lust for women and Richard's lust for power, Shakespeare produces an interior psychological dynamic for his villain-hero that can be read back into his previous life as we have seen in it in the plays so far.

Richard seeks power because he cannot have love: this is Shakespeare's own interpretation of the figure of the misshapen usurper. He re-casts More's external judgement – 'nature chaunged his course in his beginnynge, whiche in his life many thynges unnaturally committed':

> Why, Love forswore me in my mother's womb
> And, for I should not deal in her soft laws,
> She did corrupt frail Nature with some bribe

> To shrink mine arm up like a withered shrub;
> To make an envious mountain on my back
> Where sits Deformity to mock my body
>   (3.2.153–8)

The conviction that he is beyond love fuels the need for a compensatory power:

> since this earth affords no joy to me
> But to command, to check, to o'erbear such
> As are of better person than myself,
> I'll make my heaven to dream upon the crown
>   (3.2.165–8)

This, the sexually frustrated envy of the malcontent, is conventional psychology for Shakespeare's time and, as the lack of self-worth born of lovelessness, conventional psychology for the modern period too. In a theatrical context, it can also be made to make sense of the transition from the loyal young warrior son of York to the conniving Machiavel of the action from here on.

The Richard of the first scenes in which he appears lives within the all-male collective of his father and brothers. His identity is subsumed within the cause of the house of York. In contention on the battlefield, he can win his father's all-important praise by outdoing his brothers; when others lose hope, he can be the one to rally their spirits and send them back to the fight. Such contention is sanctioned under the name of the father. But with the father dead, and power won for his brother Edward, the bond of male solidarity is gone and Richard's energies are displaced into deadly sibling rivalry. This may give something like a deep structure to Richard's misogyny. There is envy of Edward's womanising; there is a jealous hatred of the reproductive powers of his potent male brothers – 'and all the unlooked-for issue of their bodies' (3.2.131). But there may also be resentment at the loss of the world without women within which the young Richard lived and thrived.

If so, then the wooing of Lady Anne in *Richard III*, one of Shakespeare's most notable additions to the Richard legend, involves a complicated sort of revenge. There is of course the triumph of persuading over to his side the very wife of his murdered enemy, Edward Prince of Wales, and in the presence of the corpse of her dead father-in-law, Henry VI whom he had also killed. It is, as such, a sort of black mass of courtship. The demonstration of his own power is at the same time a demonstration of the ridiculous weakness of women:

> Hath she forgot already that brave prince,
> Edward, her lord, whom I, some three months since
> Stabbed in my angry mood at Tewkesbury?
> (1.2. 244–6)

Actors have varied in the degree and nature of fascination that Richard is shown to exercise over Anne in this scene, from the mesmeric hypnotism of an Olivier, through the boyish urchin charm of Ron Cook playing the part in the BBC television version, to the very physical wooing of Aidan McArdle with its threats of rape in the 2001 *This England* version of *Richard III*. Ian Holm in the Barton and Hall *Wars of the Roses* was much less caricatured than other Richards, and with his sensitive young face he seemed genuinely to convince Anne (Janet Suzman) of the sincerity of his love. She came to relent to the point of a trembling, hand-to-hand, mouth-to-mouth slow motion approach to a kiss. It was only at the last second of their lips meeting that his mouth was seen to bite fiercely at hers in a shocking reversal to the mood thus far. It was a kiss to be repeated exactly at the end of the sequence where he attempts a replay of his wooing of Anne with Queen Elizabeth, and his line on her exit was a spitting away of the contact with her mouth: 'Relenting fool and shallow, changing woman' (4.4.436). In this Richard misogyny was a convulsive drive of his nature: an aggressive need to prove his contempt for such women as could be fooled into thinking him capable of love, but beyond that, an animus against the female sex itself.

Richard is the most strongly characterised character in Shakespeare's first history play series, allowing an actor to build and develop a role across the three plays in which he appears. But the very histrionicism of the part also in a sense destabilises any fixed hold on it as a 'character'. It is a donné of Richard that he could pretend to be what he was not: 'a deep dissimuler, lowlye of countenaunce, arrogante of herte, outwardely familier where he inwardely hated, not lettynge to kisse where he thought to kill' (Bullough, III, 253). He can mimic bluff brotherliness with Clarence as convincingly as he can the unrequited lover with Anne, can assume the right unctuous tone of good will towards all the world required for Edward's deathbed peacemaking:

> I do not know that Englishman alive
> With whom my soul is any jot at odds
> (2.1.70–1)

The need to act all these roles so that they carry conviction is what makes it the virtuoso actor's part it is. But it also raises doubts about any one interpretation of where this Protean ability comes from. The compelling power of Richard's later performance of himself calls in question whether the earlier self is not equally a performance. The Richard of the battlefield sequences, the Richard who cannot weep at the news of his father's death, *can* be played as true son of his father, brother of his brothers, who is going to grow into the misogynist psychopath when the wholeness of homosocial bonding is removed. But this previous self could conceivably be just as simulated as the show of loyalty to Edward and his infant son that is revealed in an aside as a Judas kiss (*3 Henry VI*, 5.7.33–4). Certainly his failure to weep at the death of his father, readable as a key traumatic symptom, is turned into just one more rhetorical effect in his purely manipulative courtship of Anne (*Richard III*, 1.2.163–8). What might be postulated as the origins of Richard of Gloucester, an emotional maiming equivalent to the literal crippling figured in the childhood callipers of the television image, could also be merely the early shows of the consummate Machiavel not as yet self-declared.

In his major soliloquies Shakespeare's Richard is given a master-motivation, a burning, ultimately self-destructive need for power born of envy, sexual frustration, self-loathing. It is never more brilliantly expressed than in the Dantean image of the figure lost in the wood, a Dante who will never find a guide out of his inferno:

> And yet I know not how to get the crown
> For many lives stand between me and home:
> And I, like one lost in a thorny wood,
> That rents the thorns and is rent with the thorns,
> Seeking a way and straying from the way,
> Not knowing how to find the open air
> But toiling desperately to find it out,
> Torment myself to catch the English crown;
> And from that torment I will free myself,
> Or hew my way out with a bloody axe.
>
> (*3 Henry VI*, 3.2.172–81)

Yet, while this vividly renders a choking claustrophobia of the inner life, that same soliloquy can turn into the showy melodrama of the gleeful villain:

> I can add colours to the chameleon,
> Change shapes with Proteus for advantages,
> And set the murderous Machiavel to school.
>
> (3.2.191–3)

Here Richard is performing More's monster. Throughout the soliloquies of *Richard III* there is a comparable self-advertising outwardness in the character's self-analyis. It is a register developed out of the language of the Vice, most obviously caught in the knowingness of Olivier's 'I am determined to prove a villain', well rendered also in the Charles Addams-like caricature of Andrew Jarvis's ESC performance. Soliloquy, which by convention may be taken to represent the truth of inner revelation, becomes in Richard just one more site for performance.

This style of knowing self-send-up serves the play *Richard III* extraordinarily well, dramatises More's study in tyranny. It creates problems only in the phase where the tyrant begins to lose control, and the focus is turned in to the guilty self that is intended as the inner mirror of the tyrant in the last phase of mad manic energy. The ghost scene, for all its stylised symmetry and Senecan idiom, can be easily naturalised. Andrew Jarvis, for instance, was shown tossing from side to side, falling out of his military camp-bed, as each of his victims appeared with some deadly dream-reprise token of their murders. The gentle and pious Henry VI (Paul Brennen) sat in a chair confronting Richard, as Richard had confronted him in the Tower, exactly re-enacting the murder in reverse when he lunges at Richard with the same flick-knife action with which Richard killed the King. Hastings (Roger Booth), buttoned up in black overcoat as in life, marched up to Richard carrying the Gladstone bag containing his own head, presented as trophy earlier. When Anne (Francesca Ryan) invoked despairing defeat for him in the battle – 'fall thy edgeless sword, despair and die' – it was with an obvious anatomic gesture to his impotence in the marriage bed. This sort of dream symbology of guilt that bound together memories of Richard's murders throughout the action could make immediate sense to a modern audience.

The difficulty comes when Richard wakes and speaks his last soliloquy that must articulate this inner landscape of panic. It is here that the outwardness of the conception of character makes inwardness so hard to achieve.

> What? Do I fear myself? There's none else by.
> Richard loves Richard, that is, I am I.
> Is there a murderer here? No. Yes, I am.
> Then fly. What, from myself? Great reason why:
> Lest I revenge? What, myself upon myself?
> Alack, I love myself. Wherefore? For any good
> That I myself have done unto myself?

> O no. Alas, I rather hate myself
> For hateful deeds committed by myself.
>
> (5.3.185–93)

Strong acting can carry a performer through this speech. It came across
especially well in Aidan McArdle's 2001 RSC performance where he emphasised its extroverted histrionicism, searching the rows of the audience
that surrounded him in the Swan on the line 'Is there a murderer here?'
But there is nonetheless a jerky awkwardness of the internal catechism
managed within the stiffness of the rhyming couplets. Only once does it
gather into a natural rhythm in the articulation of complete despair:

> There is no creature loves me,
> And if I die, no soul will pity me.
> Nay, wherefore should they, since that I myself
> Find in myself no pity to myself?
>
> (5.3.203–6)

Shakespeare has not yet found the rhetoric of the collapsed self that he
uses to such fine effect in Richard II's last prison speech. There can be no
such fully convincing language for Richard III, in part because the very
construction of the role denies him inwardness. With Richard the inner
is itself another outer in the multiplex of selves constituting the character.

No character in the first history plays series is tailored to the needs of
a single play, as no single play is conceived wholly as a unit on its own:
the chickens coming home to roost in *Richard III* have long been flying
through the night skies of the *Henry VI* plays. Humphrey of Gloucester,
Richard of York, King Henry and Queen Margaret go on from play to
play in a continuing narrative that demands their continuing presence.
They are lives in history of whose experience and actions some sense
must be made, piecing together people out of their chronicle doings,
animating the (often inconsistent) legends of their afterlives. These are,
necessarily, characters in the rough. But they represent, at least potentially, the emergence of character in action, and that potential has been
realised in the modern productions that have given coherent and consistent development to figures who in origin may have been gapped and
discontinuous. This is true even of Richard of Gloucester/Richard III,
the character who comes closest to 'character' in the first history play
series. For actors who have been able to build towards *Richard III* through
2 Henry VI and *3 Henry VI*, having the longer run at the part has added
force and depth to the portrayal of Richard, and it is clear from such

performances how carefully Shakespeare trailed the later play he must already have planned to write. The very cannibalisation of the *Henry VI* play materials into the Cibberised *Richard III* shows how strongly the earlier Richard foreshadows the later: Richard is not one-play-bound. But neither is he clearly and cleanly 'characterised'. If we insist on judging by Shakespeare's later practices of characterisation, then the *Henry VI – Richard III* plays can only be read as prentice-work in which the playwright has not yet mastered his later skills. If we can see them, as this book tries to do, as the uniquely original theatrical enterprise of the serial dramatisation of history, then the emergence of character this serialisation demanded is a phenomenon worth attention in itself.

CHAPTER FIVE

Curses and prophecies

Curses proliferate in *Richard III* and for much of the action we watch them take inexorable effect. Like a snarling and battered Ate, Queen Margaret presides personally over the system of retribution in which the crimes piled up over the preceding plays are expiated. Herself the subject of the Duke of York's curse at Wakefield, as her Yorkist adversaries are swift to point out, when she tortured him with the handkerchief soaked in his son's blood, she ploughs on undeterred through a series of curses that leave her enemies all but paralysed. The King and his family, Rivers, Dorset, Hastings, standers-by at the murder of her son Edward, are doomed to pay for their misdeeds; Buckingham, as yet innocent of the taint of Yorkism, is warned of his peril if he colludes with the guilty. And for Gloucester, chief offender, arch-criminal, is reserved the peroration of Margaret's denunciatory wrath. It is in vain that Richard, with characteristic quick-wittedness, attempts to side-step the curse by naming Margaret herself as she is about to conclude her execration of him. The cheap trick is felt as the useless dodge it is; the juggernaut of Margaret's cursing will crash on through the action of the play, mowing down its chosen targets, as many of them will acknowledge on point of death.

Given the appalling crimes of which Margaret herself is guilty, given her extreme and relentless partisanship, it is odd that her curses are proved so spectacularly effective. Why should divine providence become, as Wilbur Sanders puts it so elegantly, 'a supernatural agency under contractual obligation to exterminate the house of York'?[1] But then throughout the series of plays the working of curses and prophecies provokes questions about the operations of providence that extend out into the most long-running and hotly contested of critical debates about the histories. To what extent, and on what scale, is an audience intended to see providential patterns of causality being accomplished through the series of history plays? Tillyard's concept of the 'Tudor myth', the guilt of Henry IV's usurpation of the throne from Richard II being punished with the divine retribution of the fifteenth-century dynastic wars before the coming of Henry VII as God's saviour to England, informed the work of a generation of scholars – and of theatrical producers of the history plays. It was then challenged from a variety of points of view,[2] most fully and systematically by H. A. Kelly with his book *Divine Providence in the England of Shakespeare's Histories*. Kelly's book demonstrated in detail that the chroniclers, from whom Tillyard had maintained Shakespeare derived his shaping ideology, in fact reflected a whole set of different and contending historiographical 'myths'. Going back to the annals and contemporary accounts on which the synthetic chronicles of Hall and Holinshed were ultimately based, Kelly showed how successive generations of historians had trimmed their pious accounts of divine providential intervention in England's affairs to suit the current political regime, and that a 'Lancaster myth' and a 'York myth', as well as a 'Tudor' myth, could be detected unreconciled in the palimpsests of the later chronicles.[3] Later scholars have suggested that the history plays in fact stage conflicts between different orders of historical interpretation, an older providential scheme of things in tension with a more modern Machiavellian concept of causality.[4]

The business of reading supernatural signs was a difficult one in sixteenth-century England, as Keith Thomas's book *Religion and the Decline of Magic* helped to show. According to Thomas's master-thesis, the Reformation removed from the Church its institutional control of magic, diffusing it instead unpoliced and unmanaged into a semi-secularised world.[5] Protestant theology stressed the providential nature of everything in the world: nothing happened without God's permission. Thomas cites the Elizabethan bishop Thomas Cooper: 'That which we call fortune . . . is nothing but the hand of God, working by causes and for causes that we know not', and John Knox to similar effect: 'Fortune and adventure . . . are the words of Paynims, the signification whereof ought in no wise to enter into the heart of the faithful.'[6] Equally, however, the inscrutability of God's providence was repeatedly asserted. While all forms of disaster, natural and man-made, were regularly attributed to divine retribution for sin, men were constantly cautioned against assuming that they could know the secrets of providential causality and its manifestations. A specifically Protestant distrust of miracles, the belief that the age of miracles was over, co-existed with a devout faith that God might, if he so wished, intervene supernaturally to effect his will.

It is this ambiguity that produces the characteristic stance of Edward Hall, the most zealously post-Reformationist of the chroniclers, towards prophetic signs and omens. So, for example, Hall records, at the time of the Duke of York's formal challenge for the crown in 1460, the supposed supernatural signs of a crown falling down untouched in the House of Commons, and simultaneously a crown falling from the top of the castle of Dover. These were interpreted, says Hall with a snort of disbelief, 'as a signe and prognosticacion, that the Crowne of the Realme should bee divided and changed, from one line to another. This was the judgement of the common people, whiche wer neither of Gods privitie, nor yet of his privie counsaill, and yet thei wil say their opinions, whosoever saie nay' (Hall, fol. clxxxi). This is typical in its theological disapproval of those who claim to be 'of Gods privitie', and its class-specific contempt for the 'common people' who believe in such vulgar superstition. But that does not stop Hall from recording such supernatural omens, or from larding his chronicle with pious commentary on the providential nature of the history he records.

It is this doubleness in the interpretative stance of the chroniclers that has provided support for both sides in the debate over providence in Shakespeare's histories. At times the chronicles might highlight the ineluctably destined course of historical events as tokens of God's divine will manifested in the world, at others they might cast scorn on those who presumed to understand such tokens. There was inherent doubt, not whether there was a providential dispensation in human affairs, but how its signs might be construed. And that left room for a Machiavellian reading of the 'natural' causes of historical action. The Reformation left the issue of the powers available to evil agents in doubt also. The ministers of Satan could do nothing without the allowance of God, but who knew how much power and for what reason God might allow them? Therefore it was not safe to imagine that witches, conjurers and false prophets could *not* predict the future or ill-wish their victims. Banquo in this, as in so much else, was orthodox in his beliefs:

> oftentimes to win us to our harm,
> The instruments of darkness tell us truths,
> Win us with honest trifles, to betray's
> In deepest consequence.
>
> (1.3 123–6)

In this context my concern is not with the doctrines themselves but with Shakespeare's dramatic manipulation of them, with theatrical function rather than theological significance. With the use of curses and prophecies in the first series of history plays, as later with ghost folklore in *Hamlet*, the secularised milieu of the theatre allowed Shakespeare to pick and choose, mix and match among the available beliefs of the time. Sometimes the emphasis was on the knownness, even the fatedness, of the events to come. In such cases prophecies acted as a proleptic prefiguring of the shape of the future. Sometimes it was the occluded nature of the signs that was highlighted, prophecies as riddles to be puzzled out, dreams as omens to be decoded. And the cursing of enemies, as spectacularly in the case of Margaret in *Richard III*, might have apparent consequences, even though those doing the cursing could have little warrant for supposing God was on their side. Here, as throughout the book, my concern is not only with the theatrical practices of the texts as history play series created in Shakespeare's time, but with the subsequent theatrical practices of modern productions of those plays: the inflexions they give to the dramatic rendering of prophecy and curse, the ways they deal with the archaic nature of these tropes for sceptical, rationalist modern audiences. This chapter considers prophecies and curses as they help to shape and bind the action of the *Henry VI – Richard III* plays, providing point and direction both locally and within the series as a whole.

PROPHECY AND PROLEPSIS

It is not hard to foretell the future when it is already in the past. Shakespeare at the outset of the *Henry VI* plays figures forth the shape of things to come, a shape that pre-exists, known to his audience as history.[7] The very first scene of *1 Henry VI* functions as overture to the play, if not the series as a whole. No sooner is the breath out of the dead king's body, at his very funeral, the quarrelling begins that is to tear England apart. And in what follows, there is a sort of fast-forwarding through the action to come. Theatrically conventional messengers appear from France at symmetrically spaced intervals bringing news of fresh disasters. The war is going badly, the first messenger reports; dissension at the top makes for poor morale among the troops:

> Amongst the soldiers this is muttered:
> That here you maintain several factions
> And, while a field should be dispatched and fought,
> You are disputing of your generals.
>
> (1.1.70–3)

The warrior-king has just died, the factions have just emerged, yet there has been time for rumours of them to reach the camps in France and breed muttering discontent. Editors of the text painstakingly point out the liberties taken with chronology in the account of the towns lost to the enemy:

> Guyenne, Compiègne, Rheims, Rouen, Orléans,
> Paris, Gisors, Poitiers, are all quite lost.
>
> (1.1.60–1)

This not only backdates to 1422 events that were not to take place for years to come; Rheims did not fall until 1429, Gisors and Rouen only in 1449, Guyenne in 1451.[8] The lines anticipate battles that are still to be fought out in the play that follows: the struggle for Orléans will occupy much of the rest of the action of Act 1 and on into Act 2. Even after their victory at Bordeaux, climax/catastrophe of Act 4, the French are only heading hopefully towards Paris:

> And now to Paris in this conquering vein:
> All will be ours, now bloody Talbot's slain.
>
> (4.7.95–6)

In Act 3 Paris is still sufficiently securely in English hands to provide the setting for the re-coronation of Henry VI.

As the traditional dumbshow pre-enacted in mime the drama that was to follow, so *I Henry VI* 1.1 is a miniature of the play as a whole. We do not actually see Talbot, the English champion and protagonist, but we hear of him in full glory at the Battle of Patay from the last and fullest of the messengers' speeches. What is more, we hear of him going down to glorious defeat, as he will terminally at Bordeaux. Outnumbered, surrounded, performing deeds of desperate valour, the invincible Talbot, here as later, is betrayed by those who should be supporting him, not overcome by his cowardly and treacherous enemies. At Patay it is the English Sir John Fastolf who causes his defeat by running away; at Bordeaux it will be his feuding co-commanders, York and Somerset, who let him down. Here 'a base Walloon, to win the dauphin's grace, / Thrust Talbot with a spear into the back' (1.1.137–8); later, it is only after he has gone down to death under the weight of overwhelming odds that the French leaders dare approach his body. By the end of the first scene, all of the central themes and tropes have been declared, with the one exception of the duel between Talbot and Pucelle, Pucelle who is to be introduced in scene 2. Philip Brockbank sums up on the first scene as it 'establishes at once that double perspective which controls the mood of the chronicle – the sense of being close to the event together with a sense of knowing its consequences'.9

The first scene provides an anticipatory induction to *1 Henry VI* and to the principle of political fission following the death of Henry V that will carry through into the later plays. The famous Temple Garden scene (2.4) is the formal point of origin for the Wars of the Roses, which will not actually break out until the end of *2 Henry VI*, and which will prove more devastating to the kingdom than anything caused by the faction-fighting of the older Gloucester–Winchester generation. The scene initiates a dramatic idiom that is to become a staple of the histories, as characters articulate darkly the course of the action that we know, but they can only intuit, lies ahead. So Warwick, as he dons the white rose of York:

> And here I prophesy: this brawl today,
> Grown to this faction in the Temple garden,
> Shall send, between the red rose and the white,
> A thousand souls to death and deadly night.
>
> (2.4.124–7)

For an audience the lines act as a tragic anticipation/reminder of the terrible loss of life that is to follow, even though in theatrical terms not for a play and a half, seven acts later. There is no hint here of a fate deriving from earlier events, the Tillyardian curse visited on England for the sin of the original Lancastrian usurpation. On the contrary, what the scene brings out is the casualness and contingency of the feud's imagined beginning. History, in the very inevitability of its known pastness, is its own fate.

Exeter has a choric role through the *Henry VI* plays, a role that Barton and Hall, by giving him a Methuselah-like longevity, extended to stretch through from *Richard II* to *Richard III*. It is to Exeter that the two prophecies of Henry V are given in *1 Henry VI*. The first is at the end of 3.1, the scene in which Gloucester and Winchester are formally, but only formally, reconciled, and Richard Plantagenet is restored to the Dukedom of York:

> And now I fear that fatal prophecy
> Which in the time of Henry named the Fifth
> Was in the mouth of every sucking babe:
> That Henry born at Monmouth should win all,
> And Henry born at Windsor should lose all.
>
> (3.1.194–8)

In the sources this is attributed to Henry himself, but it is given all the more authority here by having been in 'the mouth of every sucking babe', associated as it is with the Psalms and the Gospels: 'Out of the mouth of babes and sucklings thou hast perfected praise' (Matt. 21 : 1 6). As the reign of Henry's disastrous boy-successor goes on, Exeter is reminded once again of the dead king's prognostications when Winchester appears in cardinal's robes in Act 5:

> What! Is my Lord of Winchester installed,
> And called unto a cardinal's degree?
> Then I perceive that will be verified
> Henry the Fifth did sometime prophesy:
> 'If once he come to be a cardinal,
> He'll make his cap co-equal with the crown'.
>   (5.1.28–33)

In the sources this is not a prophecy at all, merely a proscription on the part of the king, as Hall explains when he records the investiture of Winchester as Cardinal: 'Whiche degree, kyng Henry the fifth knowyng the haute corage, and the ambicious mynde of the man, prohibited hym on his allegeaunce once, either to sue for or to take, meanyng that Cardinalles Hattes should not presume to bee egall with Princes' (Bullough, III, 51–2). With the King dead, the political savvy of Henry V is turned into vatic foresight. The fulfilment of what retrospectively becomes prophecy is for the theatre audience one more ominous marker in a charted movement of events.

At the other end of the cycle, Henry VI is granted prophetic powers when he encounters the boy Richmond. It is in the scene where Henry is released from the Tower for his brief restoration to the throne that he sees and calls to him 'young Henry, Earl of Richmond':

> KING HENRY   Come hither, England's hope.
> *Lays his hand on his head*
>   If secret powers
> Suggest but truth to my divining thoughts,
> This pretty lad will prove our country's bliss.
> His looks are full of peaceful majesty,
> His head by nature framed to wear a crown,
> His hand to wield a sceptre, and himself
> Likely in time to bless a regal throne.
> Make much of him, my lords, for this is he
> Must help you more than you are hurt by me. (*3 Henry VI*, 4.6.68–76)

This is a moving moment, and in most productions impresses an audience as a still point of hope in the escalating mayhem that is *3 Henry VI*. The personal piety of the King gives credibility to his status as seer. The laying on of hands, an original Folio stage direction, represents a sort of apostolic succession from king to heir. This is a prophecy to match and rhyme with Henry V's premonition about his successor. We have seen fulfilled through the three plays the pattern by which all that was won by Henry of Monmouth (peace at home, conquest in France) has been comprehensively lost by Henry of Windsor. Now that same Henry of Windsor is allowed to foresee the coming of a third Henry who will reverse England's fortunes once again: 'this is he / Must help you more than you are hurt by me'.

In this case, the source does include an element of prophetic foreknowledge, but an element only. Hall is committed to the view that the coming of Henry VII was providentially ordained. 'Wee ought to beleve', he says when first introducing Richmond as a boy of nine in the chronicle, that he was 'sent from God, and of hym onely to be provided a kyng, for to extinguish bothe the faccions and partes, of kyng Henry the .vi. and of kyng Edwarde the. iii.' However, his account of the King's prophecy about Richmond is significantly different from Shakespeare's dramatisation of it. Richmond is brought to Henry in London and

when the kyng had a good space by himself, secretly beholden and marked, both his wit and his likely towardnes, he said to suche princes, as were then with hym; Lo, surely this is he, to whom both wee and our adversaries levyng the possession of all thynges, shall hereafter geve rome and place. So this holy man shewed before, the chaunce that should happen, that this erle Henry so ordeined by God, should in tyme to come (as he did in deede) have and enjoye the kyngdome, and the whole rule of the realme. (Bullough, III, 195)

Hall emphasises the King's holiness, he acknowledges God's special ordinance in the accession of Henry VII, but he carefully holds back from affirming the preternatural prophetic foreknowledge that the play gives us. Henry has a chance to observe Richmond's 'wit and his likely towardnes' so that it is partly a judgement of potential talent and ability. There is a caution in the phrasing that separates the King's showing 'the chaunce that should happen' of the Tudor accession from the fact that it is 'ordeined by God'. This is quite different from the dramatic certainty of the king/prophet in 'Come hither, England's hope'. Hall, even when closest to the providential design built into his narrative, is minding his theological ps and qs about prophecy.

Theatrical codes in relation to prophecy, omens and dreams, here in Shakespeare's early history plays, and indeed through virtually all the drama of the period, work counter to the orthodoxy of serious discourse on the subject at the time. Keith Thomas shows how widespread the interest in prophecies was in the sixteenth century, particularly those with political application; and the more the interest, the harder government tried to suppress them, and sophisticated intellectuals to discredit them.[10] Henry Howard's 1583 *A defensative against the poyson of supposed Prophecies*, later drawn on by Shakespeare for *Antony and Cleopatra* and *Macbeth*, may be taken as representative.[11] Howard, who was to flourish politically in the reign of James and be rewarded with the title of Earl of Northampton, under Elizabeth was suspected of Catholic sympathies with Mary Queen of Scots. The polemic orthodoxy of the *Defensative* may have been intended to ward off such accusations, but if so it was unsuccessful: the book was considered to show signs of 'seeming heresies' and of treason 'though somewhat closely covered', and Howard spent the following two years in prison or under house arrest.[12] Howard's title-page makes clear the political motivation in denouncing such prophecies as 'causes of great disorder in the common wealth'. For him

the most pestilent and bitter roote, from whence the Prophesies have drawn their head, and received, as it were, their life and soule is curiositie to searche and hunt for deeper knowledge of the future causes and affaires of the Common wealth, then it pleaseth God to discover and reveale by ordinarie meanes: As how long the Prince shall raigne? Who shall succeede and by what meane? What houses shall recover or decaye?[13]

Howard scoffs at those who believe in prophecy, offers naturalistic explanations of dreams and omens, while castigating those who presume to know the secrets of God's providence. While he does not deny that God may allow special knowledge to some of his chosen ministers, he regards this as the more unlikely in an age of Christian faith when the well-established Church needs no miracles to enforce belief.

As against such a sustained attack on the delusiveness of prophecy, supported by a full apparatus of Biblical and classical citations, in the Elizabethan theatre prophecies, omens, dreams virtually always come true. If it is a basic dramaturgical principle in later periods that a gun should never appear on stage unless it is going to be fired, an unfulfilled prophecy in Shakespearean drama would have had customers looking for their money back. What is more, in the theatre, unlike in treatises such as Howard's, those who disbelieve in prophecy are almost always

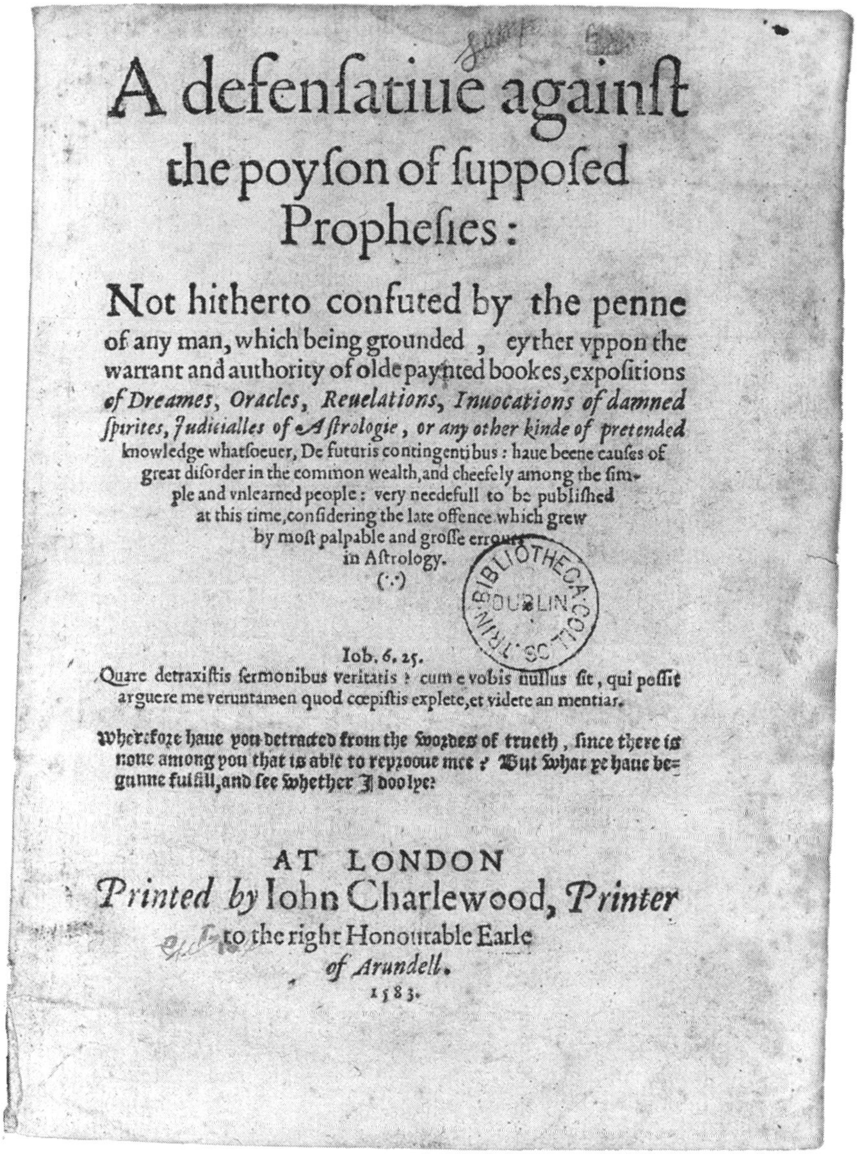

A defensatiue againſt
the poyſon of ſuppoſed Propheſies:

Not hitherto confuted by the penne

of any man, which being grounded , eyther vppon the
warrant and authority of olde paynted bookes, expoſitions
of Dreames, Oracles, Reuelations, Inuocations of damned
ſpirites, Judicialles of Aſtrologie, or *any other kinde of pretended*
knowledge whatſoeuer, De futuris contingentibus : haue beene cauſes of
great diſorder in the common wealth, and cheefely among the ſim-
ple and vnlearned people : very needefull to be publiſhed
at this time, conſidering the late offence which grew
by moſt palpable and groſſe errours
in Aſtrology.
(·.)

Iob. 6. 25.

Quare detraxiſtis ſermonibus veritatis : cum e vobis nullus ſit, qui poſſit
arguere me veruntamen quod cœpiſtis explete, et videte an mentiar.

Wherefore haue you detracted from the wordes of trueth , ſince there is
none among you that is able to reprooue mee ? But what ye haue be=
gunne fulfill, and ſee whether I doo lye?

AT LONDON

Printed by Iohn Charlewood, *Printer*
to the right Honourable Earle
of Arundell.
1583.

Plate 9 Henry Howard [Earl of Northampton], *A defensative against the poyson*
of supposed Prophecies, title-page

discredited. Omens, prophecies, dreams may be *mis*interpreted; they are
often constructed specifically to that end – more of that shortly. But they
do not lie, and those sceptics who dismiss them as nonsense do so at their
peril. It is in this spirit that Shakespeare makes use of the prophecies of
future events recorded in the chronicles. He ignores the official cautions
with which such prophecies are surrounded by the chroniclers. Instead
within the *Henry VI* plays they become sure signs of the onward shape of
the action, that pre-written narrative that is England's history.

PROPHECIES: DREAMS, OMENS, RIDDLES

In *1 Henry VI* all the prophecies are clear, definite fingerposts that
mark off the march of events towards disaster. The king's prevision of
Richmond's glorious future in *3 Henry VI* is an equally unmistakable
pointer to the 'happy ending' of the coming of the Tudors. But in
2 Henry VI the omens for the future are cryptic clues, needing to be decoded to yield up their true meaning. To begin with there are the dreams
of the Gloucesters, Duke and Duchess, in 1.2. The Duchess's dream is
easy enough to read, and an exception to the proposition that premoni-
tions always come true in the theatre. Her dream of being crowned in
Westminster with Henry and Margaret kneeling in obeisance to her is
pretty clearly a wish-fulfilment fantasy, and like most such fantasies is not
going to happen in reality. It is offered as antidote to the 'troublous dream'
of her husband, and this an audience is invited to listen to with serious
attention:

> Methought this staff, mine office-badge in court,
> Was broke in twain; by whom I have forgot,
> But, as I think, it was by th' cardinal;
> And on the pieces of the broken wand
> Were placed the heads of Edmund, Duke of Somerset,
> And William de la Pole, first Duke of Suffolk.
>
> (1.2.25–30)

This makes several sorts of sense, psychological and theatrical. Gloucester has plenty of good reason to be anxious about his position at court, as
the conspiracies of the first scene have made clear to an audience. The
Cardinal, his inveterate enemy from back to the beginning of *1 Henry VI*
in play time, is the likeliest author of his downfall. In the event, Winchester
will play a key role in bringing about his disgrace and death, but many

others are involved also: hence, at the level of premonition, the uncertainty as to just who is responsible for the breaking of his staff – 'as I think, it was by th' cardinal'.

Humphrey's dream is ominous, an intimation of his fall to come. In the following act we will see Henry ask him to hand over his badge of office as Protector, following on the disgrace of his Duchess:

> Stay, Humphrey, Duke of Gloucester. Ere thou go,
> Give up thy staff.
>
> (2.3.22–3)

The earlier dream-image of the staff broken in two gives added weight to the theatrical ceremony of Gloucester's resignation of it:

> My staff? Here, noble Henry, is my staff:
> As willingly do I the same resign
> As e'er thy father Henry made it mine;
> And even as willingly at thy feet I leave it
> As others would ambitiously receive it.
>
> (2.3.32–36)

The due decorum of government, bound in by loyalty and legitimate succession, is here abrogated. With the plurality of the ambitious 'others' eager to snatch up the staff, it will soon be broken between them, so that the dream-image of the staff destroyed is premonitory not just of the fall of Gloucester but of the very principle of law that he represents.

However, what follows in Gloucester's dream takes an audience on beyond the coming conspiracy against the Protector, which will occupy virtually all the first half of the play, to the retribution on the conspirators worked out in the second half of the action. The heads that are placed on the 'pieces of the broken wand' are those of Somerset and Suffolk. They are among those who bring about his downfall, who seek to share the power he currently enjoys. But also condensed into what Freud called the 'dream-work' are the decapitated heads of these two ambitious nobles, heads that an audience is to see in all their gory actuality in Acts 4 and 5. In both cases, not only do we witness the killing of Suffolk (4.1) and Somerset (5.2), but their heads reappear in subsequent scenes: the head of Suffolk, cradled by the anguished and mourning Margaret in 4.4, and the head of Somerset as Richard's trophy in the opening scene of *3 Henry VI*. The dream of Gloucester encodes in a symbolic shorthand key theatrical events that will take an audience through the present play and into the next in the series.

The dream in 1.2 gives one set of clues as to what is to come; the prophecies, commissioned by Eleanor in 1.4, add in another. The questions asked by the conjuror Bolingbroke of the spirit that voices itself through the witch Margery Jourdain are just the sort of 'poyson of supposed prophecies' decried by Howard, enquiries as to 'how long the Prince shall raigne? Who shall succeede and by what meane? What houses shall recover or decay?' In the sources the Duchess of Gloucester stood accused of the more active and malevolent sorcery of practising upon a wax image of the King, but this sort of infernal political opinion poll was quite bad enough. The answers that Eleanor gets to her questions are equivocal ones, as one might expect from such oracular predictions of the future, notorious from antiquity for their capacity to be read more than one way:

> BOLINGBROKE [*Reading from a scroll*] 'First, of the king: what shall
>   of him become?'
> SPIRIT The duke yet lives that Henry shall depose:
>   But him outlive and die a violent death.
>   [*As the spirit speaks, Southwell writes the answer*]
> BOLINGBROKE 'What fate awaits the Duke of Suffolk?'
> SPIRIT By water shall he die and take his end.
> BOLINGBROKE 'What shall betide the Duke of Somerset?'
> SPIRIT Let him shun castles:
>   Safer shall he be upon the sandy plains
>   Than where castles mounted stand.   (1.4.28–36)

Once again we hear of the deaths of Suffolk and Somerset, whose heads appeared on Gloucester's broken staff, and true to the riddling character of prophesies we can be sure that they will be fulfilled in some tricky unexpected way. As indeed they are, when Suffolk is killed by the pirate Wa[l]ter Whitmore, and Somerset at St Albans by the Castle – 'mounted' as an ale-house sign. For the rest of the action Suffolk and Somerset are doubly marked men.

The use made of the first prophecy about the fate of the king is more complicated. It is fairly obviously constructed both to give Eleanor the answer she wants to hear, and to reveal the truth the audience can guess at and will see fulfilled. Eleanor wants to think that her husband the Duke of Gloucester will depose Henry; given that Humphrey is a generation older than his nephew, Henry might well outlive him but in this reading he will come to an unnatural end. Of course it is Gloucester who will be deposed by Henry rather than the other way round. These questions and answers are written down, no doubt to be used as evidence against the Duchess, but also for a second re-reading of them which allows for a secondary ambiguity in relation to the prophecy about the kingship. One of the captors of the Duchess is York, who appears very oddly here in company with Buckingham. It is politically confusing to find York in alliance with the Lancastrian Buckingham, and the last time we saw him he declared his strategy was 'To make a show of love to proud Duke Humphrey' (1.1.238). Several modern productions – Barton and Hall's *Wars*, the *Plantagenets* – tidied up here, by having Suffolk come on in place of Buckingham and York, Suffolk who had told Margaret in the preceding scene that he 'had limed a bush' (1.3.83) for the Duchess of Gloucester. This makes one kind of theatrical sense. What Shakespeare wanted, however, at the expense of such clear narrative continuity, is to have York read out the prophecies with the different meanings they have for him.

York is not as credulous as Eleanor; he immediately sees the ambiguous reversibility of subject and object in 'The duke yet lives that Henry shall depose', and cites the most famous classical example of such oracular double-dealing, the prophecy to Pyrrhus from the Pythian Apollo: '*Aio te, Æacida, Romanos vincere posse*' (1.4.60). Because of Latin's use of the accusative and infinitive construction in indirect speech, this can tell Pyrrhus, descendant of Aeneas, either that he will conquer the Romans (as he hopes) or that they will conquer him (as turns out to be the case). Still, for all York's scepticism, the prophecy here speaks to an audience of the events of the first act of *3 Henry VI* where, in the Parliament-scene, York will in fact depose Henry, only to die a violent death shortly afterwards, leaving the king as survivor, even though Henry too of course will die by violence. (A violent death is a fairly safe prediction for almost any of the male characters in these plays.)

A scene such as this, with its use of the supernatural, poses certain problems for modern producers as to how seriously it should be portrayed, problems which in a way are only an extension of the controversial character of prophecy in Shakespeare's own time. Eleanor has been tempted to dabble in the occult as part of a political conspiracy against her husband. There is every reason for regarding with cynicism the 'prophecies' produced as a result, and the practices that accompany them. Such cynicism was reflected in the BBC Television production of Jane Howell, where the conjuring-scene was very obviously a hocus-pocus, with an assistant farcically banging on a sheet of 'thunder' to create atmosphere, sometimes at the most inappropriate times such as the line in Bolingbroke's invocation: 'Deep night, dark night, the silent of the night' (1.4.15) – crash, bang. In this production there could be no serious idiom of the supernatural. When York and Buckingham read over the written prophecies after the arrest of Eleanor and her conjuring crew, the camera did hold York in close-up reverie on the prediction 'The duke yet lives...', and there was a moment when both York and Buckingham considered the prophecies in silence. But this was immediately turned to laughter, breaking the spell, as these two hard-headed politicians returned to their normal scepticism.

By contrast with this sort of cool handling of the conjuring, the *Plantagenets* version of the scene gave it full-dress treatment. The original Folio stage direction, apparently deriving from Shakespeare's 'foul papers', read '*Here doe the Ceremonies belonging, and make the Circle, Bullingbrooke or Southwell reades,* Coniuro te, &c. *It Thunders and Lightens terribly*' (F, *The second part of Henry the Sixt*, TLN 643–6). Adrian Noble, in the *Plantagenets*, had to invent the 'ceremonies' that Shakespeare could count on his theatre company knowing, and expanded the 'Coniuro te, &c' into a series of magic invocations in Italian, Old English and Latin (*Plantagenets*, 62). The attempt here was to induce a willing suspension of disbelief and recover the full theatricality, if not the sense of danger, that an original audience might have experienced. For Shakespeare's contemporaries, prophecies were often subject to political manipulation, they might well be regarded with distrust; on the other hand, witchcraft and the invocation of spirits were taken seriously enough, as we realise when the mild King Henry without hesitation dooms Margery Jourdain to the stake, her three accomplices to the gallows.

The *Plantagenets* production (followed again by the 2000 *This England* version) added one extra question and answer to the prophecies of the Shakespearean text. After the enquiries about the King, Suffolk and Somerset, Eleanor asked Margery Jourdain 'What dost thou prophesy of Gloucester's house?', and the vatic reply came 'Why, Gloucester shall be king, Gloucester king'. These lines are in fact borrowed from the Barton–Hall production, where the whole set of prophecies was re-written, cutting out the fates of Somerset and Suffolk, and making the prophecy of Gloucester becoming king the culminating line that Margery Jourdain is unwilling to speak:

[BOLINGBROKE]   *What dost thou prophesy of Gloucester's house?*
[JOURDAIN]   *Ah, Gloucester, Gloucester!*

[BOLINGBROKE]   *Nay, I bid thee answer.*
[JOURDAIN]   *Why, Gloucester shall be King, ah, Gloucester, King!*   (*Wars*, 57)[14]

Barton and Hall here, Noble in *The Plantagenets* and Boyd in *This England* following them, point an audience forward to the accession not of Eleanor's husband, Humphrey of Gloucester, as she delusively reads it, but of the fearsome Richard of Gloucester, the prospect of whose reign terrifies even the spirit that speaks through Margery Jourdain. This kind of alteration seems very much in line with the original, the riddling prophecy with a surface meaning to be immediately misread, a truer interpretation to be revealed in time. In theatrical terms it extends audience attention further into the series beyond the *Henry VI* plays on to *Richard III*. Now, in the case of both *Wars* and *Plantagenets*, this was less of a stretch because both productions collapsed the *Henry VI* trilogy into just two plays. Still, the change brings out by contrast how limited the range of action that omens and prophecies foretell in the Shakespearean texts. Gloucester's dreams, Jourdain's oracles, provide an audience with clues and pointers of events through the remainder of *2 Henry VI* and on into the opening scenes of *3 Henry VI*, with the carry-over head of Somerset, the deposition of Henry and the death of York. But that seems to be as far as it was expected detailed memory of the predicted future could carry. Prophecies and omens, clear and obscure, help to organise audience attention in the short to medium term within the series; they do not provide a master-scheme for the series as a whole.

The miraculous appearance of the three suns coming together as one in *3 Henry VI* is taken as a sign of the future, the united triumph of the three sons of York. But if three suns can appear and merge as one, they can also pull apart again. A hint of the trouble to come between the brothers emerges at the very moment of their first triumph after the Battle of Towton. Edward, now proclaimed King, hands out titles:

> Richard, I will create thee Duke of Gloucester;
> And, George, of Clarence.

Richard protests:

> Let me be Duke of Clarence, George, of Gloucester;
> For Gloucester's dukedom is too ominous.
>   (*3 Henry VI*, 2.6.103–4, 106–7)

In the ESC version at this point 'Edward and Clarence . . . laugh at [Richard's] wish for another title, chant "Duke of Gloucester, Duke of

Gloucester", knock him down, and play with him as a football."[15] In the radically rewritten text of *Schlachten!*, where the 'York-boys' were played as mafiosi thugs, the protest of 'Rich' was at his position as the bullied younger brother:

> Why is it always someone else who tells me
> What I must do, decides what I must be?[16]

He is brutally overridden, and subjected to even more physical humiliation than in the ESC production: we are being shown the origins of the psychopathological 'Dirty Rich' to come.

These represent contemporary naturalisations of the incident within a dramaturgy that has no place for the supernatural. If we go back to Shakespeare's sources, we can see that he was drawing on a tradition about ill luck following the title of Gloucester: Hall notes in relation to the death of Humphrey that he was the third of that style to die a miserable death 'and after them kyng Richard the .iii. also, duke of Gloucester, in civil warre was slain and confounded' (Bullough, III, 108). In the dramatic context, it is almost as if Richard not only fears the bad fortune attending the title but dreads the prospect of becoming the bogeyman Gloucester he is destined to be. It is in the next scene but one that the breakpoint in the character of Richard comes, and in his long soliloquy (3.3.124–95) the newly created Duke of Gloucester emerges as monster villain.

As we move into the final phase of the cycle of civil war with the coming of Gloucester, the action is overdetermined with omens of what lies ahead. Richard's physical form itself, the prodigious circumstances of his birth, make up a whole panoply of sinister signs, drawn together in King Henry's formal prophecy as he faces death (5.6.37–56). Richard can finally bear to hear him no more. 'Die, prophet, in thy speech', he says as he stabs the King, 'For this, amongst the rest, was I ordained' (5.6.57–8). Richard affects to defy augury, as he defies every other power but himself, yet the statement of his ordained role as regicide is poised between irony and acceptance. The prophecies that he uses to bring about the downfall and death of Clarence are, as far as he is concerned, mere black propaganda:

> Clarence, beware: thou keep'st me from the light;
> But I will sort a pitchy day for thee,
> For I will buzz abroad such prophecies
> That Edward shall be fearful of his life
> And then, to purge his fear, I'll be thy death.
>
> (5.6.85–9)

Richard here uses the word 'sort', meaning to 'allot, apportion, or assign' (*OED* 1), sardonically; he will take on the role of the gods in 'sorting' Clarence's fate. Yet when in *Richard III*, Clarence is about to be imprisoned because of the apparently fabricated prophecy, it has an evidently true meaning as well:

> This day should Clarence closely be mewed up
> About a prophecy which says that 'G'
> Of Edward's heirs the murderer shall be.
>
> (1.1.38–40)

The princes in the Tower will indeed be murdered, not by G for George of Clarence, but by G for Gloucester.

The most elaborate omen in *Richard III* is of course Clarence's dream. The peculiar mode of Clarence's end in the malmsey butt was well known. It made for a black joke in the *Mirror for Magistrates* where Clarence testified to the truth of his ghostly deposition: 'I can not lye, *in vino veritas*.'[17] So in Shakespeare's play Clarence's dream of death by drowning may have made immediate sense to an original audience. But the detailed construction of the dream makes it at once a culmination and a trans-formation of the mode of ominous foreshadowing in the series. There is the circumstantial build-up to the drowning:

> Methoughts that I had broken from the Tower,
> And was embarked to cross to Burgundy,
> And in my company my brother Gloucester,
> Who from my cabin tempted me to walk
> Upon the hatches. Thence we looked toward England,
> And cited up a thousand heavy times
> During the wars of York and Lancaster,
> That had befall'n us. As we paced along
> Upon the giddy footing of the hatches,
> Methought that Gloucester stumbled, and in falling,
> Struck me, that thought to stay him, overboard
> Into the tumbling billows of the main.
>
> (1.4.9–20)

This begins in the prisoner's plausible fantasy of escape, but glancingly recalls also the history of the Wars of the Roses, all those retreats to France to prepare for a new phase of the struggle, the many vicissitudes of the conflict between York and Lancaster. Clarence's relationship with his brother Gloucester is that of warrior comrades together; even in dream conciousness Clarence does not suspect Richard of treachery. Yet the language and the action of his dream know better than he does. It is Gloucester who 'tempted' him to walk on the dangerous hatches; it is while thinking to help his stumbling brother that he himself is 'struck' into the sea.

Clarence's dream, however, goes far beyond that of Humphrey of Gloucester, for instance, with its premonition of doom, because it goes on to the experience of death and the afterlife. The brilliant vision of the bottom of the sea expresses not only the horrors of mortality – 'A thousand men that fishes gnawed upon' – but the lost treasures of sunken ships that vividly bespeak the vanity of human wishes and desires. The terror of drowning is as nothing in comparison to the inferno of the mind that comes next, as the soul of Clarence is ferried into the underworld. Two ghosts are there in particular to accuse him of two outstanding sins, perjury against 'my great father-in-law, renowned Warwick', and the murder of Edward Prince of Wales:

> A shadow like an angel, with bright hair
> Dabbled in blood; and he shrieked out aloud,
> 'Clarence is come: false, fleeting, perjured Clarence,
> That stabbed me in the field by Tewkesbury.
> Seize on him, furies, take him unto torment.'
>
> (1.4.53–7)

The Senecan landscape of Hades takes on the Dantesque colouring of Christian guilt. Though Clarence will plead to his murderers for his life with a spirit and a logic granted to no one else in the play, his dream represents in a way that is also unique the full interiorisation of the principle of premonition that everywhere else in the series involves a simpler hermeneutics, a prophecy needing interpretation, signs for those with the eyes to see them.

THE EFFICACY OF CURSING

It is only to be expected, in the high declamatory style of the early histories, that the vanquished *in extremis* should curse the enemies who have brought them to death. So Joan Pucelle, at the point of being dragged off to execution, lays her curse upon her captor York and on England:

> Then lead me hence, with whom I leave my curse:
> May never glorious sun reflex his beams
> Upon the country where you make abode;
> But darkness and the gloomy shade of death

> Environ you, till mischief and despair
> Drive you to break your necks or hang yourselves!
> (5.4.86–91)

Joan from her first appearance has been hailed by the French as a prophetess. 'No prophet will I trust if she proves false' (1.2.150), declares Charles, inspired by her as they go out to fight the English before Orléans, and with the siege lifted, he urges France to 'triumph in thy glorious prophetess' (1.6.8). She is even assured of canonisation for her patriotic victory:

> No longer on Saint Denis will we cry,
> But Joan la Pucelle shall be France's saint.
> (1.6.28–9)

Shakespeare and his audience would no doubt have been astonished to learn that this prospect of Saint Joan was to become a reality in 1920. For in the play, by the time she comes to die, the hallowed status claimed for Joan by the French, suspect from the start in the play's partisan English point of view, has been thoroughly exposed. It is from the fiends that Joan derives her power, the fiends who in 5.3 appear so dramatically to refuse her pleas for further help: '*They walk, and speak not . . . They hang their heads . . . They shake their heads . . . They depart*' (5.3.12,17,19,23 SDs). What, then, if any force can be attributed to Joan's dying curse on England beyond the last vented spite of the convicted witch?

A good deal of force in many twentieth-century stagings, going back as far as F. R. Benson's historic production in 1906. The political colouring of his view of Joan's death was apparent from his production note, quoted already in Chapter 1:

the wanton aggression against France, was inevitably followed by civil disruption at home . . . the War of the Roses, were practically a punishment, for a War of greed and spoliation, which reached its climax in the murder of Joan of Arc.[18]

In the same spirit, a link between Joan's dying curse and the domestic struggle that followed in England was suggested by later productions. Barton and Hall beefed up Joan's curse with lines borrowed from the opening scene of *1 Henry VI*, Bedford's gloomy forebodings on England's fate following the death of Henry V:

> Then lead me hence; with *you* I leave my curse:
> May never glorious sun reflex his beams
> Upon *that England* where you make abode.
> Posterity, await for wretched years:

> *Thy land* be made a nourish of salt tears,
> And none but women left to wail the dead:
> *Let* darkness, and the gloomy shade of death,
> Environ you *and yours*, till *black* despair
> Drive you to break your necks or hang yourselves!
> (*Wars*, 40)

The re-written lines contrive to point up Joan's execration as a curse on England to be fulfilled long after the death of York and his descendants when, in *Richard III*, 4.4. a chorus of widows are left to mourn their murdered men.

Barton and Hall ingeniously mimic the styles of curses and prophecy current in Shakespeare's theatre in their pastiche passages. But the very coherent and systematic scheme by which these are used to support an overriding thesis about the Wars of the Roses and their origins is unlike the way the original texts function. At this stage in the debate over Shakespeare's history plays, we hardly need any further demonstration that Tillyard's concept of the curse on England is ideologically oversimplified in face of the multiple competing historiographical constructions reflected in his work. What I have been trying to bring out in this chapter, rather, is the way such a concept, so influential in shaping the Barton–Hall production, is inconsistent with Shakespeare's original theatrical practice, which does not deal in long-term causalities in its use of curses or prophecies. Retributive justice does come in the *Henry VI – Richard III* plays but occasionally, uncertainly, and only in the last phase with any marked relationship between curse and outcome. Though vengeance may descend swiftly and unmistakably on the Cardinal and Suffolk, the murderers of Duke Humphrey, elsewhere in the series curse and consequence are much more undecidable.

There is, for instance, York's dying curse at Wakefield, remembered against Margaret by her opponents in *Richard III*. York in fact calls for revenge both on Clifford the killer of Rutland, and on Margaret who has crowned him with the mock paper crown, proffered him the napkin stained with Rutland's blood to dry his tears:

> These tears are my sweet Rutland's obsequies
> And every drop cries vengeance for his death
> 'Gainst thee, fell Clifford, and thee, false Frenchwoman . . .
> There, take the crown and, with the crown, my curse;
> And in thy need such comfort come to thee
> As now I reap at thy too cruel hand. –

> Hard-hearted Clifford, take me from the world,
> My soul to heaven, my blood upon your heads.
>
> (*3 Henry VI*, 1.4.147–68)

Does an audience see the curse take effect? Clifford dies in the next act, it is true, but he dies unrepentant, regretting only his death as it will bring the downfall of the house of Lancaster. The last words of his soliloquy are defiant:

> Come, York and Richard, Warwick and the rest:
> I stabbed your fathers' bosoms – split my breast.
>
> (2.6.29–30)

The best revenge the sons of York can exact is posthumous abuse of Clifford's dead body.

There is a rough justice in Margaret's plight after Tewkesbury. She who taunted York with the death of his young son Rutland must see her own son Edward stabbed before her eyes. This could be interpreted as the fulfilment of York's curse:

> And in thy need such comfort come to thee
> As now I reap at thy too cruel hand.

But no reference is made back to the death of York, nor is the analogy between Edward and Rutland pointed up dramatically. Rather the opposite: Rutland is a pathetic child pleading for his life to the ruthless and implacable Clifford; Edward is proud and princely, goading his captors with insults, defying the sons of York to the death:

> Lascivious Edward, and thou, perjured George,
> And thou, misshapen Dick, I tell ye all
> I am your better, traitors as ye are,
> And thou usurp'st my father's right and mine.
>
> (5.5.34–7)

Ironically the only 'comfort' Margaret craves and is denied in her 'need' is the release of death. She denounces the murderers of her son out of the anguish of her mother's love, without a backward glance at what she did to York:

> You have no children, butchers! If you had,
> The thought of them would have stirred up remorse;
> But if you ever chance to have a child
> Look in his youth to have him so cut off
> As, deathsmen, you have rid this sweet young prince.
>
> (5.5.63–7)

Even more remarkably, neither Edward nor Clarence, brothers of the murdered Rutland, at this point make the obvious retort.

Against such an indistinct and uncertain pattern of crime and punishment, execration and fulfilment throughout the *Henry VI* plays, in *Richard III* the curse becomes a precise engine of destruction. When Margaret first appears in the court of the Yorkists, they cite the curse of York as the just cause of her suffering, Richard leading the self-righteous chorus:

> The curse my noble father laid on thee
> When thou didst crown his warlike brows with paper
> And with thy scorns drew'st rivers from his eyes,
> And then to dry them gav'st the Duke a clout
> Steep'd in the faultless blood of pretty Rutland –
> His curses then, from bitterness of soul
> Denounced against thee, are all fall'n upon thee,
> And God, not we, hath plagu'd thy bloody deed.
>
> (1.3.172–9)

However dubious may be the position of Richard as moral spokesman, for any audience that has seen *3 Henry VI* this so precisely recalls the scene of York's torture that it is hard to resist its authority. But resist it Margaret does:

> Did York's dread curse prevail so much with heaven
> That Henry's death, my lovely Edward's death,
> Their kingdom's loss, my woeful banishment,
> Should all but answer for that peevish brat?
>
> (1.3.189–92)

And it is out of such a spirit of impenitence and disbelief that she builds up to her climactic denunciation of the assembled company:

> Can curses pierce the clouds, and enter heaven?
> Why then, give way, dull clouds, to my quick curses.
>
> (1.3.193–4)

What is so extraordinary in the rhapsody of cursing that follows is the exactness of the fate Margaret assigns to each of those accursed, and the rigour with which each one comes about. King Edward is to die by surfeit as King Henry died by murder; his son Edward is to die for Margaret's son Edward 'by like untimely violence'; Queen Elizabeth will outlive her glory, as Margaret has hers; those who condoned the murder of Prince Edward at Tewkesbury are to die 'by some unlooked accident cut off'. For Richard the vengeance of heaven is to be deferred 'till thy sins be ripe', when he is to be afflicted with paranoia, insomnia and tormented guilty nightmares, all of which we will see by the end of the play. Margaret's Senecan role in the play is Shakespeare's invention with no equivalent in the chronicle sources, and 'her theology', as Anthony Hammond notes in his Arden edition, is 'sub-Christian'.[19] Yet there is a specifically Christian colouring of guilt in the acknowledgement at point of death by each of those subject to Margaret's curse that it has come upon them.

The progress of the curse is cumulative through the play's action. Rivers and Grey, the first to die, remember Margaret's curse upon themselves and can only will it onward to take effect upon the others on her list:

> GREY   Now Margaret's curse is fall'n upon our heads,
> When she exclaimed on Hastings, you, and I,
> For standing by when Richard stabbed her son.
> RIVERS   Then cursed she Richard,
> Then cursed she Buckingham,
> Then cursed she Hastings. O remember God,
> To hear her prayer for them, as now for us   (3.3.14–20)

This forwarding of the curse on to others by its initial victims intermeshes with patterns of self-doom, most notably in the case of Buckingham. In the scene where King Edward arranges a solemn amnesty on past feuds between his courtiers, Buckingham makes a particularly full vow of peace:

> Whenever Buckingham doth turn his hate
> Upon your grace, but with all duteous love
> Doth cherish you and yours, God punish me
> With hate in those where I expect most love.
> When I have most need to employ a friend,
> And most assurèd that he is a friend,
> Deep, hollow, treacherous, and full of guile
> Be he unto me. This do I beg of heaven,
> When I am cold in love to you or yours.
>
> (2.1.32–40)

As he is about to be executed at the beginning of Act 5, Buckingham recalls this oath and acknowledges the divine justice of his punishment.

Here perjury is the manifestly punishable crime that it is not in the earlier plays:

> That high All-Seer which I dallied with
> Hath turned my feignèd prayer on my head,
> And given in earnest what I begged in jest.
> Thus doth he force the words of wicked men
> To turn their own points in their masters' bosoms.
>
>   (5.1.20–4)

Equally, however, he remembers Margaret's warning of him against Richard:

> Thus Margaret's curse falls heavy on thy neck:
> 'When he', quoth she, 'shall split thy heart with sorrow,
> Remember Margaret was a prophetess.'
>
>   (5.1.25–7)

Margaret's 'sub-Christian' cursing and the fully Christian confession of sin come together in the overdetermined pattern of causality typical of *Richard III*.

Buckingham dies on All Souls' day. Shakespeare intermits over twenty-one months of actual history to have the Battle of Bosworth follow on the next day, so that he can have the spirits of all Richard's victims plausibly abroad to visit him in sleep. It is Buckingham who invokes them to witness his own death:

> Hastings and Edward's children, Grey and Rivers,
> Holy King Henry, and thy fair son Edward,
> Vaughan, and all that have miscarrièd
> By underhand, corrupted foul injustice,
> If that your moody, discontented souls
> Do through the clouds behold this present hour,
> Even for revenge mock my destruction.
>
>   (5.1.3–9)

By night Buckingham will be in a position to join this troop of ghostly visitants. The gathering of the ghosts, like the gathering of the three widowed mothers/queens in the previous act with Margaret acting as curse-leader of the three, brings to a head the action of the play, and in some sense the action of the series, an effect particularly notable in the 2001 RSC production where virtually the whole dead cast of the *Henry VI* plays were assembled to assist at Richard's Bosworth defeat.

The alternate curses and blessings of Richard and Richmond accentuate the momentum of the play towards the defeat of one, the victory of

the other. What we have here is no longer the partisan, tit-for-tat cursing of Lancastrians by Yorkists, Yorkists by Lancastrians. All Richard's
murderees of both houses join in cursing him, blessing his antagonist.
The universal damnation pronounced on the tyrant by representatives
of Lancaster (Edward, Henry) and York (Clarence, the Princes in the
Tower) is the counterpart of the universal sanction for the emergent
successor who will bring unity to the two houses. The curses that have
been sprayed around over the preceding series are now concentrated on
a single object. By a process of attrition carried out by Richard himself, Richard is the sole remaining object of Margaret's original curse,
a curse now multiplied and endorsed by the curses of everyone else he
has dispatched. His death, clearing the way for a new age, is massively
overdetermined.

RICHARD III AND THE SENSE OF AN ENDING

The *Henry VI – Richard III* series starts with an ending, the death of
Henry V, and ends with a beginning, the accession of Henry Tudor. In
this it fulfils the criterion of David Scott Kastan for the 'shape of time'
in the history play: 'an open-ended and episodic structure'.[20] Although
Barbara Hodgdon's book *The End Crowns All* is specifically concerned
with the endings of the history plays, she argues that the drive towards
closure is always challenged by contradictions within the texts or the
varying productions of those texts, denying the unequivocal completion
of their closure.[21] From this perspective *Richard III* could be seen to be
problematic in that its ending seems so very final, so unambiguously
an endorsement of the providential destiny of the Tudors in concluding the civil wars the four plays have serially dramatised. Phyllis Rackin
is surely right to maintain that 'in *Richard III* Shakespeare reconstructs
the history he has already written, retroactively imposing a providential order that makes sense of the Machiavellian chaos he depicted in
the Henry VI plays'.[22] The choices for theatre directors with such an
ending seem to be, as I argued in Chapter 3 in relation to the representation of Bosworth, to give full authorisation and an aura of the
sacred to Richmond (as Barton and Hall did), or, like the ESC, to undermine his final speech by the 'selling of the President' television rendering
of it. A third possibility is to contrive an extra final image as in the
Jane Howell BBC Television version which had a hysterically laughing
Margaret cradling the mutilated corpse of Richard, a blasphemous, black
Pietà image on top of a heap of dead bodies. This is one heavy-hitting

Plate 10 Queen Margaret (Julia Foster) with the body of Richard III (Ron Cook), BBC Television Shakespeare production of *Richard III*, directed by Jane Howell, produced by Shaun Sutton 1983

way to count the cost of the war and keep Margaret as Fury/Nemesis to the end.

In order to define the sense of an ending in *Richard III*, it may help to draw an analogy with the *Oresteia*. F. R. Benson's first modern production of the three parts of *Henry VI* in 1906 'followed on from his company's triumph the previous year with Aeschylus' *Oresteia* and several reviewers made the comparison'.[23] Another Aeschylean trilogy was brought to R. W. Chambers' mind by the experience of seeing the *Henry VI – Richard III* plays in Pasadena. To see the plays produced in sequence, he said,

was to realise that Shakespeare began his career with a tetralogy based on recent history, grim, archaic, crude, yet nevertheless such as, for scope, power, patriotism, and sense of doom, had probably had no parallel since Aeschylus wrote the trilogy of which the *Persians* is the surviving fragment.[24]

Now it is virtually certain that Shakespeare would not have known the *Oresteia*. It is possible that via Thomas Legge's three-part Latin play *Richardus Tertius* he might have been aware of the classical trilogy form.[25] At most the *Oresteia* could be considered some sort of remote ancestor of Shakespeare's *Henry VI – Richard III* sequence. If a comparison with the early history play series is worth making, it is rather by way of illuminating the theatrical interrelation between the several parts in Aeschylus and Shakespeare, and how they progress to a conclusion in the *Eumenides* and *Richard III*.

In one thing at least the *Oresteia* resembles Shakespeare's set of four histories: no one play until the last is complete in itself. In the last words of the *Agamemnon*, Clytemnestra speaks hopefully, but evidently unrealistically, in declaring that the murder of Agamemnon and Cassandra represents a conclusive happy ending for herself and Aegisthus:

> I
> and you together will make all things well,
> for we are masters of this house.[26]

An audience knows that Orestes is waiting to enter the story. At the conclusion of the *Libation-bearers* the Chorus lists what is by now the sequence of three horrors of the house of Atreus: the father eating his children in the banquet of Thyestes, the murder of husband by wife, the murder of mother by son.

> When will it find completion? When will it end?
> When will the fierceness of our ruin
> fall again to its sleep?
> (*Libation-bearers*, 1074–6)

The answer to the Chorus' question comes in the *Eumenides*, when Orestes is tried and formally exculpated from the guilt of having killed his mother. The cycle is at last over. Similarly the *Henry VI* series rolls on from play to play, plunging further down into chaos, revealing new depths of fratricidal violence, until in *Richard III* a new order of things can be declared.

The curse on the house of Atreus is not one sequence going back to one identifiable cause. Before the banquet of Thyestes, glanced at but not expanded on in the *Agamemnon*, was the seduction by Thyestes of his brother Atreus's wife. And there are proximate causes as well as final causes that are difficult to evaluate. One of Clytemnestra's motives for killing her husband was his sacrifice of their daughter Iphigenia to make possible the war against Troy, an understandable if not necessarily a justifiable motive. But how much choice did Agamemnon have in the matter? A famous crux – 'he put on the harness of Necessity' (*Agamemnon*, 220) – suggests that he both willed the impious act of killing his daughter, and that the gods made him an offer he could not refuse. In the *Henry VI* plays short-term causes and effects, figured as curses and prophecies, may be relatively clear, but they so overlap and overlay one another as to make larger patterns no more readable than they are in the *Oresteia*. In the tropes of action that doom old honourable England – Salisbury, Bedford, Talbot – to go down to defeat, allow a new generation of political feudsters and overreachers to hound to death the last pillar of upright law, Humphrey of Gloucester, in all of these who is to say what forces are operating? Are there any principles beyond a neutral dynamics of power that produce the bloodlusts of the second generation of civil warriors, the child-killing Clifford, the sadistic Margaret, the conscienceless sons of York? A final phase must come to resolve into clarity these partial patternings, these dark tangles of evil begetting evil.

In *Richard III* such a phase takes the Manichean form of a separation into light and darkness: the wholly good Richmond, saviour of England, faces and defeats the wholly evil Richard on whom all the sins of the foregoing generations of feuding are settled. In the *Libation-bearers* Orestes himself must take the parts both of scapegoat and saviour. He willingly, with due deliberation, kills his mother, knowing what he does, knowing the consequence, and yet, as madness is about to descend upon him, proclaims the justice of what he has done and his sanction in the command of Apollo. In the *Eumenides* it is gods against gods who must decide the outcome. Orestes' matricide is, as it were, a test-case in the trial of strength between the law of the Furies and that of the Olympian deities, Apollo and Athena. And if the victory is declared for the younger (male) principle of the Olympians, the reconciliation of the end is only achieved by an accommodation with the older (female) order of the Furies who become the Eumenides, the kindly goddesses. Comparably, Richmond's victory at the end of *Richard III* must be founded on a union of the two contending houses, himself as last Lancastrian heir and his (unseen and voiceless) female consort Elizabeth of York.

Local and immediate political motives informed the *Oresteia*, as they informed the *Henry VI – Richard III* plays. No doubt there was a special significance in Aeschylus' focus on the perpetual alliance between Athens and Argos promised as reward for Athena's clearing of the Argive leader Orestes, and in the setting up of the court of the Areopagus to hear its first murder trial.[27] The politics of fifth-century Athens may have been a founding fact of the *Oresteia* just as the 'Tudor myth' of late sixteenth-century England may have been for Shakespeare's plays. But to say that these political ideologies inform the plays is not to say they determine them, or represent the end for which they were conceived. Philip Edwards speaks well of the aspirational nature of the coming of the perfect king in Shakespeare's histories:

The belief that the king is come who will alter our lives and protect us is transformed into the hope that he will come. The happy endings become not statements that the course of history has changed, but fragile moments of expectation.[28]

The politics of *Richard III* is thus best conceived as a potentially Utopian politics rather than the propaganda of Tudor absolutism. So too with the *Eumenides*. The conversion of the Furies into the Kindly Goddesses, the vision of a perpetually peaceful and fertile Athens that they will guard from underground, is a vision of what hypothetically might be, not the idealisation of a given political present state. Shakespeare need not have believed that with the coming of Henry Tudor all divisiveness was at an end and perfect peace reigned. His late collaboration with Fletcher on *Henry VIII* shows his awareness that power politics ran on uninterruptedly into the Tudor reigns. In the triumph of Richmond and his final speech are voiced an imagination of the end of strife and struggle, a coming of national harmony:

> We will unite the white rose and the red.
> Smile heaven upon this fair conjunction,
> That long have frowned upon their enmity.
> (5.5.19–21)

As the *Oresteia* moves from one imagined order of things to another equally imagined, so from the *Henry VI* plays to *Richard III* Shakespeare moves from history into myth.

The comparison of the *Henry VI – Richard III* plays with the *Oresteia*, different as they are, reveals the theatrical interdependence of the several plays in both, and the way they both progress from dark adumbrations of the relation between past and future towards a clarified vision, the sense of an ending. To associate Shakespeare with Aeschylus may also help to accentuate the double origins of Shakespeare's early histories with their classical inheritance crossed with a secularised Christianity. If the use of curses and prophecies in these plays brings out the tensions between official scepticism and disapproval of such phenomena and the popular belief on which Shakespeare capitalised theatrically, it illustrates also the way in which Christian and classical modes of signification could co-exist and interpenetrate. Margaret is indeed a Fury – no chance there of her turning kindly goddess – and her Furious curses must have their fated effect. Only as they take hold do they grow into something that could be construed as Christian Providence. Curses and prophecies, with their propulsion of an audience forward towards their fulfilment, bring us at last in *Richard III* not to an absolute and unequivocal closure, but more notionally to the sense of an ending.

PART III

Richard II – Henry V

CHAPTER SIX

Looking back

There is one sonorous prophecy in *Richard II*, when the Bishop of Carlisle speaks up to oppose Bullingbrook's ascent of the throne:

> My lord of Herford here, whom you call king,
> Is a foul traitor to proud Herford's king,
> And if you crown him let me prophesy:
> The blood of English shall manure the ground
> And future ages groan for this foul act.
> Peace shall go sleep with Turks and infidels,
> And in this seat of peace tumultuous wars
> Shall kin with kin and kind with kind confound.
> Disorder, horror, fear and mutiny
> Shall here inhabit, and this land be called
> The field of Golgotha and dead men's skulls.
> Oh, if you raise this house against this house
> It will the woefullest division prove
> That ever fell upon this cursed earth.
> Prevent it, resist it, let it not be so,
> Lest child, child's children, cry against you woe.
>
> (4.1.134–49)

For those who see the eight history plays as a single cycle, this provides a master plan for the whole, looking forward from the moment of the usurpation of Richard's throne by Henry IV in 1399 to the dynastic wars that tore England apart in the century following. But in comparison with the mode of prophecy used in the *Henry VI – Richard III* plays it appears very generalised and non-specific, not susceptible to the sort of demonstrable fulfilment that was normal in the earlier series. In fact, although chronologically the Bishop's speech looks forward to the Wars of the Roses, theatrically it looks back to Shakespeare's dramatisation of those wars. What could have been a more vivid illustration of the 'confounding' by war of 'kin with kin, kind with kind' than the scene in *3 Henry VI* with the father who has killed his son, the son who has killed

his father? Writing *Richard II* in 1595, Shakespeare could gesture back
to the sequence of plays on the reigns of Henry VI and Richard III,
reassembled and produced by the Chamberlain's Men in 1594 after
the re-opening of the theatres, the sequence 'which oft our stage hath
shown'.[1]

The *Richard II – Henry V* plays are not shaped to the same extent as
the earlier series by anticipatory and proleptic figures, prophecies and
curses. They work more typically by the retrospective rehearsal of what
has gone before. This would make sense if my hypothesis is correct, and
Shakespeare moved forward tentatively one play at a time with his second
English history series. There may, as a result, be relatively little seeding
of characters, laying of plot trails in advance; the individual plays may
have a much more pronounced independence of structure and formal
closure. But each sequent play is written with a full consciousness of
what has gone before, and this awareness of previous history shared by
characters and audience becomes a part of the substance of the drama.
In the *Henry IV* plays, in particular, the King's dethronement in *Richard II*
and the events that led up to it are revisited again and again. And even on
the eve of Agincourt, Henry V has not forgotten the fault his father made
in 'compassing the crown'; he can only pray that for this one occasion
God may let the memory pass.

However, the retrospective mode in this series of plays is not confined
to the troubled awareness of the consequences of usurpation. From the
start of *Richard II* itself looking back is habitual. Where *1 Henry VI* began
with the catastrophe of Henry V's untimely death plunging the country
into turmoil, the famous opening line of *Richard II* resonates with the
sense of England's past: 'Old John of Gaunt, time-honoured Lancaster'.
The previous reign, the previous monarch Edward III and his son the
Black Prince, are used recurrently through the play as emblems of an
Edenic earlier time. Associated with this idealisation of a past England
is the crusade or holy war. England's royal kings, according to Gaunt,
have been

> Renownèd for their deeds as far from home
> For Christian service and true chivalry
> As is the sepulchre in stubborn Jewry
> Of the world's ransom, blessèd Mary's son.
>   (2.1.53–6)

The crusade that Henry IV promises to lead at the end of *Richard II*,
that he keeps having to defer through the two succeeding plays of his

reign, thus becomes a figure for a desire to go back as much as a delusive prospect for the future. Henry's anxious plans for an international expedition to the Holy Land are bound to remain unfulfilled as they represent an impossible dream of turning back the historical clock.

The *Richard II – Henry V* plays, with their recurrent awareness of past times, raise issues about historical periodisation. Some scholars have argued that the series shows a self-conscious dramatisation of the movement from late medieval feudalism to an early modern monarchical system.[2] Others have denied to the plays this sort of historical perspective, maintaining instead that the histories are based in a mythological order of things. The recessive mode of looking back can be seen as symptomatic of the state of fallen man, the always imagined perfection of past time a secular substitute for the lost garden of Eden.[3] There is the possibility that what has been taken to be Shakespeare's evocation of historical process is actually a back projection of modern ideas of period. So, for instance, the high formal style and elaborate ceremonies of the opening scenes of *Richard II* in nineteenth- and twentieth-century productions provided the basis for a show of 'medievalism' with all its associated pageantry and glamour. Real horses and lances, sumptuous heraldic costuming were the order of the day from Beerbohm Tree's 1903 production down to the BBC Television version of 1978. Recent productions have set their face against such period-piece styling. The 2000 *Richard II* at Stratford, directed by Steven Pimlott, set the play in a white box with modern-dress costumes to clear it entirely of its associated medieval trappings. *Schlachten!* evoked in its first section, *Richard Deuxième*, a court world at once primitive and decadent, the King's French-speaking affectations and clownish histrionicism in marked contrast to the stark rituals of power over which he presided.

The object of this chapter is to explore the range of uses to which the retrospective mode is put in the *Richard II – Henry V* sequence, both as it figures the sense of time in history and as a theatrical experience for audiences. To begin with, there is the nostalgia that suffuses *Richard II* and recurs occasionally in the later plays as well. What is the designed effect of the characters looking back regretfully to a past era of greatness and glory in such marked contrast to the present? How may the playing of this in performance relate to the historical awareness of period succeeding period? In the *Henry IV* plays there are a number of times when scenes, incidents, events represented earlier are recalled and replayed. How sharply conscious will an audience be of ways in which history is being rewritten at such moments? What kinds of ironic awareness may play about the contrast between the previously performed scenes and their recollected versions? The deposition of Richard by Henry Bullingbrook is not only the main subject of *Richard II*; it preoccupies the characters of the two *Henry IV* plays, not least King Henry himself. One of the striking features of Bullingbrook in *Richard II* is the opacity of his motives in that action of deposing his cousin; as he ruminates and reflects on the past in the later plays, we are given greater access to his thoughts, and successive readings of his action. There is a case for seeing in the sequence a pattern of progressive revelation, comparable to Ibsen's technique of moving the action forward by digging through layers of misconstruction of the past. Throughout *Richard II*, *1 Henry IV*, *2 Henry IV*, the plays principally under scrutiny in this chapter, the theatrical present moment is alive with the awareness of its past antecedents.

NOSTALGIA

The event to which *Richard II* looks back most immediately is the relatively recent murder of the Duke of Gloucester. Bullingbrook accuses Mowbray of the crime in their first scene of mutual recrimination, but the unspoken subtext of that scene is the King's known involvement in having his uncle killed. Gloucester's widow makes of the death an act of sacrilege, in her bitter complaint to Gaunt in the following scene:

> Edward's seven sons, whereof thyself art one,
> Were as seven vials of his sacred blood,
> Or seven fair branches springing from one root.
> Some of these seven are dried by nature's course,
> Some of those branches by the Destinies cut,
> But Thomas, my dear lord, my life, my Gloucester,
> One vial full of Edward's sacred blood,
> One flourishing branch of his most royal root,
> Is cracked, and all the precious liquor spilt,
> Is hacked down, and his summer leaves all faded,
> By envy's hand, and murder's bloody axe.
>
> (1.2.11–21)

The twin extended simile here redoubles the imagery of the sacred. The family tree of the Plantagenets deriving from Edward III becomes a tree of Jesse, the iconographic representation of the genealogy of Christ.[4] The violent iconoclasm of hacking down one of the branches of this royal tree is matched by the desecration of smashing the relic-like vial filled with Edward's sacred blood. Gaunt is not unmoved by his sister-in-law's vehement protests, but he produces a response just as devoutly orthodox:

> God's is the quarrel, for God's substitute,
> His deputy anointed in His sight,
> Hath caused his death, the which if wrongfully
> Let heaven revenge, for I may never lift
> An angry arm against his minister.
>
> (1.2.37–41)

It hardly matters that the historical Gloucester had done a good deal to provoke his death and may have been conspiring against Richard at the time of his arrest;[5] nor yet that Gaunt himself was a fairly troublesome baron. It is Shakespeare's strategy to identify these two uncles of the King as elder statesmen, survivors of the previous age of Edward III. And the last survivors of that age are differently characterised from the comparable figures in *1 Henry VI*, where Bedford, Gloucester, Salisbury stand for the heroic reign of Henry V. They embody the glories of that reign, so suddenly brought to an end, and their removal one by one represents the extinction of soldierly strength and upright government. But the reign of Edward III is rendered as a remote pristine era subsuming into itself a timeless idyll of England; the time of Richard is by contrast a fallen latter days against which his uncles can only helplessly inveigh. The lost figure of the Black Prince helps to point the degeneracy of the present king, when York reproaches him after Gaunt's death:

> I am the last of noble Edward's sons,
> Of whom thy father, Prince of Wales, was first.
> In war was never lion raged more fierce,
> In peace was never gentle lamb more mild
> Than was that young and princely gentleman.
> His face thou hast, for even so looked he,
> Accomplished with the number of thy hours.
> But when he frowned it was against the French
> And not against his friends.
>
> (2.1.171–9)

Richard, who looks so like his father, is the simulacrum of a king, a false embodiment like Spenser's Duessa in Book 1 of the *Faerie Queene*.

In Gaunt's great paean to England it is the separateness, the specialness, the sacred status of the country that is stressed throughout. It is not only naturally embattled, moated with the sea 'against the envy of less happier lands', it is an 'other Eden', the English a chosen people. There is an implicit analogy in the fame of English kings,

> Renownèd for their deeds as far from home
> For Christian service and true chivalry
> As is the sepulchre in stubborn Jewry
> Of the world's ransom, blessèd Mary's son.

England too is a holy land. Or was. Gaunt's brilliantly managed twenty-line sentence that begins with 'This royal throne of kings, this sceptred isle' is carried forward with wave after wave of eulogy only to break with the more force on the shore:

> ... This land of such dear souls, this dear, dear land,
> Dear for her reputation through the world,
> Is now leased out, I die pronouncing it,
> Like to a tenement or pelting farm.
>
> (2.1.57–60)

Anthologised as early as 1600, Gaunt's speech has long been a set-piece of patriotic rhetoric and it has been traditionally delivered to stir audience pride: John Gielgud's stately style in the BBC Television version could be considered representative. Increasingly, however, as the post-imperial concept of English identity has become more problematic, the emphasis in performance has fallen on the sense of loss that the speech also articulates. By the Stratford production of 2000, Alfred Burke's mood in speaking Gaunt's lines was one of troubled anguish rather than patriotic fervour.[6]

England as a special place apart is not just an isolated construction of Gaunt's speech. Throughout the opening acts of *Richard II* there is an imagination of the world in which everywhere beyond England is a trackless, placeless vacancy. Mowbray is prepared to meet Bullingbrook in combat

> were I tied to run afoot
> Even to the frozen ridges of the Alps,
> Or any other ground inhabitable
> Where ever Englishman durst set his foot.
>
> (1.1.63–6)

When he is banished, he regards himself as 'cast out in the common air', speechless in being deprived of his 'native English'. 'Now no way can I stray', he declares as he leaves: 'Save back to England all the world's my way' (1.3.205–6). Bullingbrook's exit-lines are similarly fervent in their sense of deprivation:

> Then England's ground farewell, sweet soil adieu,
> My mother and my nurse that bears me yet.
> Where'er I wander, boast of this I can,
> Though banished, yet a true born Englishman.
>
> (1.3.305–8)

Where the England of *1 Henry VI* was constructed by its difference from France, where movement between the countries was a constant part of the political *va-et-vient* of the *Henry VI – Richard III* plays, in *Richard II* there is no place, there can be no place like England, or even unlike England. It is a world unto itself.

Central to this idea of the uniqueness of England is a sacred identity of land and nation. This is expressed most tellingly by Richard on his return from Ireland, when he lovingly 'salutes' his earth with his hand, playing fondly with it like 'a long-parted mother with her child' (3.2.8). The irony here, as elsewhere in the play, is that Richard is the best spokesman for those very principles of kingship and nationhood that he himself has done most to subvert. 'Landlord of England art thou now, not king' provides the peroration for Gaunt's denunciation of Richard (2.1.113). In farming the royal realm, in leasing it out, the King has traduced his own position as sovereign and the sovereignty of the relationship between king and land. In just the same way he treats Gaunt's property as convertible assets to 'make coats / To deck our soldiers for these Irish wars' (1.4.60–1). The indissoluble bond of king and country, which Richard so emphatically asserts, he himself has broken by treating his country as property he owns and can dispose of as he wishes. And that mystical relationship of king, land and people theorised by Gaunt, dramatically enacted by Richard, is in fact over by the time *Richard II* begins. What we witness in the play is a fall from an imagined earlier order of things, a fall into history.

The emblematic garden scene (3.4) shows an overgrown, disordered England:

> our sea-walled garden, the whole land,
> Is full of weeds, her fairest flowers choked up
>
> (3.4.43–4)

The 'sea-walled garden' looks back to Gaunt's 'precious stone set in the silver sea', and the Queen makes explicit the associations with Eden when she attacks the Gardener as an 'old Adam':

> What Eve, what serpent hath suggested thee
> To make a second fall of cursèd man?
> Why dost thou say King Richard is deposed?
>
> (3.4.75–7)

This is the Queen's understandably partisan view of the matter. But the play as a whole does not sanction her view of Richard's deposition as a second fall of man, nor yet the usurpation by Bullingbrook as a primal crime to be punished in England's generations to come, the perspective of the Bishop of Carlisle (and the Tillyardians). Rather the Gardener's image of the balance of power is closer to the spirit of the play's representation:

> King Richard he is in the mighty hold
> Of Bullingbrook. Their fortunes both are weighed.
> In your lord's scale is nothing but himself
> And some few vanities that make him light,
> But in the balance of great Bullingbrook
> Besides himself are all the English peers,
> And with that odds he weighs King Richard down.
>
> (3.4.83–9)

It is some such neutral political dynamics that is enacted in *Richard II* rather than the apportionment of blame to the King or the usurper. The fall of one, the rise of the other, follow through with a historical inevitability that is outside the control of either.

While the play is overwhelmingly concerned with the convulsions of the changing state in England, there is late on in the play a glimpse of a world elsewhere. Shakespeare, following Holinshed, has the about-to-be King Henry command the repeal of Mowbray's banishment in order to clear up the issue of Aumerle's complicity in Gloucester's murder:

> BULLINGBROOK ... When he's returned,
>   Against Aumerle we will enforce his trial.
> CARLISLE That honourable day shall ne'er be seen.
>   Many a time hath banished Norfolk fought
>   For Jesu Christ in glorious Christian field,
>   Streaming the ensign of the Christian cross
>   Against black pagans, Turks and Saracens,
>   And, toiled with works of war, retired himself
>   To Italy, and there at Venice gave
>   His body to that pleasant country's earth

And his pure soul unto his captain, Christ,
Under whose colours he had fought so long.   (4.1.89–100)

Holinshed merely records Norfolk's death in Venice; Shakespeare may
have gone to Stow for the suggestion that he was returning from
Jerusalem at the time (see 4.1.92–100n.). What is significant is the way
in which a whole crusading career is here imagined. Mowbray was only
banished in 1398; the parliament called by Henry at which the question of Gloucester's death was raised took place in October 1399. Yet in
Shakespeare's flexible play-time, Mowbray has been able to engage with
'black pagans, Turks and Saracens' not once but 'many a time', has worn
himself out with what sounds like half a lifetime of crusading. This is the
life of the perfect chivalric knight, graced with the equivalently perfect
death which, however, can only happen in some offstage time and place.

For Bullingbrook, Mowbray's Act 1 rival, banished at the same time
as him, his is the path not taken. Both of them were sent out into the
emptiness, the wilderness that was not-England. One repealed his own
banishment, returned to overthrow his king and take the throne. The
other turned his enforced exile into a glory and died at peace with 'his
captain, Christ'. When, at the end of the play, Henry vows atonement for
the death of Richard by making 'a voyage to the Holy Land', it is as
though he wants belatedly to do it Mowbray's way. Shakespeare had in
fact to reach forward right to the end of Henry's reign in the chronicles to
pick up this proposal for a crusade, 'a voiage which he meant to make into
the holie land, there to recover the citie of Jerusalem from the Infidels'
(Bullough, IV, 276). Linked as it is in *Richard II* to Mowbray's imagined
crusading, and to the associations of an earlier England conceived as
holy land, Henry's hope of recovering Jerusalem becomes the desire for
a time-warp that is to recur through *1* and *2 Henry IV*.

Through Adrian Noble's 1991 production of those two plays, this
motif was rendered visually by a small-scale golden model of the Holy
Sepulchre Church in Jerusalem at which the king prayed as *1 Henry IV*
opened. At the end of that scene it was then flown up, but remained
hovering overhead as reminder of the far-off goal that the king would
never reach. Such a device gave a psychological inflexion to the perpetually postponed crusade, Henry's aspired-to Jerusalem in the sky contrasted with the real earth-bound Jerusalem chamber in the palace of
Westminster where he was finally to die. In Bogdanov's *Wars of the Roses*,
the symbol of the crusade was given more far-reachingly ironic significance. In the first scene of King Bullingbrook's court (*Richard II*, 4.1),

the Regency costuming of Richard's reign had been replaced by sober-suited Victorianism, and it was a frock-coated court over which Henry presided. The only colour in the whole scene was the large crusader's flag, the flag of St George, red cross on a white ground, hanging vertically behind the small central table at which Bullingbrook sat. The crusader's flag then took on a special importance as Carlisle told of Mowbray's death after his crusading career. Later in the opening scene of *Henry V* the same flag hung behind Henry, sitting in the same position as he deliberated over the war with France. The opening credits of the video version of the whole sequence of the *Wars of the Roses* showed a crudely painted red X turning into the St George's cross flag, an ironic reminder of the disjunction between the chivalric ideals of crusading England and the bloody realities of the wars actually represented. Whatever the degree and nature of historical awareness in the succeeding plays, *Richard II* looks back to an ur-time, a time before history, when England's own sacredness as holy land made it a beacon of militant Christianity. As the time of Richard's reign is left behind, that mystical form of nostalgia is replaced by more ordinary modes of human retrospection in measurable time.

RE-WRITING HISTORY

> Open your ears; for which of you will stop
> The vent of hearing when loud Rumour speaks?

It is a brilliant device to start *2 Henry IV* with Rumour as Chorus, eye-catching ('painted full of tongues'), ear-arresting, recapitulating the story so far for those who may need reminding as to what happened at the end of *1 Henry IV*. But Rumour emblematises also the distortion of the truth in report that is one of the dramatic features of both *Henry IV* plays. Rumour, having told the news of the battle with which *1 Henry IV* ended –

> I run before King Harry's victory,
> Who in a bloody field by Shrewsbury
> Hath beaten down young Hotspur and his troops
> (1.0.23–5)

– hastily corrects himself for this unRumour-like truth-telling:

> But what mean I
> To speak so true at first? My office is
> To noise abroad that Harry Monmouth fell

> Under the wrath of noble Hotspur's sword,
> And that the king before the Douglas' rage
> Stooped his anointed head as low as death.
>
> (1.0.27–32)

In hearing this misreport, the audience is reminded of what really took place: several of the King's lookalikes were killed by Douglas, and he himself was in danger before being saved from 'Douglas' rage' by Hal. And of course it was Hotspur who went down to Harry Monmouth, not the other way round.

The skewed, false version of real events continues in the first scene with Lord Bardolph's account of Shrewsbury. He brings his co-rebel Northumberland news from the front:

> The king is almost wounded to the death,
> And, in the fortune of my lord your son,
> Prince Harry slain outright, and both the Blunts
> Killed by the hand of Douglas. Young Prince John
> And Westmoreland and Stafford fled the field,
> And Harry Monmouth's brawn, the hulk Sir John,
> Is prisoner to your son.
>
> (1.1.14–20)

Bardolph, dependent as he is on Rumour-based information, gets things the wrong way round, not only in having Prince Harry killed by Hotspur, but in making Falstaff his captive. In fact, of course, as we saw at the end of *1 Henry IV*, Falstaff having feigned death to avoid being killed or captured, claims the body of Hotspur as his trophy. There is here, though, a garble of partly true, largely false items. So, for instance, Prince John and Westmoreland have not fled, but are prominent among those who hold the field of victory at Shrewsbury; on the other hand Stafford *is* one of the notable casualties of the King's army.

The case of Douglas and 'both the Blunts' is especially interesting. Holinshed records a Sir Walter Blunt killed not once but twice in the battle. He is first dispatched as part of a violent attack 'upon them that stood about the kings standard . . . slaieng his standard-bearer sir Walter Blunt' (Bullough, IV, 190). Later, however, it is 'the earle Dowglas' who 'slue sir Walter Blunt and three other, apparelled in the kings sute and clothing' (Bullough, IV, 191).[7] Daniel in his *Civile Wars* makes sense of this by describing first the death of 'Heroycall Couragious *Blunt* araid / In habite like as was the king attirde', and then accounting for the standard-bearer

troubles, and to require some effectuall reformation in the same.

It was reported for a troth, that now when
the King hadde condiscended vnto all that was
reasonable at his hands to bee required, and seemed to humble himselfe more than was meete
for his estate, the Earle of Worcester vppon hys
returne to his nephewe, made relation cleane con-
trarie to that the King had sayde, in suche sorte,
that he set his nephewes hearte more in displea- 10
sure towardes the King, than euer it was before, driuing him by that meanes to fight why-
ther he would or not: then suddaynely blewe the
trumpettes, the Kings part cried Saint George
vpon them, the aduersaries cried *Esperance Percy*,
and so the two armies furiously ioyned. The
archers on both sides shot for the best game, laying on such loade with arrowes, that many died,
and were driuen downe, that neuer rose againe.

The Scottes (as some write) which had the 20
fore warde on the Percies side, intending to bee
reuenged of their olde displeasures done to them
by the English natio, set so fiercely on the kings
fore warde, ledde by the Earle of Stafforde, that
they made the same to draw backe, and had almost broken their aduersaries aray.

The Welchmen also which before had laine
lurking in the woddes, mountaines, and mari-

ches, hearing of this battell towarde, came to the
ayde of the Percies, and refreshed the weery people with new succours.

The King perceyuing that his men were
thus put to distresse, what with the violente impression of the Scottes, and the tempestuous
storme of arrowes, that his aduersaries dischar-
ged freely against him and his people, it was no
neede to will him to stirre., for suddainely with
his freshe battell, hee approched and relieued hys
men, so that the battell beganne more fierce than
before. Heere the Lord Henry Percy, and ȳ Erle
Dowglas, a righte stoute and hardy Captayne,
not regarding the shot of the kings battayle, nor
the close order of the rankes, preassing forwarde
togither, bente their whole forces towardes the
kings person, comming vpon him with speares,
and swords so fiercely, that the Earle of March
the Scot, perceyuing what purpose, withdrewe ȳ
King from that side of the fielde as some write,
(for his great benefite & safegard as it appeared)
for they gaue such a violent onset vpon the, that
stood about the Kings standert, that slaying his
standert bearer sir Blunt, and ouerthrowing the
standert; they made slaughter of all those that
stode about it, as the Earle of Stafforde, that
day made by the king Connestable of ȳ realme,
and diuers other.

The Prince that daye holp his father lyke a
lustie yong Gentleman, for although hee was
hurt in the face with an arrowe, so that dyuers
noble men that were about him, would haue con- 50
ueyed him forth of the fielde, yet he would in no
wise suffer them so to doe, least his departure fro
among his men, might happely haue strike some
feare into their hartes: and so without regarde of
his hurt, hee continued with his men, and neuer
ceassed, either to fight where the battell was most
hottest, or to incourage his men, where it seemed

most neede. This bataple lasted three long
houres, with indifferent fortune on both partes,
till at length, the King crying Sainct George
victorie, brake the aray of his enimies, & aduentu-
red so far, ȳ as some write, the Earle Dowglas
strake him down, & at that instāt, slew sir Walter Blunt, and three other, apparelled in ȳ kings
sute and clothing, saying, I maruel to see so many kings thus suddainely to arise. one in ȳ necke
of an other. The king indeede was raised, and did
that daye manye a noble feate of armes, for
     as it

Marginal notes:

The Earle of Worcesters double dea-ling in wrong reporting the kings wordes.

Hall. The Scottes.

Hall. The valiantie of the young prince.

The Welche-men come to ayde the Per-cies.

The Erle of Marche. Tho. Wals.

A sore battaile and wel main-teyned.

The valyant doings of the Erle Douglas.

Plate 11   Battle of Shrewsbury, Raphael Holinshed, *The laste volume of the chronicles of England, Scotland, and Irelande* . . . (London: George Bishop, 1577)

as a second, separate Sir Walter Blunt:

> Another of that forward name and race
> In that hotte worke his valiant life bestowes,
> Who bare the standard of the king that day,
> Whose colours overthrowne did much dismaie.
>
> (Bullough, IV, 214–15)

Shakespeare was not going to confuse matters at Shrewsbury by having two Blunts on the field and dramatises only Douglas' killing Sir Walter in mistake for the King, but the misrepresenting Bardolph is allowed to draw on the reduplications of Holinshed and Daniel.

What is significant in these examples of the distortions of Rumour is the criteria by which an audience in the theatre is enabled to tell true from false. What we actually see dramatised is history as it really happened, even if that includes quite unhistorical characters such as Falstaff. When we hear such events reported later in some different form, we can judge the inaccuracy of the report by contrast with the reality of what we have witnessed. This is a difficult area because Shakespeare's history plays are littered with what Kristian Smidt investigates as 'unconformities', large or small failures in narrative continuity.[8] Even within individual plays Shakespeare could be careless about details and may not have re-read his scripts to make sure the end tallied with the beginning. Could he have expected his audience to remember incidents from one play to another in the series sufficiently accurately to notice when they were misremembered? Maybe. There are at least a number of instances in the *Henry IV* plays where we seem to be asked to observe characters re-writing history, and know that is what they are doing because we have seen the orginal history dramatised in *Richard II*.

The first and most striking instance is Hotspur's recollection in *1 Henry IV* of his original meeting with Bullingbrook. It is in the scene of the Percys' initial conspiracy, following the King's demand for Hotspur's prisoners and his refusal to ransom Mortimer, a scene brilliantly worked up by Shakespeare out of Holinshed's statement about their being 'not a little fumed' with King Henry (Bullough, IV, 185). Hotspur so fumes that, for the space of some 125 lines, he cannot be got to listen to his uncle's plans for rebellion, constantly interrupting Worcester with another burst of indignant anger. He is ingenuously reproachful to Worcester and Northumberland that they conspired

> To put down Richard, that sweet lovely rose,
> And plant this thorn, this canker Bullingbrook
>   (1.3.172–3)

as though he himself had been in no way involved. We notice the new graciousness in the image of the dead king now the political case is altered. The last lash of Hotspur's self-spurring rage is devoted to remembering his first encounter with 'this vile politician Bullingbrook':

> HOTSPUR . . . In Richard's time – what do you call the place?
>   A plague upon it, it is in Gloucestershire.
>   'Twas where the madcap Duke his uncle kept –
>   His uncle York – where I first bowed the knee
>   Unto this king of smiles, this Bullingbrook –
>   'Sblood, when you and he came from Ravenspurgh –
> NORTHUMBERLAND At Berkeley Castle.
> HOTSPUR   You say true.
>   Why, what a candy deal of courtesy
>   This fawning greyhound then did proffer me!
>   'Look when his infant fortune came to age',
>   And 'gentle Harry Percy', and 'kind cousin'.
>   O, the devil take such cozeners   (1.3.239–50)

This whole passage naturalises the passing of time and the action of memory. The past reign already, just a year after the deposition, is 'Richard's time', an earlier period of people's lives. Hotspur's fits and starts, as he plausibly gropes for the lost name of the castle in Gloucestershire has an audience ready, like Northumberland, to supply it for him. For Shakespeare had highlighted the location of this scene when he dramatised it in *Richard II*, opening 2.3 with an exchange between Bullingbrook and Northumberland: 'How far is it, my lord to Berkeley now?' 'Believe me, noble lord, / I am a stranger here in Gloucestershire'. It is there that Harry Percy joins them. Where Holinshed had 'the earle of Northumberland, and his sonne sir Henrie Persie' coming together to Bullingbrook's support (Bullough, III, 398), Shakespeare marks the first meeting of the younger Percy and the royal pretender by having him initially fail to recognise the man he has come to support:

> NORTHUMBERLAND Have you forgot the Duke of Herford, boy?
> PERCY No, my good lord, for that is not forgot
>   Which ne'er I did remember. To my knowledge
>   I never in my life did look on him.
> NORTHUMBERLAND Then learn to know him now. This is the duke.
>   (2.3.36–40)

And so is ushered in the exchanges between Percy and Bullingbrook that are so satirically recalled in *1 Henry IV* 1.3.

It is noticeable, if we go back to the original scene, that it was Percy himself who initiated the image of maturation that the later Hotspur attributes to Bullingbrook. These are his lines:

> My gracious lord, I tender you my service,
> Such as it is, being tender, raw and young,
> Which elder days shall ripen and confirm
> To more approvèd service and desert.

It is in response to this quite obsequious submission that Bullingbrook responds in kind:

> I thank thee, gentle Percy, and be sure
> I count myself in nothing else so happy
> As in a soul remembering my good friends,
> And as my fortune ripens with thy love
> It shall be still thy true love's recompense.
>
> (2.3.41–9)

The phrase that Hotspur so snortingly quotes back, 'Look when his infant fortune came to age', is in fact addressed to Willoughby and Ross:

> Evermore thank's the exchequer of the poor,
> Which till my infant fortune comes to years
> Stand for my bounty.
>
> (2.3.65–7)

Now Harry Percy is quite cursorily characterised in this scene and in *Richard II* as a whole, and the Hotspur who emerges in *1 Henry IV* has a quite new individuality. The very vividness and vehemence of the scene recollected are in tune with the richly characterised Hotspur of the later play. And yet the purpose of the reminiscence must be to remind an audience of what they had watched in *Richard II* and to spot the changes. Two productions from which the lines were cut may bear out the point. They were omitted from Terry Hands' 1975 staging of *1 Henry IV*,[9] and all but edited out of Michael Attenborough's 2000 production. In the case of Hands, this was in the context of the re-grouped tetralogy that omitted *Richard II*, playing instead *The Merry Wives of Windsor* with the two parts of *Henry IV* and *Henry V*. While Attenborough's production was in the *This England* sequence of all the histories, it followed the project policy for the *Richard II – Henry V* plays of treating each play as an autonomous creation. It is easy to see how, in a very extended scene where Hotspur has

again and again interrupted Worcester, these lines could seem digressive
and be cut in the interest of narrative pace. They are significant only
for an audience watching *1 Henry IV* after having seen *Richard II* and thus
in a position to appreciate how the disenchanted Hotspur reconceives
the scene of his first meeting with Bullingbrook.

The rebels under Henry IV badly need to re-write history because
their real part in the forced deposition of King Richard does not suit their
present purposes. The *Henry IV* plays dramatise this as a psychological
and a political phenomenon. On the eve of the battle of Shrewsbury, Hotspur gives an extended account of how Henry came to take the kingship.
There the king is pointedly reminded of all he owes to the Percys –

> My father, and my uncle, and myself
> Did give him that same royalty he wears
>
> (4.3.54–5)

– while making it appear that they had nothing to do with the illegitimate
seizure of the crown. Northumberland's assistance to Bullingbrook 'when
he was not six-and-twenty strong, / Sick in the world's regard, wretched
and low, / A poor unminded outlaw sneaking home' was restricted and
conditional:

> My father gave him welcome to the shore.
> And when he heard him swear and vow to God
> He came but to be Duke of Lancaster,
> To sue his livery, and beg his peace,
> With tears of innocency and terms of zeal,
> My father, in kind heart and pity moved,
> Swore him assistance, and performed it too.
>
> (4.2.56–65)

This, according to Hotspur, created a bandwagon effect, Northumberland's name attracting the support of all 'the lords and barons of the
realm'.

> He presently, as greatness knows itself,
> Steps me a little higher than his vow
> Made to my father while his blood was poor
> Upon the naked shore at Ravenspurgh;
> And now forsooth takes on him to reform
> Some certain edicts and some strait decrees
> That lie too heavy on the commonwealth,
> Cries out upon abuses, seems to weep
> Over his country's wrongs – and by this face,

This seeming brow of justice, did he win
The hearts of all that he did angle for.

(4.3.74–84)

   The opportunistic trajectory of Bullingbrook's rise to power that
Hotspur traces here is plausible enough. The oath sworn by Henry
at Doncaster, that he came for nothing beyond his entitlement to the
Duchy of Lancaster, figures largely in the sources with due deprecation
of his subsequent perjury.[10] But we heard nothing of that oath as such in
Richard II, and no one is more assiduous in devilling on Bullingbrook's
behalf throughout the takeover of the kingdom than the same Northumberland, he who only 'in kind heart and pity moved' – forsooth – helped
out the banished exile. Equally the claim to the throne of Edmund Mortimer, Richard's proclamation of Mortimer as heir-apparent, that so
righteously exercise the Percys in *1 Henry IV*, receive no mention in
Richard II. Shakespeare is making selective use of his sources in a case
such as this, bringing forward in *1 Henry IV* matters that he left out of the
earlier play. But the effect is to allow an audience, by remembering what
'actually' happened, i.e. the parts played by the Percys in *Richard II*, to
see the speciousness of the way they re-tell that story in changed circumstances. The truth of just how Bullingbrook came to seize power may
be as yet undecidable – more of that in the next section. But the self-
interestedness of the rebels' distorted versions of those events is clearly
put before us.
   Once more, in *2 Henry IV*, there is a reprise of the past by the rebels with
their own interpretative spin on it. Mowbray, son of the banished Duke
of Norfolk, Bullingbrook's antagonist, treats us to a stirring recollection
of the tournament so dramatically broken off by the king in *Richard II*.
For Mowbray this was a tragic moment for his father, heavy with historic
consquences:

> then that Henry Bullingbrook and he
> Being mounted and both rousèd in their seats,
> Their neighing coursers daring of the spur,
> Their armèd staves in charge, their beavers down,
> Their eyes of fire sparkling through sights of steel,
> And the loud trumpet blowing them together,
> Then, then, when there was nothing could have stayed
> My father from the breast of Bullingbrook,
> O, when the king did throw his warder down,
> His own life hung upon the staff he threw.
> Then threw he down himself and all their lives

> That by indictment and by dint of sword
> Have since miscarried under Bullingbrook.
>
> (4.1.117–29)

In Shakespeare's original staging of this tournament-scene there may not have been the real-life coursers of the most elaborate of twentieth-century stagings, but Mowbray's word-picture no doubt did duty to recall for a 1590s audience the moment of suspense as the fully armed combatants prepared to joust. A generation later, the King's dramatic gesture of throwing his warder down becomes in retrospect a crucial turning-point leading on to all the disasters that followed.

Fair enough. But Westmoreland, the leader of the King's army, is there to offer an alternative view of that remembered scene.

> You speak, Lord Mowbray, now you know not what.
> The Earl of Hereford was reputed then
> In England the most valiant gentleman.
> Who knows on whom fortune would then have smiled?
> But if your father had been victor there,
> He ne'er had borne it out of Coventry,
> For all the country, in a general voice,
> Cried hate upon him, and all their prayers and love
> Were set on Hereford, whom they doted on,
> And blessed and graced indeed more than the king.
>
> (4.1.130–9)

Though Shakespeare makes apparent Bullingbrook's popularity after Coventry, what Richard saw as his 'courtship to the common people', we are given nothing in *Richard II* of the political context here sketched in by Westmoreland. He might possibly have found in Froissart the evidence for the constraints forcing Richard's decision to stop the contest. In Froissart the King is warned by his advisers that

if ye suffre these two erles to come into the place to do batayle, ye shall nat be lorde of the felde, but the Londoners and suche lordes of their parte wyll rule the felde, for the love and favoure that they beare to the erle of Derby [Bullingbrook]: and the erle Marshall [Mowbray] is soore hated, and specially the Londoners wolde he were slayne. (Bullough, III, 425)

Once again Shakespeare deploys new material from his sources, conflicting versions of the previously dramatised history, to expose the multiplicity of ways in which the story can be told.

To what end are we shown the characters of the *Henry IV* plays so refashioning the past, and what backward light does it throw upon that past? It exposes the political bias of the rebels who need to exonerate themselves from complicity in the usurpation, to unwrite their relationship with the usurper now they are disposed to regard him as such. Their evident falsifications, however, do not serve to legitimise the counternarratives of Henry and his supporters. The audience is given the primary 'truth' of what they themselves have watched happen, against which to measure the refractions of later re-writings. Such distorted recollections work also to establish the pastness of the past, transformed into that arguable form of retrospective narrative, history itself. The 'unquiet tyme of Kyng Henry the Fourth', as Hall called it, lived out the consequences of what Hotspur already in *1 Henry IV* remembers as 'Richard's time'. In the layered palimpsest of the successive history plays, the one event of the deposition/usurpation and the circumstances surrounding it are most frequently re-written. A focus on Bullingbrook, the key player in that event in *Richard II* and the title protagonist of the following two plays, may show if there is a pattern of progressive revelation in the way his ascent to the throne is viewed and reviewed.

PROGRESSIVE REVELATION

'Mark, silent king', says Richard to Henry in the abdication scene, as he smashes the mirror. Silence is indeed a salient feature of Bullingbrook in *Richard II* on all but public occasions, in all but formal speeches. He never speaks in soliloquy, never delivers a single line aside. Unlike his cousin the reigning monarch, we never see him in private, never hear him off the record. Richard performs in public with due decorum in the opening trial scene and in the tournament of 1.3. But from as early as 1.4 where he relaxes with his favourites, we are shown another Richard, flippant, edgy, cynical, that plays behind the persona of the King. And by the end of the play, when the outward world with its props and trappings are gone from Richard, we have whole fantasias of the interior:

> I have been studying how I may compare
> This prison where I live unto the world ...
>
> (5.5.1–2)

With Bullingbrook there is one glimpse of him as frazzled father of an adolescent – 'Can no man tell of my unthrifty son?' (5.3.1) – and he has to deal with an awkward family situation when his cousin Aumerle and his aunt the Duchess of York are on their knees before him pleading for mercy for Aumerle's treachery, while his uncle the Duke of York pleads equally fiercely for his son's punishment. Otherwise, there is nothing for Bullingbrook of that elaborate dramatisation of the emotions and the mind that so personalises the character of Richard.

This asymmetry of representation makes for a crucial ambiguity at the climax of the action when the two antagonists meet at Flint Castle. At this point, with York having gone over to Bullingbrook, the Welsh army of Salisbury disappeared, and Richard's own troops dismissed, the King's military power is at degree zero. He still has his title, however; 'Yet looks he like a king', says York as he appears on the castle's battlements. And looks count for a great deal in such a situation. Might it not have been possible for Richard to retain at least his titular position, even if in leading-strings to his cousin Lancaster? Historically this had happened before in his reign, as Graham Holderness points out, in 1386 when the so-called Lords Appellant (including Bullingbrook) had executed the King's favourites and taken charge of the government.[11] In the play it looks at first as if the action is headed this way, as Bullingbrook sends Northumberland to express due deference to the King:

> Henry Bullingbrook
> On both his knees doth kiss King Richard's hand
> And sends allegiance and true faith of heart
> To his most royal person; hither come
> Even at his feet to lay my arms and power,
> Provided that my banishment repealed
> And lands restored again be freely granted.
>
> (3.3.35–41)

Richard in his response seems to go along with this scenario:

> Northumberland, say thus the king returns:
> His noble cousin is right welcome hither,
> And all the number of his fair demands
> Shall be accomplished without contradiction.
>
> (3.3.121–4)

But then he turns aside to Aumerle in one of those characteristic emotional double-takes: 'We do debase ourselves, cousin, do we not, / To look so poorly and to speak so fair?' And by the time Northumberland comes back again, a riff of indignant self-pity has carried him off into high histrionics:

> What must the king do now? Must he submit?
> The king shall do it. Must he be deposed?

> The king shall be contented. Must he lose
> The name of king? A God's name let it go.
>
> (3.3.143–6)

No one else has mentioned the word deposition. Does not Richard here throw it all away? May Bullingbrook not be surprised to find the crown come tumbling into his lap without his having even to reach up for it?

This is the way it is taken in many productions. When Michael Pennington in the ESC's *Wars of the Roses* exclaimed ironically 'What must the king do now?' there were alarmed looks from Aumerle (Philip Bowen) at Richard's other flanking supporters. The King was clearly departing catastrophically from the prepared script. On the other hand it is possible to read it differently. In *An Age of Kings*, for instance, Bullingbrook's complete military hold on the situation was stressed from the point of his return to England. 2.3 was set in the rebels' embattled camp and Berkeley, York's ambassador, York himself when he followed some lines later, were led in blindfold by bands of armed men into Bullingbrook's stronghold. There was never any question in this version of the Flint Castle scene but that a coup d'état was under way, and when Richard (David William) descended into the 'base court' to meet his cousin, he had to pass through files of spears that crossed shut behind him. At the end of the scene the decisive shift in power was marked: when Richard called out 'Set on towards London', there was a pause while the soldiers looked to Bullingbrook, and the King had to turn round for confirmation of his order 'cousin, is it so?' before the army was prepared to march.

The availability of the two readings of 3.3 in performance is made possible by the opacity of Bullingbrook's motives. Shakespeare is close to his sources here. Holinshed begins by describing how Bolingbroke was invited to return to England by 'diverse of the nobilitie, as well prelates as others', promising him aid 'if he expelling K. Richard, as a man not meet for the office he bare, would take upon him the scepter, rule, and obedience of his native land and region' (Bullough, III, 397). But then on his arrival, he gave the famous oath at Doncaster 'that he would demand no more, but the lands that were to him descended by inheritance from his father' (Bullough, III, 398). Hall, who throughout seems rather more pro-Lancastrian than Holinshed, speaks of a somewhat different oath, 'that he should not dooe to kyng Richard any bodelye harme' (Hall, fol. v v). However, both offer conflicting evidence as to whether Bullingbrook intended to take the crown from the start (as he had been invited to do by his supporters), or initially intended to keep his Doncaster oath and was only carried along by the flow of events leading him to the throne. Yet, even given such indeterminacy in the sources, it would have been easy for Shakespeare to have tipped the balance with a single scene, just one speech by Bullingbrook giving an audience the inside story. The contrast between the pretenders to royal power in the earlier set of history plays is striking. From early in *1 Henry VI*, long before, historically, York had any dynastic ambitions, we are shown the stoking up of his sense of grievance against the house of Lancaster. And if an audience is made privy to the older Plantagenet's designs upon the crown well before they are publicly declared, we are constantly at the upthrust shoulder of Richard of Gloucester as he schemes and jokes his covert way towards monarchical power. Not so with Bullingbrook who wears a poker-face throughout: 'As I come, I come for Lancaster' (2.3.113).

In *Richard II* we never know what Bullingbrook is thinking; we can only guess from his formal words and his actions that often seem at odds with the words. In the two later plays devoted to Henry's reign, the usurping king, under the pressures of his 'unquiet time' and the increasing stress of isolation and illness, reflects on the events of the past not just once but several times with significant variations.

The first is at the meeting with Hal in *1 Henry IV*, the meeting already twice rehearsed in the parody plays in Eastcheap. Here we see Henry in that privacy in which he never appears in *Richard II* and we hear, as it were, the other side to Richard's sharp-eyed observation of his 'courtship to the common people' (*Richard II*, 1.4). Henry tells Hal of his public relations strategy of keeping out of sight:

> By being seldom seen, I could not stir
> But like a comet I was wondered at,
> That men would tell their children, 'This is he!'
> Others would say, 'Where, which is Bullingbrook?'

(We may remember Harry Percy unable to recognize the Duke of Hereford and being suitably impressed at finding himself in his presence.)

> And then I stole all courtesy from heaven,
> And dressed myself in such humility
> That I did pluck allegiance from men's hearts,
> Loud shouts and salutations from their mouths,
> Even in the presence of the crownèd King.
> <div align="right">(<i>1 Henry IV</i>, 3.2.46–54)</div>

How well this corresponds to Richard's antagonistic account of Bullingbrook's behaviour as he left the lists at Coventry:

Off goes his bonnet to an oysterwench.
A brace of draymen bid God speed him well
And had the tribute of his supple knee,
With 'Thanks, my countrymen, my loving friends',
As were our England in reversion his,
And he our subjects' next degree in hope.

(*Richard II*, 1.4.31–6)

In its original context this might have appeared merely the paranoid fears of rivalry. With the hindsight afforded by *1 Henry IV* it seems Richard's suspicions of Bullingbrook's motives in pressing the flesh were right on the mark.

King Henry's reminiscences are intended to act as a wholesome corrective to his son's promiscuous mixing with the people.

Had I so lavish of my presence been,
So common-hackneyed in the eyes of men,
So stale and cheap to vulgar company,
Opinion, that did help me to the crown,
Had still kept loyal to possession,
And left me in reputeless banishment,
A fellow of no mark and likelihood.

(*1 Henry IV*, 3.2.39–45)

Henry is of course unaware that Hal, in his Eastcheap slumming, has his own public relations campaign mapped out, a subject to which I shall be returning in the final chapter. The King's analysis here is that of the political commentator, picking out the factors that made for him and against Richard. He does not necessarily admit that he was planning to help himself to the crown when he talks of the 'opinion that did help' him to it. His objective is a lesson to his son in the political management of his person. And yet there is a sense of a compulsive reliving of the past in his extended recollections of the foolish behaviour of the 'skipping King'. He rides over Hal's promises of reformation – 'I shall hereafter, my thrice-gracious lord, / Be more myself' – to launch into a further bout of recriminations based on comparisons with the earlier situation:

For all the world
As thou art to this hour was Richard then
When I from France set foot at Ravenspurgh

(3.2.93–5)

The increasingly melancholy recollection of the past is a notable feature of the sick king of *2 Henry IV*. Some productions antedate this sickness

Plate 12 King Henry (David Troughton), RSC production of *2 Henry IV*, directed
by Michael Attenborough, Stratford 2000

to the first part. In David Giles' BBC Television version, from the beginning of *1 Henry IV*, the King (Jon Finch) was shown uneasily feeling
his gloved hands. The reason for this was revealed in the scene of his
interview with Hal (David Gwillim) where Henry was shown anointing
his hands for the leprosy with which some sources not Shakespeare –
claimed he was punished by God. The disfigurement progressed through
the plays as an outward manifestation of the remorse and guilt wracking
the usurping king. Less melodramatically, in the 2000 Stratford productions of the *Henry IV* plays, Henry (David Troughton) showed an
acute physical discomfort in wearing the crown itself, having to struggle
painfully to put it on or off. That is one way of playing the character.
And yet in *2 Henry IV*, 3.1, the first time we actually see the King in
that play, in the grip of insomnia, desperately aware of the troubles of
kingship, it is with an almost fatalistic pessimism that he contemplates
the past rather than with a personal sense of responsibility. 'O God, that
one might read the book of fate / And see the revolution of the times'

he exclaims.

> if this were seen,
> The happiest youth, viewing his progress through,
> What perils past, what crosses to ensue,
> Would shut the book and sit him down to die.
>
> (3.1.44–5, 52–5)

It is the thought of Northumberland's rebellion against him, and the Earl's previous changes in political alliance, that occasion this despairing meditation.

> 'Tis not ten years gone
> Since Richard and Northumberland, great friends,
> Did feast together; and in two years after
> Were they at wars. It is but eight years since
> This Percy was the man nearest my soul
> Who like a brother toiled in my affairs
>
> (3.1.56–61)

Turning to Warwick, he then goes on to recall a prophecy of Richard in a speech that closely recalls lines from *Richard II*:

> But which of you was by –
> You, cousin Nevil, as I may remember –
> When Richard, with his eye brimful of tears,
> Then checked and rated by Northumberland,
> Did speak these words, now proved a prophecy:
> 'Northumberland, thou ladder by the which
> My cousin Bullingbrook ascends my throne'? –
> Though then, God knows, I had no such intent
> But that necessity so bowed the state
> That I and greatness were compelled to kiss. –
> 'The time shall come', thus did he follow it,
> 'The time will come that foul sin, gathering head,
> Shall break into corruption.' So went on,
> Foretelling this same time's condition
> And the division of our amity.
>
> (3.1.64–78)

It does not matter that neither Warwick nor Henry was actually present at the encounter between Richard and Northumberland in *Richard II* 5.1. The audience will have forgotten that, but they will remember the words they heard in the earlier play, words the King is here recalling almost literally. These are the speeches interlined with the original words from *Richard II* given first:

> Northumberland, thou ladder wherewithal
> 'Northumberland, thou ladder by the which
> The mounting Bullingbrook ascends my throne
> My cousin Bullingbrook ascends my throne'
> The time shall not be many hours of age
> 'The time shall come', thus did he follow it,
> More than it is ere foul sin gathering head
> 'The time will come that foul sin, gathering head,
> Shall break into corruption.
> Shall break into corruption.'

The variations between the original and the reported lines are not here significant, as they are when Hotspur recalls his first meeting with Bullingbrook. Instead it is as though Shakespeare is doing an actor's memorial reconstruction of his own lines, getting the run of them right, with some ad lib variations. This is in marked contrast to *Richard III*, where prophecies are repeated word for word as the guilty victims acknowledge their fulfilment. Even though Henry is depressed at how accurately Richard predicted his falling-out with Northumberland, he is at pains to interject to correct one part of the King's statement, the implication that he had been planning to ascend the throne:

> Though then, God knows, I had no such intent
> But that necessity so bowed the state
> That I and greatness were compelled to kiss.

Even here, even sick and discouraged, Henry sticks to his official line on the deposition: I never planned it, it all just happened.

It is not until he is on his deathbed, in the last private conversation with his son, that Henry finally admits his guilt in the usurpation, and the connection between that guilt and his unhappy reign:

> God knows, my son
> By what by-paths and indirect crooked ways
> I met this crown, and I myself know well
> How troublesome it sat upon my head.
>   (4.2.311–14)

But his speech brings a quite new revelation about the past requiring us in the audience to re-read it. He urges on Hal the necessity to consolidate the power he has established:

> all my friends, which thou must make thy friends,
> Have but their stings and teeth newly ta'en out,

By whose fell working I was first advanced,
And by whose power I well might lodge a fear
To be again displaced; which to avoid
I cut them off, and had a purpose now
To lead out many to the Holy Land,
Lest rest and lying still might make them look
Too near unto my state.

(4.2.332–40)

This is a very different version of Henry's motives for the crusade than either the act of atonement for Richard's murder promised at the end of *Richard II*, or the sanctified war promised repeatedly through *1* and *2 Henry IV*. Does this reveal the true truth at last, like the truth of Henry's acknowledgement of the 'by-paths and indirect crooked ways' by which he got the crown? Is it intended to unwrite retrospectively those other professions of honourable intentions in leading the crusade?

Maybe, maybe not. It depends on how we understand the workings of the dramatic principle of progressive revelation. I suggested an analogy at the start of this chapter with the Ibsenian action that goes forward in time by successive excavations of the past. *Ghosts* begins in Act 1 with the memory of the supposed pillar of society Chamberlain Alving, in whose honour the Orphanage as charitable monument is to be dedicated. By Act 2 we know from Mrs Alving that this memory was a fraud: Alving was a lecher and a drunk whose imaginary reputation she concocted to conceal his true viciousness. In Act 3, however, there is a further revision of their past marriage. Mrs Alving has by then come to believe that it was she who killed the 'joy of life' in Alving, who turned him into the reprobate he became. Yet, however sincerely Mrs Alving holds this final view of her life and her husband's, however valid a reading it might be in moral terms, it does not wholly undo the impression left on an audience by images of the dissolute man who seduced his own maid, and whom Oswald can only remember from the childhood incident when his father urged him to smoke his pipe, and then laughed at him when he was sick. Reinterpreting the past does not necessarily erase the theatrical effect of earlier interpretations.

And so it may be with Bullingbrook/Henry IV. The impassive pretender of *Richard II* who never discloses to what he pretends is replaced by the reminiscing king of *1 Henry IV* who shows in retrospect a much greater degree of self-awareness, and eventually by the harried, sickening monarch of *2 Henry IV* who is brought close to confession on his death-bed. Yet the crusade may not have been just a blind, a device to 'giddy busy minds / With foreign quarrels' as he urges his son to do, advice that can be seen to lie ironically over the French wars to come in *Henry V*. The image of the King desperate to undo the past by an act of reparation, the way he goes on clutching at the idea of a redeeming crusade long after it becomes obvious it is not going to happen, retains much of its force even when the Machiavellian reading of it has been admitted. It is significant that when he learns of the name of the chamber in which he is to die, he reacts with pious resignation rather than despair:[12]

> Laud be to God, even there my life must end.
> It hath been prophesied to me, many years,
> I should not die but in Jerusalem,
> Which vainly I supposed the Holy Land.
> But bear me to that chamber, there I'll lie:
> In that Jerusalem shall Harry die.
>
> (4.2.362–7)

What Shakespeare contrives to suggest in King Henry's successive revisions of his past is the maze of motives, the multiple ways a life may be constructed in looking back.

CHAPTER SEVEN

Hybrid histories

'There is no certain evidence', wrote F. P. Wilson, 'that any popular dramatist before Shakespeare wrote a play based on English history.'[1] There *were* English history plays before Shakespeare; he may no longer be seen as the absolute inventor of the form.[2] But there was no precedent for the sort of history Shakespeare wrote in the *Henry VI – Richard III* series, nor yet in *Richard II*. This is a form of drama that sticks to its chronicle narrative source throughout. There are changes, of course, inventions and elaborations, but there is virtually no deviation from dramatising the story the chronicles provide. Shakespeare's practice in this was radically unlike that of his contemporaries. Some of the pre-Shakespearean plays that superficially looked like histories were nothing of the sort. It is easy to see, for instance, why the early reader of Greene's *James IV* should have crossed out the title *The Scottish History of James the fourth, slaine at Flodden* and written in over it 'or rather fictions of English and Scottish matters comicall'.[3] The play in fact has nothing whatever to do with history, the plot being lifted straight out of a *novella* by Cinthio. Marginally more historical, but a real mish-mash of a play was Peele's *Edward I*. This combines patriotic pageantry (Edward's return home from the crusades), a semi-comic treatment of the 'life of *Lleuellen*, rebell in Wales' which mysteriously turns into a Robin Hood play, ballad-derived material about the sinking of Queen Elinor at Charing Cross and her miraculous reappearance at Queenhithe, and a spectacular final scene with the Queen's deathbed confession to her husband in disguise – all this plus the knockabout comedy of a singing, wenching Friar.[4] More typical, perhaps, was the anonymous untitled play sometimes called *Woodstock*, sometimes known as *1 Richard II*. The noble hero, 'Plain Thomas' of Woodstock (the murdered Gloucester of Shakespeare's *Richard II*) is opposed by Richard's heavily satirised favourites including the corrupt Lord Chief Justice Tresillian who employs a Vice-like clown Nimble as his agent. The hybrid history play that antedated Shakespeare was a form sufficiently capacious to find room for romance, legend, folklore and freewheeling, prose-speaking comic characters with only the loosest ties to the plot.

By contrast with this sort of history, the *Henry VI* plays, *Richard III* and *Richard II* are quite remarkably homogeneous. A brief diversion such as the Countess of Auvergne episode in *1 Henry VI* – the sort of incident that is everywhere in other early histories – is remarkable in Shakespeare for its anomalousness. There is throughout these plays no romantic material extraneous to the historical narrative of the sort that occupies so much of *Edward III*, for instance, in Edward's wooing of the Countess of Salisbury, and there is no prose comedy introduced for its own sake: the Jack Cade scenes of *2 Henry VI*, though in prose and comic in their own black way, are tightly knitted into the main action. In his later history plays, however, Shakespeare seems to have fallen back on the older plays and their mixed form. Already for his *King John* he rewrote the *Troublesome Raigne*, creating the seriocomic Bastard out of the earlier play's Philip Faulconbridge – that is assuming it is an earlier play. In the two parts of *Henry IV* and in *Henry V* Shakespeare undertook what Giorgio Melchiori rightly calls a 'remake' of *The Famous Victories of Henry the Fifth*.[5]

The *Famous Victories*, again only available in a reduced text and difficult to date, was probably staged in some form in the 1580s. It is a characteristic hybrid history in its mixing of styles and subjects, literally the 'mingling kings and clowns' that Sidney so scornfully derided in his *An Apology for Poetry*.[6] The action covers both Henry's wild youth, in which he is a very boisterous madcap prince indeed, and the famous victories of the title, culminating in the wooing of Princess Katherine of France. And the clown, just as in Sidney's complaint, is 'thrust in . . . by head and shoulders to play a part in majestical matters'. Derick, played originally it seems by the famous clown Tarleton, appears at first as the victim of a robbery by one of Prince Henry's men Cuthbert Cutter, joins the army when the king goes to France and ends up on the battlefield of Agincourt collecting shoes off the dead French soldiers with his friend John Cobbler. This play, unlikely as it seems reading the almost scenario-like text that has come down to us, not only provided Shakespeare with his ground-plan for the two *Henry IV* plays and *Henry V*; he was to borrow lines, copy individual scenes from it. (John Barton's *When Thou Art King*, the 1970 three-part touring adaptation of Shakespeare's Henry plays, in turn borrowed back again from the *Famous Victories*.[7])

The indecorum of plays such as *Famous Victories*, so painful to the neo-classically-minded Sidney, probably caused their audiences no problems.

The sudden and implausible conversion of Henry from swaggering thief to devout warrior king, Derick clowning up the main action throughout, worked within established theatrical conventions going back to morality plays and the Tudor interludes. Shakespeare's adaptation of this mixed form within his history series made for very different effects. Where the *Famous Victories* in its madcap prince section showed nothing of the historical events of the reign of Henry IV, Shakespeare continued with his serious dramatisation of the chronicle in his *Henry IV* plays. This made for a potential tension between the 'history' mode of the top-line narrative, and the undersong of the comic fiction. The diversifying life of the comedy produced a dramatic texture at odds with the carefully controlled blank verse representations of the high historical action. While the onward momentum of the 'unquiet reign' of Henry IV carried the plays through the first Percy rebellion, which ended at Shrewsbury, to the later revolts by the Archbishop of York and Northumberland, another order of development, non-linear and non-causal, governed the growth of the comic situations and characters. The hybrid history, under Shakespeare's hand, kept changing the form of its hybridity, taking him at one point outside the historical series altogether into the non-historical comedy of *The Merry Wives of Windsor*, before mutating once again into the epic history of *Henry V*. The aim of this chapter is to explore these processes of change in the plays, including the outgrowth *Merry Wives*, and the effects produced in the *Henry IV – Henry V* series of these diverse modes of dramatic representation.

THE NAMING OF PARTS

Shakespeare took over from the *Famous Victories* the character of Sir John Oldcastle as the leader of Prince Henry's rogue companions. Oldcastle is hardly characterised in the play; he is not fat, he is not especially corrupt, and he certainly does not act to mislead the Prince, who seems to be going to hell in a handbasket without much need for assistance. His only role is to aid and abet the Prince in his robbing and drinking, and to be aided and abetted in his turn by the other two rogues identified only as Tom and Ned. Shakespeare must have been aware from his reading of the chronicles of the historical figure of Sir John Oldcastle, friend of Henry V and eventually Lollard martyr, but in keeping the *Famous Victories* name for the first version of his character later to be rechristened Falstaff, he was probably only counting on the audience recognition created by the earlier play. He found himself in trouble as a result. Although the details

of what happened are still in doubt, it is clear that the change of name
was an enforced one, as explained in a 1625 letter by one Dr Richard
James:

in Shakespeare's first show of Harrie the Fifth, the person with which he undertook to play a buffoon was not Falstaffe, but Sir Jhon Oldcastle, and . . . offense
being worthily taken by personages descended from his title . . . the poet was put
to make an ignorant shift of abusing Sir Jhon Fastolphe . . .[8]

Why should the use of Sir John Oldcastle's name in the *Famous Victories*
have produced no apparent reaction, while Shakespeare's play provoked
such indignation at the misrepresentation of the historical original?

The answer, I believe, lies in the much greater historicity of *1 Henry IV*.
This is a play that opens with King Henry pursuing his plans for a crusade, receiving news of the victory of Henry Percy over the Scots at
Holmedon, defeat for Mortimer by Glendower in Wales. It is dated to a
given year and shows what purport to be the leading events of that year.
And then: '*Scaena Secunda. Enter Henry Prince of Wales, Sir Iohn [Oldcastle]*'
(F, *The First Part of Henry the Fourth*, TLN 112–13). It is clear from the
first line of 1.2 that this is prose comedy, that Sir John is there as one
of the Prince's riotous companions, as he was in the *Famous Victories*.
But his fictional status, so obvious in the previous play, is blurred by his
contiguity to the historically 'real' scene that has come just before. In
these circumstances the clownish stage Sir John could be reassimilated
back up into fifteenth-century history, and become the real-life Oldcastle here outrageously traduced. Of course, it did not help that Oldcastle's reputation had been controverted between Protestant and Catholic
polemicists, canonised by the one as a martyr of the Reformation before his time, vilified by the others who were able to draw upon plays
such as Shakespeare's as evidence: 'Sir John Oldcastle, a ruffian-knight
as all England knoweth, and commonly brought in by the comedians on
their stages: he was put to death for robberies and rebellion under the
foresaid King Henry the Fifth.'[9] By 1604 the Jesuit Robert Persons was
thus able to cite the stage robberies of the fictional Oldcastle as some of
the crimes for which the real Oldcastle was executed. It is no wonder
that Shakespeare hastened to substitute the name of Falstaff, and in the
Epilogue to *2 Henry IV* to protest that 'Oldcastle died martyr, and this
is not the man.' Yet even in reaching for the name of Falstaff, remembering the minor character of the cowardly knight that had figured in
his own *1 Henry VI*, Shakespeare could not escape the charge of historical misrepresentation, for 'Sir Jhon Fastolphe', according to Dr James,

was 'a man not inferior of virtue though not so famous in piety' as Oldcastle.[10]

When changing the name of Oldcastle, Shakespeare also changed the names of his two companions. The characters, who were called knights but named only as plain plebeian Ned and Tom in *Famous Victories*, in Shakespeare's original version of *1 Henry IV* had the aristocratic names of Harvey and Russell, and Russell at least a knighthood.[11] Whether there was pressure to alter these names too, or whether Shakespeare took proactive precautions in case there might be, Harvey and Russell were changed to Peto and Bardolph, Peto a Warwickshire name apparently without historical associations, and Bardolph the name of a minor player in the later rebellions of Henry IV's reign. In the texts as we have them, Bardolph and Peto are servants of Sir John Falstaff, of a distinctly lower class than their master, who remains a knight, even if a thoroughly unworthy member of his order. So, for instance, according to the class conventions of comedy, they are expected to be cowards during the Gadshill robbery, whereas Falstaff as a knight should at least put up some show of defence. When Hal doubts if he and Poins will be able to overpower the trio of Falstaff, Bardolph and Peto, Poins reassures him: 'Well, for two of them, I know them to be as true-bred cowards as ever turned back, and for the third, if he fight longer than he sees reason, I'll forswear arms' (*1 Henry IV*, 1.2.146–8). So in place of the historically sensitive Oldcastle accompanied by grandly named and knighted companions, the altered play yields the disreputable knight Falstaff and his neutrally lower-class followers Bardolph and Peto.

While moving away from names that exposed the play to political backlash from aristocratic descendants of their real-life counterparts, Shakespeare in *1 Henry IV* kept on the whole to plausible-sounding names, even for the characters of his underplot. Poins, or Poyntz, was apparently a family 'of high antiquity' in Gloucestershire.[12] But in *2 Henry IV*, as the comedy surrounding Falstaff grew and blossomed, there was an influx of new characters with specifically comic type-naming: the constables of the watch Fang and Snare; Pistol and Doll Tearsheet; Shallow and Silence; the whole crew of the Gloucestershire recruits, Mouldy, Bullcalf, Wart, Feeble, Shadow. But, as Anne Barton comments on the use of such nomenclature in a history play, 'Removal from its comic context complicates comic naming, yet also sheds light on the way it works.'[13] To follow through the comic cast of *1 Henry IV* as it is enlarged and changed in *2 Henry IV*, transferred with further changes to Windsor for *Merry Wives*, before appearing as an Eastcheap rump

Flow of recurring characters

Character	1 Henry IV	2 Henry IV	Merry Wives	Henry V
Oldcastle/Falstaff	x	x	x	[x]
Poins	x	x	[x]	–
Peto	x	x	–	–
Bardolph	x	x	x	x
Pistol	–	x	x	x
Quickly	x	x	x	x
Doll Tearsheet	–	x	–	[x]
Page/?Robin/Boy	–	x	x	x
Nim/Nym	–	–	x	x

Key:

x   appearance
[x] reference
–   non-appearance

in *Henry V*, provides an insight into the theatrical dynamics of comedy and the way in which that interacted with Shakespeare's hybrid history form.

A table showing the flow of the recurring characters may help here (see above). In spite of the difficulties of dating, I am assuming an order of composition in which *Merry Wives* was written after *2 Henry IV* and before *Henry V*,[14] partly on the basis of the way the characters appear and disappear. There is a thickening of the comic cast in *2 Henry IV* with the introduction of major new figures, Pistol, Doll Tearsheet and Shallow; on the other hand Poins, the companion of the Prince who had no marked comic feature of his own, is phased out after the second act. The popularity of Falstaff and his companions was such that a separate comedy was called for – whether or not by the royal command of the Queen, as legend has it. *Merry Wives* opens as though it were a continuation of the action of *2 Henry IV*, Shallow loudly complaining of being abused by Falstaff. It is, as it turns out, not the unrepaid thousand pounds of the previous play he is aggrieved about, but the liaison of the comic actions is made. Falstaff's men Pistol and Bardolph duly appear in attendance on him, even though in the new plot of *Merry Wives* they are supernumeraries, and Falstaff in fact discharges them early on. In place of the rather nondescript Peto, there is the humours character Nim. Mistress Quickly reappears but in a quite different situation as the housekeeper of Dr Caius. With the decision to have Falstaff die offstage in *Henry V* and to reduce Doll Tearsheet to a mere mention, Shakespeare is left with a number of the old crew: Bardolph, Pistol, Nim (re-spelled Nym), the Boy and Quickly. He sends the men off to France, as Derick the clown of *Famous Victories* went before them. But they are there only to be disposed of, killed off one by one to make room for a new cast of comics led by Fluellen.[15] By the conclusion of the action, with Nym hanged after Bardolph, the Boy murdered in the attack on the English camp, Doll or Nell Quickly – it doesn't seem to matter which – reported dead of venereal disease, it is only a very seedy and humiliated Pistol that survives.

The continuity requirements for characters in a historical narrative do not apply to comic figures. Within chronicle material as Shakespeare dramatised it, a character is introduced, comes to prominence in his or her portion of the action, and when that part is played out, he/she exits or dies. Such characters are governed by the linear movement of time in which they are embedded as history. Not so with clowns and comics. They can come back indefinitely, in the same or different situations, for as long as audiences continue to laugh, and they disappear from the stage, on whatever pretext or on nonc, as soon as the audiences are no longer laughing. It looks as though in *1 Henry IV* Shakespeare took over the situation of the *Famous Victories*, that is a madcap prince with three boon companions. The piquancy of the humour lay not in the individual characters as such but in the spectacle of the prince behaving in riotously unprincelike ways. However, with the enormous popular success of Oldcastle-turned-Falstaff, and the less than compelling chronicle material remaining for a *2 Henry IV* – ten years of the king's reign after Shrewsbury in 1403, but a fairly messy time of minor rebellions – there was a need to capitalise upon the comedy. Hence the second-phase comic characters of the play. Falstaff had satirically described his appalling recruiting practices on the road to Shrewsbury in *1 Henry IV*; so show him actually at work in *2 Henry IV*. And provide a couple of gullible country justices in charge of mustering men for him to con down in Gloucestershire. The geographical unlikelihood of marching to York from London via Gloucestershire has been pointed out, and used as evidence of an earlier single *Henry IV* play subsequently expanded into two.[16] But the logic does not necessarily hold because comic situations and characters are not bound by such laws of verisimilitude. If it is implausible that Falstaff should visit Shallow in Gloucestershire on his road to York in *2 Henry IV*, what on earth would 'Robert Shallow esquire . . . In the county of Gloucestershire, Justice of Peace and Coram' be doing in Windsor?[17] Similarly, no one mentions Doll

Tearsheet in the Eastcheap tavern scene of *1 Henry IV*, though from Mistress Quickly's comment in *2 Henry IV* it seems as though Doll and Falstaff are long-term sparring partners: 'By my troth, this is the old fashion: you two never meet but you fall to some discord' (2.4.45–6). Doll is like Pistol, Shallow and Silence marked off by a generic name; they all belong to the revised scheme of things in *2 Henry IV*, where additional self-generated comic characters satellite out from the original set-up.

Where in *2 Henry IV* there was space for an open-plan comedy of mood and atmosphere enlivened by a rich mix of freewheeling figures, *The Merry Wives of Windsor* tightened down into a comedy of intrigue, ordered by plotting symmetries. Falstaff courts the two wives simultaneously, Mistress Page and Mistress Ford, whose husbands are designed to contrast trust with jealousy. There are three suitors for Anne Page's hand, Caius favoured by the mother, Slender by the father, and Fenton by Anne herself. There are three successive humiliations of Falstaff in Acts 3, 4, 5. The eccentrics carried over from the *Henry IV* plays can only operate on the peripheries of this sort of plot. Shakespeare attaches *Merry Wives* to the offstage historical action by the thinnest of mooring lines. Page, good middle-class father that he is, objects to Fenton as a potential son-in-law on grounds of class and reputation: 'The gentleman is of no having, he kept company with the wild Prince and Poins. He is of too high a region' (*Merry Wives*, 3.3.64–6). It is impossible to scrutinise this as a date-marker. Fenton 'kept company' – past tense – 'with the wild Prince and Poins': does that imply that the Prince is no longer wild, maybe even that we are now in the reign of Henry V? These are unsafe deductions. The purpose is to locate the nature of Fenton's ineligibility from Page's point of view, the penniless young gentleman, louche associate of royalty, with the most far-off reminder to the audience of the Hal–Poins friendship of *1* and *2 Henry IV*.

They say that, in soap-opera, when an actor's contract is up there is nothing further medical science can do. How punitive is Shakespeare's killing off of his comic characters in *Henry V*, or is it merely a question of disposing of superfluous personnel, the brutal equivalent of the soap-opera car-crash? The general design seems to be one of systematic riddance. The cursory treatment of Doll Tearsheet and of Nym, for example, is suggestive. Pistol, in fiery defence of his newly married bride, the 'quondam Quickly', tells his thwarted rival Nym to look elsewhere: 'to the Spital go, and from the powdering tub of infamy fetch forth the lazar kite of Cressid's kind, Doll Tearsheet, she by name, and her espouse' (*Henry V*, 2.1.59–62). Given the occupational hazards of Doll's profession, this is a likely enough situation for her to be in. In the final act Pistol relates his news 'that my Doll is dead i'th'Spital of a malady of France' (5.1.72). Though this tallies perfectly with the earlier reference, editors have been bothered by Doll Tearsheet being referred to by Pistol as 'my Doll' and have emended to 'Nell' so that this becomes news of the death of Quickly. They may be right: it seems odd that, in this last appearance of the last Eastcheap survivor, with all the others accounted for, Pistol's wife of Act 2 and our old acquaintance from two previous plays should be left out. But the interest in these characters has gone by now, and they are huddled off any which way. Similarly Nym, very briefly established as a humours character in *Merry Wives*, shows up in *Henry V* to provide an antagonist to Pistol, a third comic coward on the French battlefields. That function served, he does not even rate a separate death like Bardolph, but is accounted for only in the Boy's final speech when we are told that Bardoph and Nym 'are both hanged' for thieving (4.4.57).

The end of the Boy himself seems hardest to reconcile with an authorial policy of unwanted character disposal. His last lines make it absolutely clear that he is about to fall victim to the (historical) attack by the French troops on the undefended English camp. 'I must stay with the lackeys with the luggage of our camp. The French might have a good prey of us if he knew of it, for there is none to guard it but boys' (4.4.58–61). Every modern production makes of his death a moment of pathos, whether discovered by Fluellen at the opening of 4.7 – 'Kill the poys and the luggage' – or in some versions by the king himself further into the scene: 'I was not angry since I came to France / Until this instant' (4.7.45–6). Yet it is odd that there is no signal for this either in the lines or the stage directions. It is as though the Boy, assigned as page to Falstaff by Hal in *2 Henry IV*, possibly named as Robin in *Merry Wives* if he is the same Boy there, shrewd observer of the battlefield antics of his rogue companions at Harfleur and Agincourt, is here assimilated into the nameless category of boys so treacherously massacred by the French.

A closer look at three of the most important comic through-characters, Pistol, Quickly and Bardolph, may help to illuminate the way in which they are handled and the issues arising from their serial appearances in the sequence of plays. Pistol is the most straightforward of the three. He is given the careful build-up belonging to a new comic star in *2 Henry IV* with the prolonged dispute between Falstaff, Doll and Quickly as to whether he should be let in, or barred as a 'swaggerer'. At first entrance he seems to correspond to Falstaff's reassuring description of him: 'He's no swaggerer, hostess, a tame cheater, i'faith, you may stroke him as gently as a puppy greyhound' (2.4.77–8). Editors have been puzzled by the fact that his characteristic histrionic idiolect is not assumed until some forty lines after his entrance:

> These be good humours indeed! Shall pack-horses
> And hollow pampered jades of Asia,
> Which cannot go but thirty miles a day,
> Compare with Caesars, and with Cannibals,
> And Troyant Greeks?
>
> (2.4.130–4)

But it is good strategy to make an audience wait for the comic pistol to go off. Thereafter, Pistol is invariably that great stand-by of theatrical comedy, the character who recycles old theatrical materials, as quick to quarrel and as prone to quote in the varying milieux of *Merry Wives* and *Henry V* as in *2 Henry IV*. He was ready to hand when Shakespeare – for whatever reason – decided not to have Falstaff continue his career as *miles gloriosus* in France. And his final face-off with Fluellen over the leek represents the triumph of the reformed over the unregenerate comic cast in *Henry V*, equivalent to the reform of the king himself.

Mistress Quickly has a more complex evolution over the four plays in which she appears. She is the all-but-nameless Hostess of *1 Henry IV*, acquiring a name only in passing from the greeting of the Prince at his entrance in 3.3: 'What sayest thou, Mistress Quickly? How doth thy husband? I love him well, he is an honest man' (3.3.73–4). By *2 Henry IV* she has not only lost the offstage honest husband so as to make possible the constantly renewed promises of marriage by Falstaff, but she has acquired a new comic idiom of her own. It is not only her mistaking words – Falstaff is decried as 'honeysuckle villain . . . honeyseed rogue' (2.1.38–9), her shots at 'homicidal' and 'homicide' – but the wonderful comic garrulity that allows her to sketch in by the way a whole social scene of London life in her recollection of one of Falstaff's proposals:

thou didst swear to me upon a parcel-gilt goblet, sitting in my Dolphin chamber at the round table by a sea-coal fire, upon Wednesday in Wheeson week, when the prince broke thy head for liking his father to a singing man of Windsor – thou didst swear to me then, as I was washing thy wound, to marry me, and make me my lady thy wife. Canst thou deny it? Did not goodwife Keech the butcher's wife come in then and call me gossip Quickly, coming in to borrow a mess of vinegar, telling us she had a good dish of prawns, whereby thou didst desire to eat some, whereby I told thee they were ill for a green wound? And didst thou not, when she was gone downstairs, desire me to be no more so familiarity with such poor people, saying that ere long they should call me madam? (2.1.67–78)

Out of this tumbling tale emerges a life of novel-like density implied as hinterland to the dramatised action: the rough-and-tumble of Falstaff and Hal's continuing relationship, Falstaff's knightly airs, the social advancement that marriage to him would mean for Quickly, her Eastcheap neighbourhood peopled by the likes of goodwife Keech the butcher's wife.

In her new capacity as Caius's housekeeper in *Merry Wives* Quickly keeps her confused vocabulary and some of her compulsive talking, but she has apparently never met Falstaff before, and is no longer either married or widowed, professing herself a maid (2.2.32–7). She certainly serves as maid-of-all-work to the plot, scurrying to and fro with the messages so vital to keeping the farce going. Like everyone else in the play she becomes a mere agent of the plot. The degree of Quickly's disreputability keeps changing through the plays. In *1 Henry IV* she runs the Eastcheap tavern with her husband, for whose honesty we have the word of the Prince of Wales. In *2 Henry IV* she procures Doll Tearsheet as an afterdinner treat to allure Falstaff back, after he has bamboozled her into dropping her legal charges against him. By the end of the play she is on her way to jail in company with Doll, both of them arrested for the murder of a man they seem to have mugged: 'the man is dead that you and Pistol beat amongst you' (5.4.14–15). She can still be rehabilitated to the quite innocent role of comic go-between in *Merry Wives*. But in *Henry V* there are broad hints as to the nature of the lodging-house that she and her second husband Pistol now keep: 'we cannot lodge and board a dozen or fourteen gentlewomen that live honestly by the prick of their needles but it will be thought we keep a bawdy house straight' (2.1.28–31). There may be a strategic blackening of Quickly along with the other Eastcheapers to distance them from the reformed Prince/King. But it is not consistent or systematic, and leaves Shakespeare free to deploy her to quite other ends in *Merry Wives*. Mistress Quickly has neither a logically developing moral character nor a coherent *curriculum vitae*.

With Bardolph there is one thing stable and certain – his nose, a challenge and opportunity for make-up artists in every production of the plays. Though never more than a supporting part, because of his nose he becomes a landmark figure right through the plays, the only comic to appear virtually unchanged throughout all four. Shakespeare invented him, but contrived twice to stitch him in to the received source

narrative. One of the best-known legends of Prince Henry's youth was
the striking of the Lord Chief Justice on the bench when he refused to
release one of the Prince's servants, with the boldness of the magistrate
in sending the Prince to prison for it. Shakespeare chose not to show this
scene, unlike the *Famous Victories*, which has its Harry catch the Justice
a resounding box on the ear in defence of the evidently guilty thief
Cuthbert Cutter. In *2 Henry IV* this incident is only reported obliquely
when the Lord Chief Justice is introduced at first entrance by the Page:
'here comes the nobleman that committed the prince for striking him
about Bardolph' (1.2.42–3). Bardolph, familiar already from *1 Henry
IV* and already associated with Hal, becomes the Prince's servant who
occasioned the row with the Lord Chief Justice.

In dramatising the end of Bardolph in *Henry V*, Shakespeare again
found means to write him in to the source story. Holinshed records how
on his first arrival in France, the king 'caused proclamation to be made,
that no person should be so hardie on paine of death, either to take anie
thing out of anie church that belonged to the same, or to hurt or doo anie
violence either to priests, women, or anie such as should be found without weapon or armor, and not readie to make resistance' (Bullough, IV,
386–7). This is saluted in the margin as 'A charitable proclamation', done
'Princelie and wiselie'. It is under this decree that the soldier who becomes Bardolph is hanged. For on the way to Calais, in spite of the short-
ness of provisions, the English army maintained the discipline Henry
imposed:

in this great necessitie, the poore people of the countrie were not spoiled, nor
anie thing taken of them without paiment, nor anie outrage or offense doone
by the Englishmen, except one, which was that a souldiour tooke a pix out of a
church, for which he was apprehended, & the king not once remooved till the
box was restored, and the offendour strangled. (Bullough, IV, 389)

Once again Holinshed gives his marginal approval: 'Justice in warre'.

Shakespeare makes of this the incident in *Henry V* where Fluellen
refuses Pistol's urging that he petition for clemency for Bardolph who
has stolen a 'a pax of little price'. Fluellen goes on to tell the King
about the – to him unknown – situation, in terms that make Bardolph's
identity obvious to Henry, and give him the opportunity to intervene to
save his life if he wishes. In the battle, the King is told, the Duke of Exeter

hath lost never a man, but one that is like to be executed for robbing a church,
one Bardolph, if your majesty know the man. His face is all bubuckles and
whelks, and knobs, and flames o'fire, and his lips blows at his nose, and it is like

a coal of fire, sometimes plue and sometimes red. But his nose is executed and his fire's out.

This is the last time anyone will make a joke about Bardolph's nose for the King replies firmly: 'We would have all such offenders so cut off' (3.7.84–91). Where the Prince was prepared to strike the highest law officer in the land in defence of this man, the King dooms him to death.

Many modern productions highlight Henry's personal responsibility for Bardolph's death. In Terry Hands' 1975 version, the King gave the order for the execution to the accompaniment of a drum-roll, a moment anticipated right back in the Hands staging of *1 Henry IV*. There in the tavern scene, with the exchange over what the 'exhalations' of Bardolph's face portended –

> BARDOLPH Choler, my lord, if rightly taken.
> PRINCE No, if rightly taken, halter. (2.4.268–9)

– there was a 'mock hanging of Bard[olph] accompanied by Poins drumming on the table'.[18] Kenneth Branagh's film went even further, hanging Bardolph on camera with close-ups of the anguished features of Richard Briers; in the immediately ensuing interview between Henry and Mountjoy, the feet of the hanged man were seen dangling on the edge of the shot throughout. Even in interpretations such as Branagh's that are sympathetic to the King, the need to kill his old acquaintance is seen as a desperately painful duty, part of the appalling burden of kingship. At the moment of execution, the film inserted flashbacks to jolly Eastcheap scenes figuring a laughing Bardolph to mark the point. For more severe readings of Henry, the hanging of his friend is the measure of the King's militaristic brutality.

Many changes in attitude between the late sixteenth and the late twentieth century obviously condition such modern versions of this scene. We do not take capital punishment for theft as normal, we do not have an Elizabethan audience's class-conditioned sense of the positive desirability of hanging thieves, we are unlikely to view sacrilege with quite the horror of the devout King. But there is more to the matter than this. Bardolph is not only the 'friend' of the King (whatever degree of friendship would have been considered possible in Shakespeare's time between men as widely separated in rank); he is the old acquaintance of the audience, an acquaintanceship built up over four plays. An actor written out of the script of a soap-opera may have to be killed off, but so to dispose of one of the regulars in a sitcom is something else again.

Situation comedy characters are expected to recur within the situation in which they live, and not to live, much less die, beyond it. As they continue to return, they accumulate audience recognition and affection. Some such credit accrues to the Eastcheap characters in modern serial productions of the *Henry IV – Henry V* plays, and partly accounts for the sense of shock at their being so violently removed. Shakespeare's practice with his rolling comic cast was evidently much more casual, with no scruples about changing their characters to suit different theatrical needs or any squeamishness about disposing of them at will by hanging, murder or venereal disease. But this *ad hoc* comic characterisation within the hybrid history mode produced a complexity of dramatic texture deriving from the conflicting conventions of history and comedy.

HYBRID CHARACTERS: HOTSPUR AND FALSTAFF

With the Hotspur of *1 Henry IV*, a new dimension to characterisation appears in Shakespeare's histories. At his first appearance, in his vivid recital of the battlefield encounter with the court popinjay (1.3 28–68), there comes into being a personality fully formed. He is unlike the earlier Harry Percy of *Richard II* in having a kind of gratuitous individuation, over and above what is necessary for his part in the play. Hotspur's role in the thematic design of *1 Henry IV* is clear enough. He is the chivalric hero whose compelling, but ultimately inadequate, understanding of honour –

> By heavens, methinks it were an easy leap
> To pluck bright honour from the pale-faced moon
> (1.3.199–200)

– is intended to contrast with the socially organic valuation of honour that Hal, to whom Hotspur is the foil, must discover. Yet, as he goes hotspurring through the play's action, there is an energy and definition to the part that threatens to unbalance that careful conceptual opposition. One theatrical marker of Hotspur's hypercharacterisation is the old tradition of playing him with a speech impediment. This had its origins in a misreading of Lady Percy's line in *2 Henry IV* – 'speaking thick, which Nature made his blemish' (2.3.24). A phrase that just means 'speaking fast' gave rise to a variety of speech mannerisms for Hotspur. Laurence Olivier in a 1945 Old Vic production 'spoke quickly, even incomprehensibly, with a stammer which culminated in his last broken line, "food for w– w –"'.[19] The clear-speaking Scottish Sean Connery in *An Age of Kings* had a consistent trouble with 'w's, only occasionally showing earlier, but surfacing twice in the one line of his final speech, 'They wound my thoughts worse than thy sword my flesh' (5.4.79), as his strength ebbed towards death. The idiosyncracy of the speech hesitation in performance is an emblem of the distinctiveness of the character.

The rebels, with Hotspur as their *de facto* leader, are generally seen as occupying a separate space in the play, between the domain of law and government of the King's court and the Eastcheap territory of misrule.[20] Yet the characterisation of Hotspur and the rebel space he so vividly fills are affected by the existence of a contiguous comic mode. In 2.4 Hal parodies the dialogue between Hotspur and his wife that we have just witnessed in 2.3.

I am not yet of Percy's mind, the Hotspur of the north, he that kills me some six or seven dozen of Scots at a breakfast, washes his hands, and says to his wife, 'Fie upon this quiet life, I want work.' 'O my sweet Harry', says she, 'how many hast thou killed today?' 'Give my roan horse a drench', says he, and answers, 'Some fourteen', an hour after . . . (2.4.88–93)

This wickedly hits off Hotspur's appetite for slaughter, his delayed response to questions, Lady Percy's wifely concern, not to mention his roan horse. But the satiric lampoon here chimes with a more delicate kind of comedy in the scene parodied. Hotspur is akin to a comedy humours character, the creature of his one dominant feature, headlong, impulsive, martial ardour. He is defined by that one characteristic, and like any other humours part, we do not expect him – do not want him – to change or develop, only to go on exhibiting his irrepressible self in a continuing variety of situations.

A kind of creeping comedy moves through the rebel conspiracy in Hotspur's wake. There is his reading of the letter from the non-supporter whom he has tried to draft into the rebellion (2.3.1–29). This is included to illustrate Hotspur's tendency to jump the gun, to ignore his uncle Worcester's specific instructions: 'No further go in this / Than I by letters shall direct your course' (1.3.286–7). The unwise approach to the wrong person will expose the conspiracy before it is well under way, as even Hotspur realises. 'You shall see now in very sincerity of fear and cold heart will he to the King, and lay open all our proceedings!' (2.3.25–6). Yet the exasperated commentary of Hotspur throughout makes of this a comic speech, well caught by Adam Levy's performance in the 2000 RSC production, where Hotspur hectored the absent non-supporter in the person of the scrumpled-up ball of paper that had been his letter. In the negotations with his wife Kate that follow, there is opened up a personal, even a domestic scene in which the comically conceived Hotspur is convincingly at home. And the Percys carry this atmosphere with them into the quite different scene of the rebels' meeting in Wales.

Glendower, Mortimer and Hotspur meet to carve up Britain – quite literally. We see them with the map before them, their several portions predrawn by the Archdeacon of Bangor. The scene had its origins in a Holinshed account of how the rebel leaders

> by their deputies in the house of the archdeacon of Bangor, divided the realme amongst them, causing a tripartite indenture to be made and sealed with their seales, by the covenants whereof, all England from Severne and Trent, south and eastward, was assigned to the earle of March: all Wales, & the lands beyond Severne westward, were appointed to Owen Glendouer: and all the remnant from Trent northward, to the lord Persie. (Bullough, IV, 185)

Consider the likely effect of this sort of national dismemberment on a 1590s audience. Richard II had been ringingly denounced as 'landlord of England', not the sovereign king he should be. But the conspirators here are no more than robber barons quarrelling about their share of the booty they have not yet taken. The division of the kingdom, from *Gorboduc* to *King Lear*, was the ultimate evil in the monitory political orthodoxy of the time. It is noticeable that throughout this scene there is no real attempt to sustain the pretence of Mortimer as pretender to the throne. If Mortimer were really the realm's legitimate heir it would be for Hotspur and Glendower to bow the knee in homage, not haggle over how much of the country was to fall to each of them. It is only necessary to contrast the treatment of Richard Duke of York as royal pretender in the *Henry VI* plays, the formal submission to him of Salisbury and Warwick when they recognise his lineal right (*2 Henry VI* 2.2.59–63), to see how nugatory is Mortimer's technical position as claimant.

Mortimer, instead of being placed as the threatening counter-king to Henry IV in this scene, is cast as Glendower's emollient and submissive son-in-law, the besotted, monolingual husband of his melodious Welsh wife. The set-off between the Percys, with their rough and offhand affection, and the Mortimers, their romantic wooing mediated through Glendower as Welsh/English interpreter, tunes the drama to comedy. Lady Mortimer's evocative invitation to her husband –

> She bids you on the wanton rushes lay you down,
> And rest your gentle head upon her lap,
> And she will sing the song that pleaseth you
>
> (3.1.207–9)

– is mischievously matched by Hotspur's bawdy proposition to Lady Percy:

> Come, Kate, thou art perfect in lying down.
> Come, quick, quick, that I may lay my head in thy lap.
>
> (3.1.221–2)

And there is comedy too in what is the central energising dynamic of the scene as a whole, the clash of personalities between Hotspur and Glendower.

Once again Worcester is quick to point out the serious political consequences of Hotspur's misbehaviour with their most important Welsh ally:

> In faith, my lord, you are too wilful-blame,
> And since your coming hither have done enough
> To put him quite besides his patience.
> You must needs learn, lord, to amend this fault.
>
> (3.1.171–4)

'Well, I am schooled', says Hotspur penitently. But of course he never is. Hotspur is incapable of schooling, educationally irremediable. 'I cannot choose' (3.1.142), he confesses, when reproached with his provoking of Glendower. The airs and graces of the great magician, his boastful self-assertion, for Hotspur are nothing but pretentious pomposity, and he can never resist letting the air out of the old windbag. Hotspur's inability to alter his own nature, this essentially comic trait, has consequences for the dramatic representation as a whole.

We cannot take Glendower seriously because Hotspur does not. Though the part can be played with more dignity than it often is, the dramatic dialogue repeatedly makes Glendower a comic butt, as when the neck of his mage's rhetoric is so deftly broken by Hotspur's cant-cutting directness:

> GLENDOWER I can call spirits from the vasty deep.
> HOTSPUR Why, so can I, or so can any man,
> But will they come when you do call for them?   (3.1.50–2)

The sense of danger and menace that ought to emanate from these rebel conspirators, intent as they are on the breaking up of Britain, is drained away, leaving something more like a social occasion going disastrously, hilariously awry. Mortimer, evidently nice young man that he is, is never going to take over any kingdom. Hotspur could not in reality care less whether the course of Trent is changed to give him more land; he has only started the argument out of a spirit of perverse contentiousness: 'in the way of bargain . . . I'll cavil on the ninth part of a hair' (3.1.133–4). The spirit of Hotspur, for whom all life is a strenuously competitive game, turns rebellion into gamesmanship.

Hotspur and the rising he leads are part of the continuing historical narrative of the play series, the fractious fallout from the fracturing of authority represented by Henry's usurpation. *1 Henry IV* is planned to climax with his death at Shrewsbury, the duel between himself and Hal fitting end to his 'ill-weaved ambition', his defeat fulfilling the Prince's promise to his father: 'I will redeem all this on Percy's head' (3.2.132). Hotspur is a great part for any actor at a rising point in his career, witness some of the outstanding performances it has inspired. However, if he threatens to upstage Hal, the technically central part of the play, it is not just because his is theatrically the fatter role. What the semi-comic character of Percy, in his *1 Henry IV* likeness, brings to the play is an amplitude of dramatic life beyond the conventionally 'serious' main political conflict. Hotspur and his co-conspirators are not just rebels, defined by their power-seeking posture of rebellion against the king. They have marriages and married relationships, fathers-in-law and brothers-in-law; they fret and bicker, they kiss and make up, on a scale of human volatility remote from the clash of sword on sword, the confrontations of the council-table. The hybridity of the history play in *1 Henry IV* produces not only a comic underplot to the high narrative line, but a third order of dramatic representation poised somewhere between comedy and history.

Hotspur, characterised as Hotspur, appears only in *1 Henry IV*, though his loss is registered in the full elegy afforded him in Lady Percy's grieving retrospect of *2 Henry IV* (2.3.9–45). If the characterisation of him and his fellow rebels is touched by comedy and the proximity of the comic mode, then with the predominant comic character of Falstaff who survives into *2 Henry IV*, and is provisionally promised a reincarnation in *Henry V*, something like the opposite process takes place. Falstaff, by the very duration of his existence within the linear sequence of the plays, takes on a quasi-history at odds with his comic status. It is generally recognised that the fictional Falstaff inhabits a different order of time from that of the historical figures, a difference symbolised in his very opening exchange with the Prince:

> FALSTAFF Now Hal, what time of day is it, lad?
> PRINCE Thou art so fat-witted with drinking of old sack, and unbuttoning thee after supper, and sleeping upon benches after noon, that thou

hast forgotten to demand that truly which thou wouldst truly know.
What a devil hast thou to do with the time of day?   (1.2.1–5)

The time of the day, the week, the month, the year are not Falstaff's
business as he lives in a perpetual present of comic enjoyment. This
may be interpreted as the holiday time of festive comedy, the Bakhtinian
chronotope of carnival. As such it can be placed as time out, but with
the structural assurance that in due course, holiday over, the audience
will be returned to the ordered succession of time in history. However,
the ambiguity of the figure of Falstaff, which has produced such endless
controversy, stems in part from his amphibious existence in two different
dimensions of time corresponding to the different dramatic modes co-
existing in the history play series.

One way into the debate over Falstaff is to ask the question whether his
was the clown's part in the original staging of the plays. David Wiles in
Shakespeare's Clown argues forcefully that it was, that the Falstaff of *1* and *2
Henry IV* was played by Will Kemp, and that Kemp may actually have left
the company in 1599 because Shakespeare decided not to have Falstaff
return in *Henry V*.[21] Wiles points to all the features of Falstaff that correspond to the traditional clown's part, his costume, his armour – a cudgel
rather than a real sword, Wiles maintains – his associations with carnival.
In this view Falstaff spoke the Epilogue to *2 Henry IV* before stepping forward to perform the jig for which Kemp was famed. However, Giorgio
Melchiori denies that Falstaff was a part for Kemp, pointing out that in
other Shakespearean plays where there is direct evidence for the casting
of Kemp, his 'appearances on the stage . . . are always brief, and his language is that of the professional clown, chiefly based on equivocations,
lacking Falstaff's much wider range'.[22] The evidence from T. J. King's
work on the distribution of parts in Shakespeare's plays would seem to
support Melchiori's argument rather than that of Wiles. Falstaff has more
lines than any other character in *1 Henry IV*, in *2 Henry IV* and in *Merry
Wives*, and King's findings suggest that the principal actors in Elizabethan
companies took the major parts and were not necessarily typecast.[23] If
this is correct, then Melchiori's conjecture that John Heminges might
have played Falstaff – no doubt opposite Burbage as Hal – sounds plausible. Even Wiles allows that 'the Tudor Vice/clown tradition was never
more complex than when, under the pressure for dramaturgical change,
it spawned "Falstaff"'.[24] In other words, Falstaff both is and is not a
clown part.

Falstaff's class differentiates him from other clowns. The clown was
virtually always a low-life figure, a servant, apprentice or thief who

mimicked and mocked his betters. It is significant that Sir John Old-castle does not have the clown part in *Famous Victories*; this is taken by Derick who plays upon the word's double meaning, both comedian and simple countryman.[25] Derick and John Cobbler act out in comic slapstick the scene they have just watched of the Prince's boxing the Justice's ears, just as Hal and Falstaff will pre-parody in different forms the serious interview between king and prince to be staged in *1 Henry IV* 3.2. Falstaff's knighthood, however, and the range and control of his language betokening education, even learning, however misused, place him in a dramatic mode quite unlike that of regular clowns such as Derick – or Dogberry in *Much Ado*, a part that we know Kemp played. Seedy and disreputable as Falstaff is, highly indecorous companion for the Prince of Wales, he yet retains the nominal status that allows Hal to place him in command of a company of infantry. There is here per-haps a residuum of his historical origins as first Sir John Oldcastle, then Sir John Fastolf, both of them trusted military officers. It brings him, however marginally, into contact with the upper plot of king and rebels.

Sidney may have objected to the indecorum of mingling clowns with kings, but there was a decorum of sorts even in this indecorum. Derick may be there on the battlefield of Agincourt in *Famous Victories*, most un-heroically gathering up the shoes of the dead for his friend John Cobbler, but he does not appear in company with the King in his famous victory. Falstaff, however, is present at the colloquy between King Henry and the rebel deputation before Shrewsbury, and has to be shushed into silence by the prince when he attempts one of his typical jokes. 'I have not sought the day of this dislike', protests Worcester:

> KING　You have not sought it? How comes it, then?
> FALSTAFF　Rebellion lay in his way, and he found it.
> PRINCE　Peace, chewet, peace!　　　　　　　　(*1 Henry IV*, 5.1.27–9)

His clowning round the battlefield includes the equally subversive offer of his sack-bottle in lieu of pistol to Hal who, in verse-speaking heroic mode, is unamused: 'What, is it a time to jest and dally now?' (5.3.52). His pre-tend death and resurrection are true to his carnivalesque clownishness.[26] There is, though, a sort of crossover of dramatic modes when he stabs the dead body of Hotspur and claims him as victim. The grotesque im-age from the 1951 Stratford production of Anthony Quayle as Falstaff lugging off the armoured corpse of Hotspur (Michael Redgrave) catches well the nature of the collocation.

Plate 13 Falstaff (Anthony Quayle) carries off Hotspur (Michael Redgrave),
Shakespeare Memorial Theatre production of *1 Henry IV*, directed
by Anthony Quayle and John Kidd, Stratford 1951

By his association with the Prince of Wales, Falstaff acquires a time-
bound life. In *1 Henry IV* his fantasies with Hal about 'when thou art king'
yield an imagined Land of Cockaigne future in which there will be no
more gallows, and thieves will go by honorific euphemisms, 'Diana's

foresters, gentlemen of the shade, minions of the moon' (1.2.21–2). *2 Henry IV*, by virtue of the fact that it is *2 Henry IV*, concerned with the second part of the King's reign that will lead up to his death and the accession of his son, brings that futurity of 'when thou art king' into perceptible focus. In preparation for that event, Hal is kept largely away from Falstaff, and it is often observed that there is a strategic darkening of the character in his predatory anticipation of what he will do when he is all in all to the new monarch. Quite as significant, though, is the fact that Falstaff is affected by the play's universal preoccupation with time and ageing. It was one of the running jokes of *1 Henry IV* that the fat old knight should have pretended to be young. 'They hate us youth' he shouts at the travellers he is robbing on Gads Hill: 'what, ye knaves, young men must live' (2.2.69–74). The joke is continued in *2 Henry IV* – 'you that are old', Falstaff tells the Lord Chief Justice, 'consider not the capacities of us that are young' (1.2.137–8) – but it is wearing thin, and the disease-plagued Falstaff of this scene may not altogether relish the Justice's pitiless enumeration of his physical symptoms of ageing: 'a dry hand, a yellow cheek, a white beard, a decreasing leg, an increasing belly?' (1.2.143–4). Even Falstaff's whore thinks that the time for repentance may be near:

> Thou whoreson little tidy Bartholomew boar-pig, when wilt thou leave fighting a-days and foining a-nights, and begin to patch up thine old body for heaven? (2.4.187–8)

As the living spirit of Carnival, Falstaff is the body of appetite, a body that in Carnival-time is insatiable and eternal. In *2 Henry IV* he becomes a fat man towards the identifiable end of a lifespan, a lifespan that runs in parallel to history.

The comedy of Shallow and Silence contributes to this new perspective on Falstaff. In all probability the comic justices were an outgrowth of misrecruiting stories of *1 Henry IV*, as I suggested earlier, or a decision by Shakespeare to balance the city comedy of Eastcheap with the country comedy of Gloucestershire. Certainly these scenes wonderfully extend out the observation of London tavern manners into a countryside of cattle prices at the local fair, headlands to be sowed with red wheat. However, the running gag of Shallow's recollections of his all-too-brief youth in the capital told to the obligingly silent audience of Silence makes for a retrospective mode in which Falstaff, companion of that shared past time, has his part. Shallow's comic old man's trick of repeating himself makes for an insistence on mortality even before Falstaff's arrival, as he ruminates on the latest deaths among Silence's neighbours: 'And is old Dooble dead?' (3.2.43). He is doubly dead before Shallow is done exclaiming on the matter.

Significantly Dooble is remembered as a fine archer favoured by John of Gaunt: 'A shot a fine shoot. John a'Gaunt loved him well and betted much money on his head' (3.2.35–7). Shallow's intimate acquaintance with the great John of Gaunt was no doubt a fabrication of memory, as Falstaff makes clear at the end of this scene: '[he] talks as familiarly of John a'Gaunt as if he had been sworn brother to him, and I'll be sworn a ne'er saw him but once in the tilt-yard, and then he burst his head for crowding among the marshal's men' (3.2.259–62). Still this sort of reference loosely attaches the fictional comedy of Shallow and Falstaff to the successive eras of time marked out in the serial histories. In *Richard II* Gaunt was 'time-honoured Lancaster', aged spokesman for an all-but-mythical past England. Here in *2 Henry IV* men who are themselves old remember Gaunt's vigorous and powerful manhood, laying wagers at archery contests, beating back overeager onlookers at the tournament. Falstaff is similarly inscribed in the history represented by the history plays when Shallow dates his time at the Inns of Court: 'Then was Jack Falstaff, now Sir John, a boy, and page to Thomas Mowbray, Duke of Norfolk' (3.2.20–1). Difficult to imagine Falstaff a page-boy, even harder to envisage him attending on Bullingbrook's antagonist of the opening scenes of *Richard II*, but it is just such a transgeneric effort of the dramatic imagination that we are encouraged to make in these scenes. The chimes at midnight that Falstaff and Shallow heard together rang out during the lifetime of John of Gaunt, in the reign of Richard II. The comic genre scene of old men sentimentally recollecting their wild youth is placed against a sketched-in ground of the passing of historical time.

Falstaff by his association with the prince acquired a life, but he also acquired an old age and death. If Hal was to live on and be transformed into the victor of Agincourt, he had to discard Falstaff, misleader of his youth. But into what limbo of time did that consign the misleader, identified as he was with the pre-reformation prince? Falstaff as autonomous comic character could be recycled at will, as he was in *Merry Wives*, even if this has provoked critics who take as different a view of Falstaff as John Dover Wilson and Harold Bloom to call the *Merry Wives* version an imposter.[27] It is true that the *Merry Wives* character is always the butt of the jokes not their master as he is in the *Henry IV* plays, but he is as in his earlier manifestation a survivor, an escapologist. He may be stuffed in washing-baskets, ducked in the river, beaten in various degrading

disguises, but he always lives on incorrigible in spite of so many correc-
tions. Even in the Epilogue to *2 Henry IV* when the audience is given the
enticing prospect that in the continuation of the story with the French
wars of Henry V, Falstaff may 'die of a sweat', it is likely that they would
have taken it metaphorically: more of Falstaff ignobly sweating with fear
on the battlefield, rather than the fever that actually carries him away
in his bed offstage in *Henry V*. Nothing so tellingly suggests the hybrid
character of Falstaff as that death and the way it is represented.

The decision to kill off Falstaff may have been conditioned by changes
in the personnel of the Chamberlain's Men, or by a market judgement
on Shakespeare's part. He may have considered that with three plays
already as starring vehicles for the character, his audience might well be
'too much cloyed with fat meat'. But the death of Falstaff in *Henry V* is built
into the course of his life as dramatised in the *Henry IV* plays, and linked
specifically to the pastness of his relationship with Prince Hal. It is possible
to see the elimination of the other Eastcheap characters as a strategic
policy of removal, replacing them with what Paola Pugliatti calls the
'legalitarian comedy' appropriate to *Henry V*.[28] Amid the other deaths,
the hanging of Bardolph, the casual murder of the Boy, the offstage deaths
of Nym or Quickly looked at in the previous section, Falstaff represents
a special case.

The famous description of his death is always played for its full pathetic
value in modern productions. The comic Quicklyisms in the speech are
overridden or dropped: Falstaff going to 'Arthur's bosom' rather than
Abraham's, Falstaff's deathbed denunciations of women as 'devils incar-
nate' misread – 'A never could abide carnation, 'twas a colour he never
liked' (2.3.8, 27–9). There may be an element of modern sentimentalism
here, an audience in 1599 may have been tougher-minded, but it is hard
to see how that speech could be played wholly for laughs. What is more,
the play returns as though insistently to the King's past relationship with
Falstaff, and the effect of his rejection of the old man. The Eastcheapers
are all as one on this, each in his or her own idiom. When the news is first
brought in of Falstaff's illness, Quickly comments 'The king has killed his
heart.' Nym agrees: 'The king hath run bad humours on the knight'; 'his
heart', according to Pistol, 'is fracted and corroborate' (2.1.70, 97–101).
This is the way they would see it, presumably; the effect, though, is to fill
in the gap between the rejection scene of *2 Henry IV* and *Henry V* as a sad-
dened interim of decay into death. And even Fluellen, lead actor in the
legalitarian comedy that replaces Falstaff, sets up a suggestive analogy
between Henry and Alexander: 'As Alexander killed his friend Cleitus,

being in his ales and his cups, so also Harry Monmouth, being in his right wits and his good judgements, turned away the fat knight with the great belly doublet' (4.7.36–9). The comparison concedes that Falstaff was Henry's friend and that, however correct the decision to reject him, it did result in his death. And this is to be the last time that Falstaff's name is spoken in the plays.

'Hal and Falstaff do not exist as characters within a single, contained fictive universe.'[29] Wiles is no doubt right to stress the extra clown-like dimension to the character of Falstaff, whether Kemp played the part or not. He is, in every sense of the word, larger than the life of the situations into which he is cast, hence his easy translation to the comedy of *Merry Wives*. Yet Falstaff does share a fictive universe with Hal, even if it is not a single or contained one. And if Hal has to grow up, so Falstaff must grow old. The perpetually buoyant comic figure cannot wholly escape the condition of time to which the history of Prince Hal/King Henry binds him. It is this that brings him into the dimension of theatrical experience where pathos is a possibility, pathos based on the observation of human change, as comedy is founded on the assurance of changelessness. Hotspur makes a complementary figure to Falstaff. Where the status of the comic Falstaff is altered by his participation in the dramatic mode of history, the historical Hotspur is as it were contaminated by comedy. Though he is theatrically destined to die at Shrewsbury to mark the ascent of Hal's rising star, he has the inalienable and distinctive vitality we associate with comic characterisation. There is no better measure of the hybridity of Shakespeare's hybrid history in the *Henry IV* plays than these two figures who so cross between the different genres in which they are conceived.

FROM COMIC TO EPIC HISTORY

An Age of Kings showed in the final scene of *2 Henry IV* coronation crowds thronging the streets. After Falstaff, traumatised by the rejection of the King, had been carried off struggling to the Fleet, the actor playing Shallow (William Squires) came forward taking off his wig and make up, and spoke an edited version of the Epilogue in a young man's voice markedly unlike Shallow's wavering falsetto. It was a real surprise. Up to that point, the *Age of Kings* series had preserved a completely representational convention, eliding the formal features differentiating play from play. Each episode included narrative bridges pointing on towards the next. For similar reasons of continuity, Rumour was cut from the opening of *2 Henry IV*, and the episode entitled 'The New Conspiracy' continued seamlessly with the (true) news of Shrewsbury being brought to Northumberland. There seemed an asymmetry, then, in retaining the metatheatrical framing device of the Epilogue, when the equivalent Induction had been removed. Everywhere else in the series up to that point, the illusion of representation had been maintained and actors stayed within their roles. The explanation came with the opening of *Henry V* where William Squires, as actor out of part, was to speak the Choruses throughout.

The sequence *Richard II* to *Henry V* makes a bumpy ride for any-one trying to adapt it as a homogeneous serial production. Shake-speare not only reinvented his own form of history play when he cre-ated the hybrid mode of the *Henry IV* plays; he reinvented it again in *Henry V*. The epic subject of the glorious warrior king required a differ-ent sort of comedy, a phasing out of the Eastcheap lowlifes in favour of Fluellen's quaint Welsh loyalism, but it involved also a change in narrative mode. One of the striking features of the *Henry VI* plays, *Richard III* and *Richard II*, particularly by comparison with the quasi-histories written by Shakespeare's contemporaries, is the continuity of their narrative line. There may be roughnesses and 'unconformities' here and there, but on the whole event follows event, character generates action and action character, with a rigorous logic shaped out of the looser juxtapositions of the chronicles. In the epic action of *Henry V* it is very different. The Chorus is there to give the audience a slide-show of great images, a pageant of heroic tableaux. There seems to be some evidence from the Quarto and Folio texts of uncertainties, changes of mind, in the sequence of scenes in *Henry V*. It hardly seems to matter. The play does not depend on the sort of articulation of past, present and future in which the causal order of events is crucial.

The Southampton conspiracy may serve as an instance. We never hear of Cambridge, Grey and Scroop before the one scene in which they appear, they are never mentioned again after their execution. The King takes some fifty lines to berate the ingratitude of Scroop,

> Thou that didst bear the key of all my counsels,
> That knew'st the very bottom of my soul.
>
> (2.2.93–4)

Why have we never seen this bosom intimate of Henry in his com-pany before? A question not to be asked. The Southampton conspira-tors are only there to act out a detachable allegorical scene of Treachery Detected, Ingratitude Exposed, before the action moves on to France and glory. It is only necessary to glance at the rebellions of the reign of Henry IV, so carefully built up and motivated, to see the contrast in the dramatic mode of *Henry V*. From the multiply layered form of comic history in the *Henry IV* plays we move in *Henry V* into a discontinuous epic history.

The transformation of the wild Prince Henry into the great King Henry V takes place across plays that themselves shift in style. The implications of this for concepts of change and identity across the series will be considered in the next chapter. My concern here has been with the way the introduction of comedy in the *Henry IV* plays contributed to a new order of dramatic representation in the histories, a different sort of theatrical space. In the earlier popular forms of mixed-mode history plays, the separate styles co-existed easily and unselfconsciously. In Shakespeare's more complex and sophisticated hybrid history, there is constant interaction between the several species of drama from which the hybridity is generated. A changing cast of comic characters could be deployed at will across the plays as plot situation or audience demand required. Yet in so far as they continued to appear in a sequence dramatising the linear progress of history they developed something like human lives. The history plays showed a continuing narrative of England's past; with the miscellany of modes of the *Henry IV* plays England itself becomes a very different country. This is a nation not just of kings, princes and rebellious barons, but of drawers in Eastcheap, carriers on the road to London, musical concerts in Wales, doddery JPs down in Gloucestershire. Such a diversity of theatrical life-forms makes denser and more diffuse the sense of a single onward action of history. And this changes again with the epic mode of *Henry V*. The final chapter will take up the issues that arise from this sequence of changes for our understanding of the figure of Hal/Henry V.

CHAPTER EIGHT

Change and identity

> Cover your heads, and mock not flesh and blood
> With solemn reverence. Throw away respect,
> Tradition, form and ceremonious duty,
> For you have but mistook me all this while.
> I live with bread like you, feel want,
> Taste grief, need friends. Subjected thus,
> How can you say to me I am a king?
>
> (3.2.171–7)

At this stage of *Richard II*, there is still some high-horse attitudinising in Richard's posture as the king-who-is-yet-but-a-man. Sardonic irony is at play in that finely poised pun on 'subjected'. It is like Lear's angry and rhetorically intended question, 'who is that can tell me who I am?' that expects anything but the deflationary answer it gets in the Fool's reply, 'Lear's shadow'. King Richard, like King Lear, is not lightly prepared to abandon his habitual occupation of the royal role. Yet the force of the action is to drive him out of that unexamined equation of selfhood and kingship. 'Unkinged by Bullingbrook', he has to take up the shattered shards of the self and make what he can of them. The unmade King/man ends in the vortex of destructive self-scrutiny culminating in the prison soliloquy of Act 5:

> But whate'er I be
> Nor I nor any man that but man is
> With nothing shall be pleased till he be eased
> With being nothing.
>
> (5.5.38–41)

The doctrinal paradox of the King's two bodies is dramatised in *Richard II* as the descent of the royal method actor, who fully believes in his role, down to the bewildered less-than-man trying to find a part. The *Henry IV – Henry V* plays trace an almost exactly opposite pathway. The Prince of Wales whom we meet in *1 Henry IV* is all too much like other men, all too little like the king he is born to be. Yet by the final play of the sequence he is to enact sovereignty with a grace, an authority, given to no other English king. Falstaff's Hal, the man whom the Eastcheap drawers call 'a Corinthian, a lad of mettle', is to be transformed into the mirror of all Christian Kings. The unkinging of Richard is the central subject of a single play; *Richard II* is built around that process with a concentrated unity unlike anything else in Shakespeare's histories. But the transformation of Hal from man to monarch, previewed in *Richard II*, twice enacted in *1* and *2 Henry IV*, consummated in *Henry V*, is rendered complex and problematic by the extended sequence of its dramatisation. Issues of change and identity, by definition encoded in the concept of the king's two bodies, take on a different dimension in this multiple theatrical version of the wild prince becoming great king.

'I shall hereafter, my thrice-gracious lord, / Be more myself' (3.2.92–3) promises the repentant Hal to his father in their climactic interview in *1 Henry IV*. The implication of the promise is that Hal's true self is the prince, his father's son and heir. But both the wild youth and the eventual glorious warrior king are pre-inscribed in the legend. In the *Famous Victories* the two personae are dramatised successively with equal gusto, and with no sense of the need for characterological continuity between the two. Shakespeare gives to Hal the early soliloquy, 'I know you all, and will a while uphold / The unyoked humour of your idleness' (1.2.155ff.), to suggest the later self lurking behind the madcap mask. Still for some considerable 'while' what an audience is to be shown – and demands to be shown – is the 'idle' Hal, and there remains the question of how that holiday figure relates to the working king of the later phase.

The issue of the two parts of *Henry IV*, and whether they were designed as such, arises here also. By the end of *1 Henry IV*, the Prince seems a wholly reformed character, reconciled to his father, having won his spurs at Shrewsbury with the conquest of Hotspur. Yet by the start of *2 Henry IV* it is all to do again: Hal has been sent to prison for striking the Lord Chief Justice; he is still regarded as being under the sway of Falstaff; he is once again the despair of the King, his succession dreaded by his brothers. It makes a crucial difference if this backsliding is regarded as a planned stage in Shakespeare's representation of the figure of Hal or merely an accidental effect of the need to replicate the formula of the earlier play. And then there is the question of the transformed king of *Henry V*. Does the changed dramatic mode of the last play in the series make it possible to say we are dealing with the same character? Is Henry V recognisably the

Hal of the *Henry IV* plays turned monarch-like, or is he in fact someone else again, the king that the new form of epic history demands?

One way to approach these questions is to look at the range of images used to figure the change from prince to king throughout the series. Again and again, prospectively in the *Henry IV* plays and retrospectively in *Henry V*, the phenomenon of that change is represented in a variety of ways. By interrogating the implications of these several images we can explore the different interpretative models available within the plays. An older generation of critics commonly saw within the Henry plays a process of education, the education of a perfect king. But what ideas of character development, psychological schemes of growth and change, are workable within these hybrid histories, including the problematically two-part *Henry IV*? Looking at some of the performance possibilities in serial productions of the plays may help to illustrate the continuities and discontinuities in attempting a through-conception of Hal/Henry.

There is more at issue here than the matter of theatrical character, and whether it can be tracked consistently across the three plays. For the change that Henry undergoes is the change consequent upon becoming king. *Henry V* returns as if insistently to the question of the King's personal responsibilities for what he has to do in his royal office. But such is the integration of self and public function in the play that it is hard to know quite what person is there to take responsibility. As Graham Bradshaw puts it, 'we repeatedly see Henry's virtuoso performances as he stages a royal "self"', but are not allowed to see – and consequently want all the more to know – whether there is still a human face behind the royal mask.'[1] 'Still' here implies that a human face was visible earlier, that the royal role in *Henry V* represents an occlusion of the private personality manifest in the Hal of the previous plays. Such is the assumption of many critics in interpreting the play, and indeed of producers producing it: hence the inserted flashbacks to the *Henry IV* plays in both the Olivier and the Branagh films. It is the aim of this, my last chapter, exploring the implications of the seriality of the histories, to look at the sort of identity, the nature of the changes, enacted in the figure of Hal/Henry V as man and king across the three plays in which he appears.

METAPHORS OF METAMORPHOSIS

For the chroniclers, Henry's reform was an all-but-miraculous alteration that took place the moment he came to the throne. Hall called him 'almost the Arabical Phenix', presumably not only because he was 'emongest his predecessors a very Paragon' (Hall, fol. xxxiii v) but because he rose from the ashes of his previous self. Similarly Holinshed commented that on his accession 'this king even at first appointing with himselfe, to shew that in his person princelie honors should change publike manners, he determined to put on him the shape of a new man. For whereas aforetime he had made himselfe a companion unto misrulie mates of dissolute order and life, he now banished them all from his presence' (Bullough, IV, 280). Behind Holinshed's wording here lies the conception of being born again in Christ, St Paul's injunction to the Ephesians to 'put on a new man' (Eph. 4: 24). The legends of Prince Henry's wild youth went well back in the chronicle accounts, and made a set-piece wonder of his remarkable transformation into the king he was to become.

It is there in essence already in Shakespeare from the very first time we hear of the Prince in *Richard II*. When Bullingbrook asks for news of his 'unthrifty son', it is significantly Harry Percy who has sighted him most recently:

> PERCY   My lord, some two days since I saw the prince
>   And told him of those triumphs held at Oxford.
> BULLINGBROOK   And what said the gallant?
> PERCY   His answer was he would unto the stews
>   And from the commonest creature pluck a glove
>   And wear it as a favour, and with that
>   He would unhorse the lustiest challenger.   (5.3.13–19)

Hal is later to confess that he has 'a truant been to chivalry' (*1 Henry IV*, 5.1.94), but here he shows himself to be a positive rebel against its values. He will fight, not for the chastest and most beautiful lady, as in the courtly ritual of the tournament, but for the lowest whore from the brothel, provocatively championing such unreconstructed lust over the sublimated sexuality of the chivalric knight. (It is noticeable, however, that Shakespeare in the *Henry IV* plays chooses not to associate Hal with whoring: Doll Tearsheet is a stranger to him.) Bullingbrook is disgusted by this latest token of his son's unprinceliness, but not altogether despairing of him:

> As dissolute as desperate! Yet through both
> I see some sparks of better hope in him
> Which elder years may happily bring forth.
> (5.3.20–2)

Shakespeare's madcap Prince of Wales is never to be shown without a hint or reminder of his potential for reform, as his counterpart in *Famous Victories* was. Here the image of the 'sparks of better hope' suggests the smouldering fire that may yet take light, a more homely form of ignition than Hall's 'Arabical Phenix', but suggestive of the improvement to come.

The Prince's own vision of his reformation involves an image of the sun:

> I know you all, and will a while uphold
> The unyoked humour of your idleness.
> Yet herein will I imitate the sun,
> Who doth permit the base contagious clouds
> To smother up his beauty from the world,
> That when he please again to be himself,
> Being wanted, he may be more wondered at
> By breaking through the foul and ugly mists
> Of vapours that did seem to strangle him.
>
>   (*1 Henry IV* 1.2.155–63)

This is interestingly comparable to Richard's extended imagination of his kingly presence as sunrise on his return from Ireland. 'Knowest thou not', he haughtily tells Aumerle who is anxious about the Bullingbrook rebellion,

> That when the searching eye of heaven is hid
> Behind the globe and lights the lower world
> Then thieves and robbers range abroad unseen
> In murders and in outrage boldly here.

But now that he, the sun-king of England, has returned from 'wandering with the antipodes', the thief Bullingbrook will be exposed, unable 'to endure the sight of day' (*Richard II*, 3.2.36–52). For Richard the equation of king to sun yields a concept of the supremacy of royal power as inevitable as the natural succession of day to night. And a faulty equation it proves to be, for all the grandeur of its articulation here. What is striking by contrast in Hal's soliloquy is the notion of the sun's management of its appearance. If he is temporarily obscured, it is because he 'doth *permit* the base contagious clouds' to cover his glory; he remains at perfect liberty to shine out 'when he please again to be himself'. It is the capacity for agency in Hal's sun/prince that differentiates it from Richard's purely determined solar system.

King Henry uses ironically similar imagery about public appearance in his reproaches to his son in Act 3 of *1 Henry IV*. It was by scarcity value that Henry attracted attention in his rise to power:

> By being seldom seen, I could not stir
> But like a comet I was wondered at
>
>   (3.2.46–7)

By contrast Richard who had 'enfeoffed himself to popularity' was

> seen, but with such eyes
> As, sick and blunted with community,
> Afford no extraordinary gaze,
> Such as is bent on sun-like majesty
> When it shines seldom in admiring eyes
> (3.2.76–80)

Father and son speak the same language, even if they apply the sun imagery of public relations differently. But Hal changes the idiom altogether in this scene when he promises his father to make good his past misdemeanours:

> I will redeem all this on Percy's head,
> And in the closing of some glorious day
> Be bold to tell you that I am your son,
> When I will wear a garment all of blood,
> And stain my favours in a bloody mask,
> Which, washed away, shall scour my shame with it.
> (3.2.132–7)

The word 'redeem', coupled with the imagery of cleansing blood, enforces the idea of Christian conversion implied in Holinshed's phrase about putting on 'the shape of a new man'. The changed Prince will be a man new made. But the literal meaning of buying back in 'redeem' is activated later in the speech where he elaborates on the significance of his promised defeat of Hotspur:

> Percy is but my factor, good my lord,
> To engross up glorious deeds on my behalf
> (3.2.147–8)

Hal's antagonist is his agent because all the martial feats, which he has, so to speak, bought in, will become Hal's own when he conquers Hotspur. The reformation is to be a most advantageous trade-off:

> I shall make this northern youth exchange
> His glorious deeds for my indignities.
> (3.2.145–6)

The emphasis in all the images of Hal's coming transformation, looked at so far, is on the miraculous change ahead, when the sun comes out from behind the clouds, the battlefield victor appears renewed by the blood of conquest, the underdog – 'your unthought-of Harry' – replaces Harry Hotspur as the champion of chivalry. But there is another perspective that considers the apparently misspent youth itself, and sees its longterm

usefulness. The fullest statement is that of Warwick, cheering up the King
in 2 *Henry IV* when he fears the worst for his son's accession, given the
looseness of his behaviour as Prince:

> My gracious lord, you look beyond him quite:
> The prince but studies his companions
> Like to a strange tongue, wherein, to gain the language,
> 'Tis needful that the most immodest word
> Be looked upon and learnt; which once attained,
> Your highness knows comes to no further use
> But to be known and hated.
>
> (4.2.67–73)

This is generally linked by commentators to the scene in *1 Henry IV*
where Hal, after his session with Francis and his fellow-drawers, boasts
that 'I can drink with any tinker in his own language during my life'
(2.4.15–16). For Stephen Greenblatt, Warwick's speech demonstrates
Hal's mission to control and master the lower classes whose language
he is learning, akin to the thieves' slang glossaries of Elizabethan cony-
catching pamplets.[2] But there is another more beneficent view of the
utility of Hal's time in Eastcheap offered in Falstaff's paean to sack. The
Prince is contrasted with his 'sober-blooded' brother John of Lancaster
who 'drinks no wine':

Prince Harry is valiant, for the cold blood he did naturally inherit of his father
he hath, like lean, sterile and bare land, manured, husbanded and tilled, with
excellent endeavour of drinking good and good store of fertile sherris, that he is
become very hot and valiant. (2 *Henry IV*, 4.1.464–9)

Hal overcomes Hotspur at Shrewsbury not in spite of his drinking sessions
in Eastcheap but because of them. Though this is comically placed in
the spirit of Falstaff's praise of folly speech, there is here available a
conception of the Prince's sensual indulgences as humanising influences
rather than merely bad habits to be forsworn.

   With Henry's accession as king, there is a reversion to the language
of miracle and Christian redemption in the metaphors of his alteration.
Most daring is the image with which he reassures the court in his speech
immediately following his father's death:

> And, princes all, believe me, I beseech you,
> My father is gone wild into his grave,
> For in his tomb lie my affections.
>
> (2 *Henry IV* 5.2.121–3)

With the body of the dead king is the wildness of the wild prince, also now dead. In his newly acquired body as the king, Henry stands passion-free, purged of his past bodily weaknesses. The Archbishop of Canterbury in *Henry V* sounds the same note, though giving it, as might be expected, a more explicitly religious turn:

> The breath no sooner left his father's body
> But that his wildness, mortified in him,
> Seemed to die too. Yea, at that very moment
> Consideration like an angel came,
> And whipped th'offending Adam out of him,
> Leaving his body as a paradise
> T'envelop and contain celestial spirits.
>
> (1.1.25–31)

Explanations, readings, interpretations are indeed not wanting in the series of plays for the change from wild prince to responsible monarch. The problem, rather, is the sheer plurality of ways of seeing that change and their contradictory implications. Within the conventions of Elizabethan drama no rational explanation for instantaneous conversion was thought necessary. The *Famous Victories* is typical rather than anomalous in representing Harry's repentance as a sudden and completely unprepared turnaround. Shakespearean characters in the comedies and romances are quite as suddenly metamorphosed. Celia and Rosalind in *As You Like It* are astonished to discover that the stranger who tells them the story of his rescue from serpent and lioness by Orlando is none other than his wicked brother Oliver:

> CELIA Are you his brother?
> ROSALIND   Was't you he rescu'd?
> CELIA Was't you that did so oft contrive to kill him?
> OLIVER 'Twas I; but 'tis not I. I do not shame
>   To tell you what I was, since my conversion
>   So sweetly tastes, being the thing I am.   (4.3.132–6)

There is no real strain put on the idea of identity by the formulation ''Twas I; but 'tis not I.' The self, radically fractured by conversion, is easily acceptable here as in many more plays of the period, Shakespearean and non-Shakespearean. However, in playing out Hal's transformation in the form of the history, and in a series of histories at that, Shakespeare opened the way for developmental interpretations which would make sense of the movement from prince to king. In the several manifestations of the madcap Hal predestined to become the glorious Henry V, as they are played out theatrically in the linear sequence that mimics historical time, actors, audiences, critical readers seem challenged to find a consistent psychological profile or political strategy. To do so involves plotting a graph of changing significance over the series of plays, trying to establish the nature of the prince/king's identity out of the metaphors of his metamorphosis.

DEVELOPMENT

If there was one germ of historical fact that grew into the legend of the wild prince, it may have been his estrangement from his father. In the later years of Henry IV's reign, when the King was increasingly ill, Prince Henry came to dominate the council that was largely composed of close associates and supporters of his own. There was even a suggestion that the King abdicate in his favour. The King's reaction to such an idea of standing down came in November 1411, when, without warning or explanation, he dismissed the Prince and his supporters from the council. Henry's brother, Thomas of Clarence, was promoted in his place.[3] There may be a fossil record of this incident in *1 Henry IV* when the King reproaches Henry with his misbehaviour –

> Thy place in Council thou hast rudely lost,
> Which by thy younger brother is supplied
>
> (3.2.32–3)

– though Shakespeare follows the legendary tradition in attributing the demotion to the Prince's wildness rather than his political ambitions. The Prince of Wales was precocious, a successful military campaigner from his early teens: he was only sixteen when he fought at Shrewsbury. It seems that, as with other charismatic heirs-apparent to the throne, a court party may have grown up around the Prince in opposition to the King.

There are two stories in Holinshed suggestive of the alienation of father and son and their subsequent reconciliation. One is the incident of the stolen crown dramatised in *2 Henry IV*. The other, which Shakespeare did not use, though the *Famous Victories* dramatist did, was the description of the Prince's surprising appearance at court with a very large train of followers dressed in 'strange apparell' (Bullough, IV, 193), proffering the King a dagger to kill him if his father suspected him of disloyalty. 'The king mooved herewith, cast from him the dagger, and imbracing the prince kissed him, and with shedding tears confessed, that in deed he had him partlie in suspicion, though now (as he perceived) not with just cause, and therefore from thencefoorth no misreport should cause him to have him in mistrust' (Bullough, IV, 194–5). There are hints of this in *1 Henry IV* with Hal's dismissal of the 'smiling pickthanks, and base newsmongers' who have misrepresented him to his father, his horrified indignation at the King's supposition that he might join with Percy and the rebels:

> Do not think it so, you shall not find it so;
> And God forgive them that so much have swayed
> Your majesty's good thoughts away from me!
>
> (3.2.129–31)

It makes for a second reconciliation at Shrewsbury when Hal intervenes to save his father from Douglas.

> KING ... Thou hast redeemed thy lost opinion,
>   And showed thou mak'st some tender of my life
>   In this fair rescue thou hast brought to me.
> PRINCE O God, they did me too much injury
>   That ever said I hearkened for your death.   (5.4.47–51)

The king is dead – long live the king. The suspicion of the reigning monarch is that his son and heir must look forward to that moment and thus to his death; the aim of the Prince is to convince his father that he remains loving and loyal. It is in this spirit that Hal in *2 Henry IV* restores to the King the crown he has prematurely taken:

>   There is your crown;
> And He that wears the crown immortally
> Long guard it yours. If I affect it more
> Than as your honour and as your renown,
> Let me no more from this obedience rise
>
> (4.2.271–5)

This is the second reconciliation of king and prince, providing the climax of Shakespeare's second *Henry IV* play, as Hal's rescue of his father at Shrewsbury confirming his earlier professions did for *1 Henry IV*. But the separation of father and son that makes reconciliation necessary is structurally built in to both plays, and signalled already from Bullingbrook's first querulous enquiry in *Richard II*:

> Can no man tell of my unthrifty son?
> 'Tis full three months since I did see him last.
>
> (5.3.1–2)

Hal, through most of the *Henry IV* plays, occupies his own space apart in Eastcheap rather than attending at court as his father's heir apparent. For the Prince thus to behave in markedly unprincely ways is a threat to the authority of the King, whose image he should replicate, as well as to the future order of the kingdom. The two manifestations of Hal's riotousness that Shakespeare chose to represent (in however toned-down a form in comparison with the boisterousness of the *Famous Victories*), the robbing of money that should be going to the King's exchequer, and the striking of the King's highest magistrate the Lord Chief Justice, are challenges to the principle of the patriarchal order that the monarchy embodies. The suspicion of rivalry underlies the estrangement of king and prince in the two *Henry IV* plays; Hal, low-lifing it in Eastcheap, is in rebellion against the law of the father.

In this configuration, Falstaff, leading misleader of Hal's youth, stands as Lord of Misrule, counterking, pseudofather. At least as far back as J. I. M. Stewart, Falstaff has been perceived as a sacrificial substitute for Henry IV: 'Hal, by a displacement common enough in the evolution of ritual, kills Falstaff instead of killing the king, his father.'[4] For C. L. Barber, Hal's image of his father 'going wild into his grave' is a conceit that 'hints at the patricidal motive . . . the complement to the father–son atonement'.[5] Modern productions have built upon the psychological reading of the father–son relationship, and used it to make of Hal's development a staged adolescence. In Terry Hands' 1975 RSC productions Emrys James played Henry as a despotic, possessive parent. As one reviewer of *1 Henry IV* described it, 'he tyrannises over [Hal] not only mentally, but physically, grasping him in a savage embrace, kissing him mouth to mouth, a contact from which the prince shudderingly drags himself away'.[6] Alan Howard's Prince had to come through a bad relationship with his father before he was able to take on the burden of the kingship, a role theatrically signalled in his coronation appearance 'like a robot, masked and glistening from head to foot in yellow metal'.[7] Even at this point, it seemed, the severance from his substitute father was as difficult for him as earlier contact with his real parent had been. 'The new King . . . dressed head to foot in gold . . . covers his face in agony with his hands as Falstaff confronts him with his acclamation, and it is clearly a wretched duty to turn the old man away.'[8] In the 2000 production directed by Michael Attenborough it was the lack of physical warmth that marked the failure of the father–son relationship. At the climax of their reconciliation scene in *1 Henry IV*, 3.2, David Troughton as the King visibly held back from an impulse to embrace

Plate 14 Falstaff (Desmond Barritt) and Hal (William Houston) in RSC production of *1 Henry IV*, directed by Michael Attenborough, Stratford 2000

Hal (William Houston), at just the point where Emrys James had savaged Alan Howard with his kiss. In this staging, the contrasting ease of bodily contact was stressed in the opening Eastcheap scene where Houston lolled comfortably against the massive figure of Desmond Barritt's Falstaff. The rivalry between the father and father-substitute was caught in a glancing moment before Shrewsbury, where the exiting King unhappily eyed Falstaff moving to Hal with his request for protection in the conflict to come: 'Hal, if thou see me down in the battle and bestride me so, 'tis a point of friendship' (5.1.121–2). It is just such informal intimacy that Henry could not manage with his son.

The most radical version of this psychological modelling of Hal in his transformation from prince to king came in *Schlachten!* There Falstaff was not a substitute father but mother, the drag queen La Falstaff (Roland Renner). In the dramatic opening tableau to *Heinrich 4*, he/she was highlighted upstage in a vivid red dress with full train and female wig of gold tresses down to his/her shoulders, wearing a golden crown far more

Plate 15 Heinz (Wolfgang Pregler) and La Falstaff (Roland Renner) in *Schlachten!*,
Deutsches Schauspielhaus, Hamburg, directed by Luk Perceval

elaborate than the plain metal version which was the standing prop for
the real crown throughout. Later, a bespectacled Heinz (= Hal), played
by Wolfgang Pregler, initially wearing nothing but underpants and a
pair of wings, was cuddled beneath La Falstaff's cloak. It is this unlikely
specimen that Heinrich 4 (Bernd Grawert) brutally shaped up for battle
with wings stripped off, crown shoved down upon his head. And the
militarist make-over took effect. When finally La Falstaff came forward
to kiss Heinz congratulations on his accession to the throne, the new king
stared straight out to the audience and delivered an adapted version of
Warwick's speech about the Prince studying 'his companions / Like a
strange tongue':

> Ich habe Euch und Eure Sitten durchaus
> Studiert wie eine fremde Sprache

In response to all La Falstaff's endearments, he would only repeat
automaton-like his formal title:

> Mein Nam ist Heinrich, fünfter dieses Namens.[9]

La Falstaff was forced to take off wig and crown in a formal humiliation of the rival king/queen.

Jean Howard and Phyllis Rackin in *Engendering a Nation* also see Falstaff as 'characterised in feminine terms' in their view of the *Richard II – Henry V* series as representing the emergence of a 'performative masculinity' typical of a new modern era.[10] Tom Lanoye and Luk Perceval, in their adaptation and casting of these plays in *Schlachten!*, made this a systematic thematic progression. Roland Renner played Richard Deuxième as a blatantly bisexual figure, before going on to appear as La Falstaff. In *Der Fünfte Heinrich*, La Falstaff, changed into a formal dress suit, seated in an armchair with microphone in hand, was given a highly adapted version of the Chorus's speeches ironically recast as a forsaken love-song to his Heinrich. Just once in the production, at a significant moment, he was given a wordless gesture of contact with the King, after the siege of Harfleur.

The French in the besieged city had been presented in grossly caricatured form occupying a central stage pit crammed with old furniture, a vaulting-horse, assorted junk. When Harfleur duly surrendered in response to the King's threats, the English army ignored his orders to show mercy and proceeded to sack the city violently and comprehensively, just as Henry had threatened to do. Everything in the 'city' was smashed to pieces, a host of small dolls torn apart, and the grotesquely doll-like Cathérine (Nina Kunzendorf), who represented France, anally raped. At the end of all this, Henry stood visibly appalled and it was at this moment that La Falstaff, in a gesture of sympathy, came forward and handed him a bottle of beer before leaving him again to himself. For an extraordinarily long-held period of silence, Henry did nothing but pace up and down, contemplating the reality of what his soldiers had done. He finally began to drink the beer, which twice fizzed up over his hand, until at last he swilled it down spilling some of it over his neck. This was a stage emblem in little for the tour de force that followed as Henry, at first bewailing the role of kingship in a version of the 'ceremony' speech, gradually rebuilt his confidence until he was able to move not only into the St Crispin's day speech, but a solo performance of Agincourt, miming the parts of both English and French. He ended up in triumph atop the vaulting-horse, with a shower turned on him to provide a parody version of Branagh's rain-drenched, mud-bespattered victor-king.

This bravura tour de force of a solo Agincourt had obvious advantages for a production of *Henry V* staged with all of nine actors; the very different published version, which included far more of Shakespeare's text, suggests how it may have been reached by a process of theatrical rationalisation.[11] But it represented a fitting climax to the psychodrama of Heinz/Heinrich as this production had envisaged it. The timid, gentle, homosexual young prince is forced by his father into the mould of martial hypermasculinity. He imagines that war can be conducted by rules of order and chivalry, and is aghast at what actually happens at Harfleur. Still he can go on by a process of self-intoxication to work himself back into the role of macho hero, a role he can play out in his own head without the need to confront the reality of battle. That is one through-line for the role of Hal/Henry V, re-imagined polemically, tendentiously, from a modern anti-authoritarian point of view. But it could be achieved only in an adaptation drastically reducing the original texts. Whereas the bulk of *Richard II* had been retained as a full-length play in *Schlachten!*, the two parts of *Henry IV* with *Henry V* were boiled down to a single relatively brief playing unit. Significantly this involved the cutting of the comedy from all three plays, and the excision of all Hal's Eastcheap companions but Falstaff. True to the exclusive concentration of *Schlachten!* on a drama of power and gender, all the theatrical multiplicity of social and political representations in the *Henry IV – Henry V* plays had to go. It is this multiplicity that makes developmental models of the part of Hal/Henry so hard consistently to sustain while remaining responsive to all of the several texts.

One scene may serve to illustrate the intractability of the problem, the scene between Hal and Poins in *2 Henry IV* that Erich Auerbach used to illustrate Shakespeare's mixed style, his rendering of the 'most varied phenomena of life'.[12] In a developmental scheme of things, this could be made to stand for a transitional moment in the experience of Prince Hal, pointing the way forward and back, showing the emotional realities behind his gamesplaying. It is the first time an audience has seen him in *2 Henry IV*. He has just returned from campaigning in Wales – that was where he was headed with his father at the end of *1 Henry IV*, and in the immediately preceding scene we have heard Gower report to the Lord Chief Justice that 'The King, my lord, and Harry Prince of Wales / Are near at hand' (2.1.106–7). So his opening remark can be taken literally: 'Before God, I am exceeding weary'; this could plausibly be the aftereffect of the strenuous march from Wales back to London. In the 1951 Stratford production 'to indicate that Hal has just returned from Wales, we show him having just taken off his riding gear and about to dress, with Poins' assistance, in something rather gay and jeune premier'.[13] But as the scene continues in bantering repartee with Poins, the nature of the weariness becomes more elusive. The play is upon the incompatibility of high rank and ordinary human weaknesses, ordinary human desires:

> POINS ... I had thought weariness durst not have attached one of so high blood.
> PRINCE Faith, it does me, though it discolours the complexion of my greatness to acknowledge it: doth it not show vildly in me to desire small beer?
> POINS Why, a prince should not be so loosely studied as to remember so weak a composition.
> PRINCE Belike then my appetite was not princely got, for by my troth, I do now remember the poor creature small beer. (2.2.2–10)

Does the exchange show a satiric mockery of the pretended greatness of great men as liable as any other to thirst after small beer? Or is this the weariness of the prince who knows that his position will oblige him eventually to give up such simple creature comforts: 'But indeed these humble considerations make me out of love with my greatness' (2.2.10–11).

Underlying this is the more fundamental question of his basic attitude towards Poins, or indeed any of his 'low' companions. There appears to be a completely class-conditioned contempt in the terms in which he refers to Poins throughout this scene: 'wits of no higher breeding than thine', 'one it pleases me for fault of a better to call my friend', 'such vile company as thou art' (2.2.28, 30–1, 37). (It is a class contempt evidently shared by E. M. W. Tillyard who refers to 'people as thick-witted as Poins' in his commentary on this scene.[14]) But this could be played as part of the accepted bantering of the relationship, ironic mockery like Hal's obviously self-satiric 'What a disgrace it is to me to remember thy name – or to know thy face tomorrow – or to take note how many pairs of stockings thou hast' (2.2.11–13). The scene could well show the pathos of Hal's isolation as he hesitates to confide his grief at his father's sickness – 'shall I tell thee one thing, Poins?' – with the realisation that Poins, like everyone else in this group, would think him 'a most princely hypocrite' if he expressed such feelings, assuming he cannot wait to become King. There is an edgy negotiation between prince and friend/follower with the revelation in Falstaff's letter that Poins has boasted that Hal is to marry his sister:

> PRINCE ... But do you use me thus, Ned? Must I marry your sister?
> POINS God send the wench no worse fortune, but I never said so.
> (2.2.105–7)

Perhaps Hal does feel something like friendship for Poins, but the fact of his rank is always there, and at a moment like this it intrudes to demonstrate that for them real intimacy, based on equality, is never possible.

This can be an important scene for the building of the character of the Prince over the two plays. It is the last time we see him alone with Poins, the character with whom he has apparently been closest in *1 Henry IV*, if only in conspiring against Falstaff. It shows him between the battlefield of Shrewsbury and what is going to prove his last appearance in Eastcheap. It intimates an encroaching sense of the public part that will be finally thrust upon him with his father's death, a reluctant uneasiness at the crossways between low private and high public life. Yet to read it in this way is to presuppose a consistent, developing characterisation of Hal running across the two plays. And to make such an assumption is to tangle with the whole series of critical and interpretative problems attending on *1* and *2 Henry IV*.

To start with, there is the status of the two-part play itself. The options range from Dr Johnson's crisp affirmation, 'two only because too long to be one',[15] a view enthusiastically endorsed by Dover Wilson, to those who see Part 2 as an unpremeditated sequel with 'pot-boiler written all over it',[16] with variant theories such as that of Harold Jenkins arguing for an original single play expanded to two in the course of composition,[17] or G. K. Hunter's concept of a 'diptych-unity'.[18] This is not merely a technical problem, an ultimately indeterminable issue of Shakespeare's original intentions only. A staged reformation of the madcap prince over two plays makes for a quite different effect than a planned and accomplished reformation, re-run a second time to meet unexpected theatrical demand. If the latter construction is accepted, then the scene with Poins becomes only accidentally significant. In the re-creation of the formula of *1 Henry IV*, Shakespeare was bound at this point to have another major Eastcheap scene in which Hal and Poins together try to catch out Falstaff, and therefore needed a preparatory scene setting up that situation – here the disguise as drawers to eavesdrop unawares on his conversation. That might have been the real purpose of *2 Henry IV*, 2.2, with all the banter about small beer and silk stockings, the revelation of the King's sickness, incidental theatrical filler and joiner.

Whatever the origins of the two-part play, even if it shows the structural signs of follow-up sequel, modern serial productions are almost bound to seek a developing logic of character and narrative. So, for instance, Hal has several times been shown as something less than the unequivocally heroic victor at Shrewsbury. Alan Howard in 1975, it appears, hardly fought fair in his final duel with Hotspur. It was after Hotspur had disarmed Hal in the fight, according to the prompt-book, that 'Hal grabs sword from Hot[spur].' When Hal succeeded in hitting his opponent in the stomach and he had fallen to his knees, 'Hal takes off Hot[spur's] helmet – slashes him on face w[ith] dagger.' Such catch-as-catch-can brutality culminated in a heavily ironic piece of business on the line normally treated as a chivalric gesture of victor to vanquished: 'let my favours hide thy mangled face', says Hal covering up the dead Hotspur. Here the prompt-book stage direction indicated 'Hal wipes blood from Hot[spur's] face onto his own.'[19] This seems a markedly unheroic prince, but the intended effect is suggested by Irving Wardle's approving review: 'The production wholly achieves its first purpose in showing Howard's mooncalf Hal developing step by step to the modest chivalry of Shrewsbury.'[20] Modest indeed, one might feel; yet in a 'step by step' progress that was intended to come to its destined goal in *Henry V* with the full heroism of Agincourt, there is a plausible theatrical pacing in showing the still emergent Hal having to use dirty dodges to win against the battle-hardened Hotspur.

The English Shakespeare Company production equally looked for coherent development between the two parts in supplying a narrative bridge accounting for Hal's 'relapse'. Hal is reconciled to his father in *1 Henry IV*, 3.2, a reconciliation confirmed by the battlefield; yet they are estranged again by the start of *2 Henry IV*. Why? Michael Bogdanov supplied an explanation by reversing the order of two scenes at the end of *1 Henry IV*. In the original text 5.4 ends with Falstaff coming on carrying the body of Hotspur, claiming credit for his death to Hal and his brother John of Lancaster. Neither of the princes seems really to believe him – 'This is the strangest tale that ever I heard', 'This is the strangest fellow, brother John' – but Hal goodhumouredly offers to back up Falstaff's story:

> For my part, if a lie may do thee grace,
> I'll gild it with the happiest terms I have.
>
> (5.4.145–9)

5.5 then follows with the King wrapping up, dealing with the outstanding rebels, setting off with Hal to fight against Glendower and the Earl of March. The ESC production brought the king on *before* Falstaff's arrival. Hal is just modestly claiming credit for the killing of Hotspur, brandishing his victorious sword on the phrase 'the noble Percy slain' (5.4.19), when on comes Falstaff with his trophy, the newly re-slain Hotspur, on his back. The king takes Falstaff's word at face value and stalks away from Hal, who splutters aghast at the misunderstanding. The play ends with the corpse of Hotspur, bundled unceremoniously on to a cart by Falstaff, being wheeled around the stage as a dirge is played on the recorder. It is with this very same image that the ESC's *2 Henry IV* was to begin, preserving narrative continuity, and giving a plotted reason for the King's renewed distrust of his son, a disillusioned Hal's regression to his old Eastcheap ways.

This is the thinking of the realist novel tradition. Shakespeare, even if he did plan the two plays together, may not have felt the need for such tightly causal narration. The narrative ellipsis that left an audience to work out for themselves, if they could be bothered, why the Prince relapsed, was probably easily accepted in the theatre. But modern critical interpreters as much as modern theatre directors are disposed to try to make sense out of the sequence of what happens over the two-part play, or indeed over the series of three plays in which Hal/King Henry appears. The idea of the progressive education of the perfect king is one example. Eschewing a realistic or psychological reading of Hal, Dover Wilson and Tillyard pointed to a morality play structure in which the Prince must first learn the significance of the chivalric idea of honour, then be tutored in the civic principles of law by the Lord Chief Justice, antitype to the anarchic Falstaff. In the new historicist school, the ideology may have been transvalued, the conservative order, so idealised by the Tillyardians, now the deplored manifestation of an oppressive state power, but the idea of process is similar. In *1 Henry IV*, according to Stephen Greenblatt, we might be 'allowed for a moment at least to imagine that we are witnessing a social bond, the human fellowship of the extremest top and bottom of society in a homely ritual act of drinking together'. But by *2 Henry IV* it is 'clear that the betrayals are systematic'. 'The founding of the modern state, like the self-fashioning of the modern prince, is shown to be based upon acts of calculation, intimidation, and deceit.'[21] What looks like subversion is contained, the audience's collusion with the status quo increasing over the play series to *Henry V*.

Through the *Henry IV* plays there is a game of 'spot the self'. Take the theatrically charged moment in the *1 Henry IV* Eastcheap play within the play, the Prince's response to the peroration of Falstaff's stirring self-apologia:

> FALSTAFF ... Banish plump Jack, and banish all the world.
> PRINCE. I do. I will.   (2.4.397–9)

From 'do' to 'will', the 'I' switches. The first is the playacting prince in his current role as his father the king, mock-banishing 'that villainous abominable misleader of youth, Falstaff'; the second is the king that is to be, serving due warning of the sentence of banishment to come in good earnest. Are the selves simultaneous or successive in time? From the first soliloquy, 'I know you all', Hal's mind seems already made up. The later judicious and judicial persona is already there, merely suspended for an interim. Yet, could this not also be a theatrically proleptic figure for a continuing internal debate: a part of Hal is determined eventually to reform, and to that extent already *is* reformed, another part remains engaged in the enjoyment of his unreformed leisure. There remains equally the question of what the Prince thinks he is doing with his time. In *Henry V*, the King responds with formal dignity to the Dauphin's tennis-ball insult:

> we understand him well,
> How he comes o'er us with our wilder days,
> Not measuring what use we made of them.
> (1.2.266–8)

We are left to puzzle out the retrospective riddle of what use he did make of them. Was it a conscious and deliberate exercise, designed, as the imagery of Warwick's speech suggested, as a sort of aversion therapy in bad-language learning? Or did it involve a more positive enlargement of his human understanding of himself and his people, manuring the lean earth of his nature with the drinking of sherris sack?

Leonard Dean puts the matter well in a thoughtful essay on the *Richard II – Henry V* series: 'the play . . . asks us to imagine through Hal an extraordinary relation to time and a unique way of being one's self'.[22] The extraordinary relation to time has to do with the fixed nature of the legend of the madcap prince turned great King, figured severally in the various metaphors of metamorphosis examined in the previous section of this chapter. Each of these is a single image complete in itself: the sun coming out from behind the clouds; the speaker of the strange tongues of low life, once fluent, avoiding the swear-words he has learned; the man new born at his father's death. Each one is satisfying in its own limited context, but they do not add up to a stage character who must be apprehended in the linear movement of theatrical action. The actor, director or interpreter seeking a line of development for Hal must pick their way as best they can through this non-developmental collocation of figures. The Prince's 'unique way' of being himself arises in part from this peculiarity of representation. But it also has to do with the very formal nature of the kingly self that he must eventually assume. *Henry V*, the final play in the series, on which I want to concentrate in my final section, makes even more problematic the matter of agency, the manifestation of the self in action, and the ironic perspective that one school of critical opinion brings to bear upon the play.

IRONY AND AGENCY

The debate on *Henry V* between the ironisers and the idealists was set going in 1817 by William Hazlitt in his *Characters of Shakespear's Plays*. The republican Hazlitt, still filled with post-1815 indignation at the restoration of the Bourbons in France, unleashed his fury against England's favourite patriotic play and its militarist hero:

Henry, because he did not know how to govern his own Kingdom, determined to make war upon his neighbours. Because his own title to the crown was doubtful, he laid claim to that of France. Because he did not know how to exercise the enormous power, which had just dropped into his hands, to any one good purpose, he immediately undertook (a cheap and obvious resource of sovereignty) to do all the mischief he could.[23]

Some sixty years later, the year before Victoria became Empress of India, the Irish unionist Edward Dowden eulogised Henry as the very type of the Imperial hero, 'Shakspere's ideal of manhood in the sphere of practical achievement':

Henry's freedom from egoism, his modesty, his integrity, his joyous humour, his practical piety, his habit of judging things by natural and not artificial standards; all these are various developments of the central elements of his character, his noble realisation of fact.[24]

The twentieth century brought variants on ironic or idealising readings. Tillyard thought Shakespeare tried to fulfil the design of his series with the 'copy-book paragon of Kingly virtue' he found in the chronicles, but his creative imagination failed him, the result being a play 'constructed without intensity'.[25] For Jonathan Dollimore and Alan Sinfield, '*Henry V* can be read to reveal not only the strategies of power but also the anxieties informing both them and their ideological representation.'[26]

If we are to see irony at work in *Henry V* where does it come from and what might its effects be? The chronicle itself left openings for ironic implications. Consider, for instance, Holinshed's account of Henry's deathbed profession of the integrity of his motives in the French wars:

he protested unto them, that neither the ambitious desire to inlarge his do-
minions, neither to purchase vaine renowme and worldlie fame, nor anie other
consideration had mooved him to take the warres in hand; but onelie that in
prosecuting his iust title, he might in the end atteine to a perfect peace, and
come to enioie those peeces of his inheritance, which to him of right belonged:
and that before the beginning of the same warres, he was fullie persuaded by
men both wise and of great holinesse of life, that upon such intent he might and
ought both begin the same warres, and follow them, till he had brought them
to an end iustlie and rightlie, and that without all danger of Gods displeasure
or perill of soule. (Holinshed, 583)

Sincere words a reader might assume, recorded as spoken by the King
going to his final account. But Holinshed is at pains to identify in a
marginal note who these 'men both wise and of great holinesse of life'
actually were, and what were their motives: 'Cheeflie Chichelie archb. of
Cantur. for dashing the bill against the cleargie, as appeares before, pag.
546'. If we turn back to pag. 546, we find the full account of the Commons
bill for the appropriation of Church property; it was to divert the King
from supporting this bill that the Archbishop was at such pains to advance
Henry's genealogical claim to the throne of France. Holinshed, with this
cross-referencing device, digs the ground from under the King's pious
professions uttered apparently in good faith.

Shakespeare seems to be following Holinshed's lead in starting his play
about the patriotic war against France with a full elaboration, taken over
in detail from Holinshed, of the self-interested motives of the hierarchy.
The extent of the confiscation of lands proposed is spelled out in terms
of the amount of worthy secular causes it would support, if effected:

> As much as would maintain to the king's honour
> Full fifteen earls and fifteen hundred knights,
> Six thousand and two hundred good esquires,
> And to relief of lazars and weak age
> Of indigent faint souls, past corporal toil,
> A hundred alms-houses, right well supplied
> (1.1.12–17)

These are details, surely, to convince any post-Reformation English
audience of the villainous, Machiavellian character of the Archbishop.

How does this ironic political context bear upon Henry himself in
modern theatrical production? Alan Howard saw the king as fully aware that the 'Archbishop is urging him to go to war, and promising him

money to do so, as a way of avoiding conflict with Church interests'.[27]
This too is how Branagh played the part in his film version. The coldly
insistent repeated question to the Archbishop –

> HENRY V May I with right and conscience make this claim?
> CANTERBURY The sin upon my head, dread sovereign!

– made it clear that he was aware of the mixed motives in the prelate's
pleading. As the camera moved from Exeter to Westmoreland and back
to Canterbury with their cumulative urging of war, the pressure mounted
but the decision remained his own. Branagh's screenplay comment reads:

Behind unfathomable eyes the young soldier king affects to weigh interests commercial, spiritual and political attendant on the enterprise. What he genuinely
feels or thinks is uncertain, but after a pause his decision is certain.
> HENRY Call in the messengers sent from the Dauphin.[28]

That is a way of reading it, and a way of playing it. The trouble is
that it is not just in this scene, at this moment, that the King's eyes are
'unfathomable'; throughout the play 'what he genuinely feels or thinks
is uncertain'. To supply an inner life for the King that could animate or
make sense of his actions, we need to go to the previous plays and the
previous characterisation of the Prince in it. So, for example, for those
who see Henry's role in the French war ironically, there are the dying
words of his father to use as evidence against him, the advice to 'busy
giddy minds with foreign quarrels'. More sympathetic interpreters read
into the King's acceptance of the hanging of Bardolph an anguished
awareness of all the force of their past associations. Branagh again: 'The
King stares at the ugly death throes of his former friend. Tears stain his
cheeks.'[29] The lines are not there, but they can be supplied as sub-text to
the apparently draconian comment, 'We would have all such offenders
so cut off' (3.7.91).

Stephen Greenblatt claimed in *Shakespearean Negotiations* that 'in the
wake of full-scale ironic readings and at a time when it no longer seems
to matter very much, it is not at all clear that *Henry V* can be successfully performed as subversive'.[30] That statement may still hold good.
In *Schlachten!* certainly there was a thorough-going subversive production of *Henry V*, but it involved a complete re-modelling of the play.
The English Shakespeare Company staging seems a fairer case to test
Greenblatt's proposition. Their Chorus – played by Barry Stanton who
had also been cast as Falstaff – was given the very minimum of rhetorical
brio. Representing Pistol and his cronies as invading English football

hooligans, having the Chorus wave a placard with the infamous tabloid headline 'Gotcher!' used after the sinking of the Argentinian ship the *Belgrano*, were provocatively topical shock tactics. Bogdanov's *Henry V* was as emphatically post-Falklands as Hazlitt's was post-Waterloo. And yet Michael Pennington's performance as Henry was not all that discernibly ironic. The scenes at Harfleur and Agincourt, indeed, with the English ducking behind sandbags under fire, evoked rather the idiom of patriotic war-movies. Even in as polemically political a production as this, the play had a tendency to revert to stock.

This is not just a case of an irreducible mass of enthusiastic martial action and emotion in the play that no amount of directorial irony can acidify. At issue is the very mode of the play, the way Henry and his actions are represented. It is Shakespeare's only fully mediated history play. The Chorus stands continuously, intrusively, between the audience and the characters and events. Now it has been frequently pointed out that what the Chorus evokes in his speeches is *not* what we see on stage, and this has increasingly been interpreted as an irony undermining the Chorus' position. For Andrew Gurr it provokes the question, 'What is there in the body of the play that the Chorus has to misrepresent?'[31] Terry Hands had an onstage Chorus (Emrys James) overridden and displaced by the characters instead of occupying his usual kind of privileged vantage-point of externality. At the start of 1.3 he is 'addressed and interrupted by Bardolph and Nym. They include him in their conversation. And as their scene, ribald and music hall, is the exact opposite of the heroic sentiments expressed by the Chorus he retreats from the unequal combat.'[32]

There are limits, however, to this sort of ironising. Whatever opportunities there may be for local skirmishing between characters and Chorus as in Hands' production, in general the Chorus has a very strong position of theatrical authority. Even for audiences less familiar with the convention than the Elizabethans would have been, the solo voice accorded him and the sheer virtuosity of the rhetoric with which his lines are endowed must lend the figure an all-but-unsinkable buoyancy. There is, no doubt, a marked discrepancy between what the Chorus invites an audience to imagine and the tacky, inadequate reality they often see. But the modesty topos that is the very staple of the Chorus' self-presentation works pre-emptively against this being used as negative ironic evidence. An audience is prepared in advance to see Agincourt travestied, played out as it will be by 'four or five most vile and ragged foils' (4.0.50). The afflatus of the choric imagination is reality-proof, having admitted to the bathetic nature of the reality it has to offer.

Ironic readings of *Henry V* must rest on logical inferences carried from one scene to another, juxtapositions and omissions, what we do not see as much as what we do see. So, for instance, there is the lacuna of Cambridge's true intentions in the Southampton conspiracy.

> For me, the gold of France did not seduce
> Although I did admit it as a motive
> The sooner to effect what I intended.
>
> (2.2.150–2)

What lies behind this is the chronicle report that Cambridge, seeing his own case doomed, chose not to proclaim his true object, to place the Yorkist claimant Edmund Mortimer on the throne, knowing that this would only ensure the death of more members of his family. By failing to elucidate this, Shakespeare suppresses from the play the whole dynastic dispute that is the preoccupying concern of all his other histories. In the 1964 RSC production, in the context of the whole history play cycle including the Barton–Hall *Wars of the Roses* of which this was the highlighted theme, the lines were emended to read as follows:

> My Lord, the gold of France did not seduce me
> Although I did admit it as a motive,
> The sooner to effect what I intended:
> What t'was, God knows, and thou and thine shall know it
> For God doth sanction what I did intend.[33]

What are we to make of the Shakespearean suppression of Cambridge's concealed motives? Andrew Gurr, in the context of a long and illuminating argument about contemporary Elizabethan sensitivity to the issue of inheritance through the female line, by which Henry claimed the French crown but the Yorkists were also to claim the English monarchy, maintains that the omission of Cambridge's true objective is a pointed one.[34] But in the theatre, however alert the audiences of the 1590s might have been to dynastic genealogy, they were hardly likely to have picked up on a single opaque line from one of an anonymous threesome of traitors safely on their way to execution. Rather than ironically calling into question Henry's position, Shakespeare could be accused of whitewashing him by not allowing even the shadow of a justification to the only conspiracy against his kingship.

In the stop-go mode of narration controlled by the Chorus, there is no continuous causal chain of action in *Henry V*, as I suggested at the end of the last chapter. And there is no coherently characterised character of the King whose agency can be satisfactorily detected throughout. Henry plays each scene brilliantly, convincingly, with grace and conviction. He is in the opening scenes the cautiously concerned monarch, prepared to go to war if necessary in the national interests, but very aware of its costs; his response to the Dauphin's tennis-balls insult is a model of restrained dignity. He can show passion in his denunciation of the traitor Scroop for his combination of personal and public treachery, but can equally quickly return to a tone of judicial impersonality in the sentence of execution. At Harfleur, he can 'imitate the action of a tiger' while acknowledging that 'In peace there's nothing so becomes a man / As modest stillness and humility' (3.1.3–4). The private Gethsemane of his soliloquies before Agincourt, the awareness of the burden of kingship, the acknowledgement before God of his father's guilt in 'compassing the crown', does not prevent him from animating his army with the apparently unshakeable confidence of the St Crispin's day speech. And after Agincourt, he is a devoutly humble victor, attributing his victory entirely to the hand of God. Henry can be bluff good companion with Fluellen, sharing a sense of Welshness with the stage Welshman. Most unexpectedly of all, he can turn into a reincarnation of Hotspur (as Dr Johnson was the first to observe) with his rough soldier's wooing of the princess he persists in his heartily English way in calling Kate.

There are gaps and interstices in this shifting sequence of roles that can be read ironically. It is often observed that the King's attempt to administer his 'little touch of Harry in the night' somewhat misfires when, in his disguise, he comes up against the stubborn arguments of Williams, who is hardly convinced by the incognito royal self-justification. Before Agincourt Henry addresses his men as a 'band of brothers':

> For he today that sheds his blood with me
> Shall be my brother; be he ne'er so vile
> This day shall gentle his condition.
>
> (4.3.61–3)

This levelling egalitarianism of the battlefield appears to have been forgotten by the time he receives the rollcall of the dead, where he reverts to a strictly hierarchical view of things. After the names of the four leading casualties have been read out, he adds only:

> None else of name, and of all other men
> But five and twenty.
>
> (4.8.97–8)

Ironies might appear to peep through the courtship-scene also, when Henry assures Katherine that he is not the enemy of France: 'in loving me you should love the friend of France, for I love France so well that I will not part with a village of it' (5.2.160–1). Underneath the charmingly gauche wooing is the fact of military occupation that conditions the whole proposed marriage.

It remains difficult to see just where such ironic awarenesses might be located theatrically. Henry himself shows none whatsoever. He plays the part of the king for all people and all occasions without any hint of self-consciousness in the shifts of mode required. In this his royal ac-torliness is markedly unlike the Hal of *1 Henry IV* who takes us behind the scenes of his staged personality the very first time we meet him: 'I know you all . . .' It marks Henry V out as antitype to Richard III, whose protean performances are accompanied always with self-undoing commentary. The fissures and joins in the assembly of royal selves that makes up Henry's part are covered up rather than highlighted by the interpolating comments of the Chorus. We are stood off from the his-tory as a convincing representation of characters and events, and shown instead an exemplary spectacle of kingship in action. There is a degree of playfulness in this, and the detachment that allows for the historically aware diminuendo of the Epilogue:

> Henry the Sixth, in infant bands crowned king
> Of France and England, did this king succeed,
> Whose state so many had the managing
> That they lost France and made his England bleed.
>
> (5.3.9–12)

But it is a metatheatricality that does not promote a dissident irony undermining the credibility and integrity of the play's central character and what he stands for politically.

The object of this section of the chapter testing ironic readings of *Henry V*, both critical and theatrical, has not been to reinstate an idealist interpretation. It is unlikely that any contemporary readers will see in the play Dowden's ideal of manhood, or any actor choose to imitate Olivier's bravura performance of the warrior king. What I have been trying to illustrate rather is the theatrical mode of the play that makes a sustained ironic interpretation problematic by removing a clearly iden-tifiable identity from the central character. In the context of the play series, we look for such an identity from the character who was Prince Hal, and attempt a perspective based on continuities between the earlier and later figures. There are plenty of materials for the construction of such a view. Critics may postulate a role-playing king having grown into the responsibilities of power through a role-playing youth, or they may see the final manifestation of power as a theatricality implicit in Hal's earlier self-stagings. An actor cast to play the part of Hal/Henry through the three plays can build for himself, must perhaps build for himself, an emotional and psychological trajectory from Eastcheap to Agincourt. The series as it dramatises the transformation of prince into king, as it explores the relationship between the private man and the public figure, seems to demand such a continuing curve of perception. But *Henry V* is so much its own thing formally, the identity of the King as king so absorbs any remaining traces of the prince as individual, that through-readings feel strained and suppositious. *Henry V* is a discontinuous continuation of the *Henry IV* plays; Henry V, a discontinuous character in himself, is not the former prince he purports to be.

Conclusion

To sit in the Swan Theatre, Stratford in December 2000, watching the Royal Shakespeare Company perform the sequence of Shakespeare's three *Henry VI* plays, or their *Richard III* sequel in February 2001, is to see a twenty-first-century theatre reinterpret the plays dramatised by a late sixteenth-century playwright out of the earlier sixteenth-century chronicles that were themselves a synthesis of the annals of fifteenth-century events. If we accept Hayden White's concept of a poetics of metahistory informing historical narratives, then the experience of the RSC series must be something like metametametahistory. This book, in allowing the modern productions/adaptations of Shakespeare's serial history plays to keep company with the original business of serialising the chronicles, has tried to promote the consciousness of the layered constructions and reconstructions involved in the staging of the histories. To what end? How might the history plays be seen differently at the conclusion of this process than at the beginning? I declared in the Introduction that looking at seriality in the histories was designed as an open enquiry, not to prove a preconceived thesis. Still, a reader has a right to expect some sort of conclusion, however tentative, to a book-length enquiry, however open.

One aim has been to restore attention and credibility to the seriality of the plays. In the reaction against Tillyard and the Tillyardian imagination of the histories as a grand narrative of England, came a distrust of what Barbara Hodgdon calls 'tetralogy thinking'.[1] In so far as the notion of the series was bound up with the concept of a single unified and determining ideology, when that fell out of fashion the identification of Shakespeare's histories as a Wagnerian-style *Ring* cycle also came to seem false and inappropriate. Hence, perhaps, the swing back in textual scholarship to disintegrationist theories of the *Henry VI* plays, or the decision by the RSC to assign separate directors, different theatre spaces, to their Stratford staging of the *Richard II* – *Henry V* plays in 2000. However, it is perfectly possible to dissociate serial dramatisation of the chronicles, serial production of the plays, from ideological uniformity, as I hope I have done in this book. From H. A. Kelly's *Divine Providence in the England of Shakespeare's Histories* to Annabel Patterson's *Reading Holinshed's Chronicles*[2] it has been demonstrated that the chronicles were not themselves by any means homogeneous, but a layered palimpsest of narratives representing different, often mutually exclusive, political viewpoints. Shakespeare, in writing serial history plays, could make theatrical capital out of this very plurality. The polyvalence of the series for later theatrical representations derives to a large extent from the mixed skein of the sources themselves.

One of the excitements for me in writing this book has been to come in close, as it felt, to Shakespeare at work, at work in the discovery of the English history play form quarried from the chronicles, changing and developing that form as his theatrical markets and his imaginative needs changed and developed. If, as I have argued, the *Henry VI – Richard III* series was an invention born out of the perceived need for readily available sequels, and the chronicles as a ready source for such, then the altered circumstances of the later 1590s, with the much greater security of a steady company affiliation, allowed for a slower rate of production, more formally distinct plays, within a more loosely conceived series. My view of the two sequences runs exactly counter to the common perception of their evolution, and indeed what one might in logic expect: that the first sequence came together accidentally, improvisationally, and that the second series was planned as a series on the model of the first. I believe that the evidence of the plays in fact points the opposite way. Although the *Henry VI – Richard III* series may be formally cruder and less sophisticated than the later histories, that does not mean that these plays were not serially conceived. On the contrary, I would argue that their serial form is a measure of their relatively primitive theatricality. *Richard II*, the two parts of *Henry IV*, *Henry V*, with their several reconceptions of the history play, show Shakespeare near the height of his imaginative powers, never content to repeat himself, producing as a result a series that is chronologically continuous but formally discontinuous.

To see any one of the plays as a serial history play is necessarily to see it differently. Take *3 Henry VI*, for instance. It can be, and has been, produced successfully on its own, but it makes another sort of sense in the continuing run of narrative, character, image. The emotional intensity of York's death-scene, a scene famous enough in its own time to elicit Greene's bitter parody of the 'tiger's heart wrapped in a woman's hide', comes oddly early, in the play's first act. It is only in the longer rhythm of the story of York, going right back to its beginnings in the Temple

Garden scene of *1 Henry VI*, that his torture and death here provides a fitting catastrophe. When an audience in 2.5 watches with King Henry the tragic pageant of the father who has killed his son, the son who has killed his father, they can recall that other father–son battlefield death, the Talbots in *1 Henry VI* – all the more so when, as in the 2000 RSC production, the two actors who played the Talbots play both parts of the later anonymous fathers and sons. Across the plays one scene speaks to the other, as the ultimate contrast of heroic chivalry in war, the ideal of patrilineal succession affirmed even at the moment of defeat, and the parricidal destructiveness of civil strife. The last major event of the play is the confrontation between Henry and Richard in the Tower. It may be a specifically modern theatrical perspective to represent the two figures as all but doubles: Ian Holm's half-loving Judas to David Warner's self-sacrificing Christ in the 1960s *Wars of the Roses*, the hairless head of Andrew Jarvis facing the bald Paul Brennen in the 1980s *Wars of the Roses*. Yet the text invites such treatment as it locks the two characters into place in the inevitability of the moment. 'Die, prophet, in thy speech', exclaims Richard, 'For this, amongst the rest, was I ordained.' The Henry we have watched through three plays was born to die as this sort of martyr-king, Richard to live on in to his own nightmare reign that will follow.

The third in line in the next series of histories, *2 Henry IV*, can also stand by way of illustration of how seriality works there. It is driven by no such onward force of events as *3 Henry VI*. On the contrary it is a repetition, a reduplication of the pattern of events of *1 Henry IV*. Out of this apparent narrative torpor arises the play's defining concern with time and tiredness. Where in *1 Henry IV* the spontaneous immediacy of the comic underplot contrasts and resonates with the dramatisation of the chronicle's past history, in the second play the comedy itself winds towards an end in parallel to the ending King's reign. *2 Henry IV* reaches back to its predecessor plays in the continuing reflections of the King on his seizure of the throne from Richard II and the consequences of that event. The audience is enabled, with him, to review and revalue the redemptive project of the crusade, first announced as atonement for Richard's murder. Meanwhile the dramatic action eddies out to a countryside distant from the court where a rump of rebellion dies, and geriatric squires reminisce about their wild youth in the capital. The play moves to its prefigured close, prefigured already in the second scene of *1 Henry IV*, the miraculous transformation of wild Prince Hal into good King Henry, but it is with no great urgency of movement. And it is without any urgency that the play looks on to *Henry V*: '*if* you be not too much cloyed with fat meat, our humble author will continue the story'. *2 Henry IV* depends for its meanings on its place in the play series, but lives as well in its own distinctive dramatic time and space, without the propelling dynamic of the continuing narrative.

The broadest ambition of this book has been an exploration of how the serial history plays have represented history theatrically over time. At the simplest level, it can be said that the seriality of the history plays reproduces the linearity of history. Any historical narrative, and especially a chronicle, involves a sequential ordering, the setting down of one event after another. To play *1 Henry VI*, followed by *2 Henry VI*, followed by *3 Henry VI*, is to feed an audience's tapeworm appetite for what happened next. By virtue of their claimed historicity, though, the history plays represent something more than the continuing story of soap-opera. They narrate not just the continuum of a *roman fleuve* but the life of a nation as imagined over a measurable stretch of its past. That pastness and the claim to non-fictional status are the defining features of the history play.

The fact that these plays purport to be historical only renders more problematic our experience of them as texts in history. Critics addressing Shakespeare in general and the history plays in particular have admitted to the difficulty. Stephen Greenblatt famously opened *Shakespearean Negotiations* with the impossible yearning – 'I began with the desire to speak with the dead.'[3] Phyllis Rackin admitted at the outset of her book *Stages of History*, 'The questions I ask are the products of my own historically specific concerns; the answers I recover, even when couched in the words of sixteenth-century texts, are the products of my own selection and arrangements.'[4] Leonard Tennenhouse, in *Power on Display*, saw his critical task 'as something akin to wriggling out of my cultural skin, much as someone might wriggle out of a particularly close-fitting turtleneck shirt'.[5] Such cultural self-flaying is hardly feasible; the best one can hope for is to wear one's historical jumper loose and sloppy. That is what I have tried to do in this book. Drawing attention to the refigurings of the history plays both as dramatisations of chronicle in Shakespeare's own time and as re-representations through the modern period has been a way of highlighting the transhistorical character of these texts. Not ahistorical, evidently, but transhistorical – an effort at the imagination of history renewed and re-created in the very different theatrical and cultural conditions of 1590s London, 1864 Weimar, the Stratford of 2000.

The chronicles presented to Shakespeare a dramatic opportunity because they allowed a late Elizabethan audience to see upon the stage the history of their own nation of a hundred years before. With the

European reconception of the nation that came with romanticism, these plays again offered a vehicle for nineteenth- and then twentieth-century theatres and audiences to re-imagine national history in action. The historical conditions of Elizabethan theatre had first made it possible for Shakespeare to mount series of history plays: a limited audience that needed to be fed a continual succession of new plays; acting troupes professionally trained to mount a shifting repertory day after day; the rivalry of a contending entertainment industry with high rewards for a popular success capable of multiple revivals – 'which oft *our* stage hath shown' – *ours*, the Chamberlain's not the Admiral's Men. Different cultural conditions, municipal or state support for canonical theatre, ensemble acting, monumental celebration of major anniversaries, the specialist audiences of theatre festivals, the influence of television, all helped to produce the modern revival of serial stagings of the history plays. Shakespeare's serial history plays thus multiply illustrate the production and reproduction of theatre in history as well as history in theatre. If this book has shown something of the nature of that multiplicity, the complex phenomenon of the plays' seriality across time, it will have achieved its aim.

Notes

I SERIALISING THE CHRONICLES

1 See Felix E. Schelling, *The English Chronicle Play* (New York: Macmillan, 1902).
2 Ibid, p. 39.
3 See, for example, Graham Holderness, *Shakespeare Re-cycled: The Making of Historical Drama* (Hemel Hempstead: Harvester Wheatsheaf, 1992), and Paola Pugliatti, *Shakespeare the Historian* (Basingstoke: Macmillan, 1996).
4 Edmond Malone, *A Dissertation on the three parts of King Henry VI* (London: Henry Baldwin, 1787), p. 19.
5 See Madeleine Doran, *'Henry VI, Parts II and III': Their Relation to the 'Contention' and 'The True Tragedy'* (Iowa City: University of Iowa, 1928), and Peter Alexander, *Shakespeare's Henry VI and Richard III* (Cambridge University Press, 1929; repr. New York, Octagon Books, 1973).
6 The term 'tetralogy' has come to be associated with this view of a fully integrated set of four plays; for this reason I have preferred to use the more neutral terms 'series' or 'sequence' throughout this book, except when citing others.
7 Tillyard acknowledges his debt to Alexander's work in *Shakespeare's History Plays* (1944; Harmondsworth: Penguin, 1969), p. 136.
8 See, for example, Andrew Cairncross's Arden editions of *Henry VI* (London: Methuen, 1962–4) or Anthony Hammond who argued in his edition of *Richard III* (London: Methuen, 1981) that it was the culmination of a *Ring*-like four-play project. There was, however, the dissenting figure of J. Dover Wilson who continued to argue for multiple authorship and revised texts in his 1952 Cambridge editions of the three *Henry VI* plays.
9 See William Shakespeare, *The Complete Works*, general editors Stanley Wells and Gary Taylor (Oxford University Press, 1986), pp. 55–124, 153–82.
10 The most recent and most measured case against this emendation is put by David Scott Kastan in *Shakespeare after Theory* (New York and London: Routledge, 1999), pp. 93–106.
11 'Prologue', *Tamburlaine the Great*, Part 2, ed. David Fuller, in Christopher Marlowe, *Complete Works*, V (Oxford: Clarendon Press, 1998).
12 The evidence for these titles is drawn from E. K. Chambers, *The Elizabethan Stage*, 4 vols. (Oxford: Clarendon Press, 1923) and from R. A. Foakes and

R. T. Rickert (eds.), *Henslowe's Diary* (Cambridge University Press, 1961). Further citations from these two sources (hereafter cited as Chambers, *ES* and Henslowe) are given parenthetically in the text.

13 *A most pleasant comedie, intituled, a knacke to knowe a knave* (London: Richard Jones, 1594), was played by Strange's Men in 1592–3; *A pleasant conceited comedie, called, a knacke to know an honest man* (London: Cuthbert Burby, 1596) was performed by the Admiral's Men 1594–6.

14 For the latter view see E. A. J. Honigmann's New Arden edition of *King John* (London: Methuen, 1954); for the alternative position and a summary of the arguments, see A. R. Braunmuller's Oxford Shakespeare edition: *King John* (Oxford, New York: Oxford University Press, 1989), p. 10.

15 *The First part of the Tragicall raigne of Selimus, sometime Emperour of the Turks, and grandfather to him that now raigneth* (London: Thomas Creede, 1594), sig. κ 3.

16 See, for example, David Fuller's introduction to the play in Marlowe, *Complete Works*, v, p. xlii.

17 Clifford Leech, 'The Two-Part Play: Marlowe and the Early Shakespeare', *Shakespeare Jahrbuch* 94 (1958), 103.

18 See Roslyn L. Knutson, 'Henslowe's Naming of Parts: Entries in the *Diary* for *Tamar Cham*, 1592–3, and *Godfrey of Bulloigne*, 1594–5', *Notes and Queries* 228 (1983), 157–60.

19 See, for instance, *The First Part of King Henry VI*, ed. J. Dover Wilson (Cambridge University Press, 1952), pp. xi–xiii.

20 For the arguments on this issue see Foakes and Rickert's Introduction to Henslowe, pp. xxx–xxxi.

21 See Stanley Wells and Gary Taylor with John Jowett and William Montgomery, *William Shakespeare: A Textual Companion* (Oxford: Clarendon Press, 1987), pp. 76–89. The most fully argued case is made by Gary Taylor in 'Shakespeare and Others: The Authorship of *Henry the Sixth, Part One*', in J. Leeds Barroll (ed.), *Medieval and Renaissance Drama in England*, VII (London and Toronto: Associated University Presses, 1995), pp. 145–205.

22 E. K. Chambers, *William Shakespeare: A Study of Facts and Problems*, 2 vols. (Oxford: Clarendon Press, 1930) produces this case of the *Civil Wars* series as evidence for the possibility of a non-chronological order of composition for Shakespeare's *Henry VI* plays: I, 293.

23 Anthony Colynet, *The True History of the Civil Warres of France, betweene the French King Henry the 4. and the Leaguers. Gathered from the yeare of our Lord 1585. vntill this present October 1591* (London: Thomas Orwin for Thomas Woodcock, 1591).

24 In one case, 27 and 29 January, the two parts are separated by the performance of another play.

25 *The First Part of Ieronimo. With the Warres of Portugall, and the life and death of Don Andraea* (London: Thomas Pavier, 1605).

26 An exception is Edward Berry who remarks that 'I assume ... though the matter has not been generally explored, that the completed series [of the *Henry VI – Richard III* plays] was performed wherever possible on successive days. That two-part plays were customarily presented in this

manner is clear from the record of Henslowe's diaries.' *Patterns of Decay: Shake-speare's Early Histories* (Charlottesville, VA: University Press of Virginia, 1975), pp. ix–x. Beyond this remark in his introduction, however, Berry does not pursue this assumption.

27 I owe this point to the anonymous reader of the book for Cambridge University Press.

28 H. J. Oliver in the New Arden edition of *The Merry Wives of Windsor* (London: Methuen, 1971), pp. lii–lvi, suggests that Shakespeare may have in fact been working on *The Merry Wives* at the same time as *2 Henry IV*.

29 See particularly Leonard Tennenhouse, *Power on Display: The Politics of Shake-speare's Genres* (London: Methuen, 1986).

30 Chambers, *William Shakespeare*, II, 325.

2 STAGING THE NATIONAL EPIC

1 See George C. D. Odell, *Shakespeare from Betterton to Irving*, 2 vols. (London: Constable, 1921), I, 75.

2 Ibid., I, 63–6, 56–9, II, 166–9.

3 See Philip Edwards, *Threshold of a Nation* (Cambridge University Press, 1979), pp. 190–3 on the connections between cultural nationalism and the theatre.

4 See Michael Bogdanov and Michael Pennington, *The English Shakespeare Company: The Story of 'The Wars of the Roses' 1986–1989* (London: Nick Hern Books, 1990), p. 158.

5 *Correspondence between Schiller and Goethe*, trans. L. Dora Schmitz, 2 vols. (London: George Bell, 1877), I, 433.

6 A. W. Schlegel, *A Course of Lectures on Dramatic Art and Literature*, trans. John Black (London: Bohn, 1846), p. 419.

7 T. M. Raysor (ed.), *Coleridge's Shakespeare Criticism*, 2 vols. (London: Constable, 1930), I, 139–40.

8 For the fullest account of this production in English, see Robert K. Sarlos, 'Dingelstedt's Celebration of the Tercentenary: Shakespeare's Histories as a Cycle', *Theatre Survey* 5(1964), 117–31. I have drawn largely upon Sarlos's article in the account of the production that follows.

9 See *The Athenaeum*, 2 January 1864, 24.

10 The summary is that of Sarlos, 'Dingelstedt's Celebration', 121.

11 Ibid. The earliest use of the term 'tetralogy' in English in connection with Shakespeare's histories which I have come across is in Richard Simpson, 'The Politics of Shakespeare's History Plays', *New Shakspere Society Transactions* 1 (1874), 441.

12 Sarlos, 'Dingelstedt's Celebration', 122.

13 *The Athenaeum*, 21 May 1864, 717–18.

14 See Odell, *Shakespeare from Betterton to Irving*, II, 301–2.

15 Sally Beauman, *The Royal Shakespeare Company: A History of Ten Decades* (Oxford University Press, 1982), pp. 32–3.

16 See W. B. Yeats, *Essays and Introductions* (London: Macmillan, 1961), pp. 96–110.

17 *Birmingham Express*, 4 May 1906.

18 *The Athenaeum*, 12 May 1906, 587.

19 *Stratford-upon-Avon Herald*, 4 May 1906.

20 Ibid.

21 Quoted by Arthur Colby Sprague, *Shakespeare's Histories: Plays for the Stage* (London: Society for Theatre Research 1964), p. 112.

22 *Stratford-upon-Avon Herald*, 11 May 1906.

23 For background see Gail Leo Shoup, 'The Pasadena Community Playhouse: Its Origins and History from 1917 to 1942', Ph.D. dissertation, UCLA, 1968.

24 See 'The Chronicle Plays of W. Shakespeare', Scrapbook of Midsummer Drama Festival 1935, in the Huntington Library.

25 *Pasadena Star-News*, 15 July 1935.

26 Note on one of the publicity photographs, Birmingham Central Library collection.

27 *Manchester Guardian*, 3 April 1952.

28 Information drawn from prompt-books in Birmingham Central Library collection.

29 Kenneth Tynan, *Curtains* (London: Longmans, 1961), pp. 181–2.

30 Ibid., p. 182.

31 *Richard II*, Shakespeare Memorial Theatre programme notes, opening performance, 24 March 1951.

32 'Shakespeare and English History as the Elizabethans Understood it', in J. Dover Wilson and T. C. Worsley, *Shakespeare's Histories at Stratford 1951* (London: Max Reinhardt, 1952).

33 Wilson and Worsley, *Shakespeare's Histories*, p. 35. The prompt-book of the production is in Shakespeare Centre Library, Stratford.

34 Harold Hobson, *Sunday Times*, 8 April 1951.

35 *The Times*, 4 April 1951.

36 Quoted in Wilson and Worsley, *Shakespeare's Histories*, p. 73.

37 Preliminary copy with notes for 1951 production by Michael Redgrave at the Shakespeare Memorial Theatre, Shakespeare Centre Library, Stratford, typescript notes on 4.1–3.

38 Ibid., typescript notes on 5.2.

39 Wilson and Worsley, *Shakespeare's Histories*, p. 35.

40 Ibid., p. 68.

41 Ibid., p. 51.

42 *Henry V*, Final Chorus, 1951 prompt-book, Shakespeare Centre Library, Stratford, typescript of the Chorus notes 'NB. Lines 8–12 by Patric Dickinson'.

43 Peter Hall and John Barton, *The Wars of the Roses* (London: BBC, 1970), p. xvi, hereafter cited as *Wars*.

44 'The Dream in the Labyrinth', one of the 'Notes by the modern Polish critic, Jan Kott', *Henry VI* programme, first performance 17 July 1964. This was the revival of the 1963 production.

45 For the political implications of this combination, see Robert Shaughnessy, *Representing Shakespeare: England, History and the RSC* (New York etc.: Harvester Wheatsheaf, 1994), p. 47.

46 Bamber Gascoigne, *Observer*, 19 April 1964.

47 Alan Brien, *Sunday Telegraph*, 7 June 1964.

48 *The Times*, 16 April 1964.

49 Bamber Gascoigne, *Observer*, 19 April 1964.

50 *An Age of Kings* was directed by Michael Hayes, produced by Peter Dews, broadcast in fifteen fortnightly parts, two of 75 minutes, all the others an hour each, from 28 April to 17 November 1960: the script was published as William Shakespeare, *An Age of Kings* (New York: Pyramid Books, 1961).

51 Edgar Wreford, Paul Daneman and Jack May were among the actors who appeared both in the Birmingham Rep and the *Age of Kings* productions.

52 *King Henry VI Part I,* ed. Edward Burns (London: Arden Shakespeare, 2000), Appendix 3, p. 320.

53 See Sally Beauman, *The Royal Shakespeare Company's Production of Henry V* (Oxford: Pergamon Press, 1976).

54 *Centenary of the Royal Shakespeare Theatre*, Souvenir Programme 1975.

55 Terry Hands, quoted in Homer D. Swander, 'The Rediscovery of *Henry VI*', *Shakespeare Quarterly* 29 (1978), 156.

56 Ibid., 149.

57 Irving Wardle, *The Times*, 13 July 1977.

58 B. A. Young, *Financial Times*, 12 July 1977.

59 Shaughnessy, *Representing Shakespeare*, p. 45.

60 *The Times*, 5 July 1965.

61 Ibid.

62 Cited by David L. Hirst in *Giorgio Strehler* (Cambridge University Press, 1993), p. 72.

63 Ibid.

64 Jean-Michel Déprats, 'Shakespeare in France', *Shakespeare Quarterly* 32 (1981), 390.

65 Cedric Messina, 'Preface', *Richard II*, The BBC TV Shakespeare (London: BBC, 1978), p. 6.

66 Ibid., p. 19.

67 See Peter Saccio, 'The Historicity of the BBC History Plays', and Martin Banham, 'BBC Television Dull Shakespeares', in J. C. Bulman and H. R. Coursen (eds.), *Shakespeare on Television: An Anthology of Essays and Reviews* (Hanover and London: University Press of America, 1988), pp. 208–20.

68 For a very appreciative account, see Dennis Bingham, 'Jane Howell's First Tetralogy: Brechtian Break-out or Just Good Television', in Bulman and Coursen (eds.), *Shakespeare on Television*, pp. 221–9.

69 William Shakespeare, *The Plantagenets* (London: Faber & Faber 1989). In this published text of the adaptation, traditional act and scene divisions are replaced by individual scene numbering within the two acts, broken by intermission, into which each play is divided.

70 The first tour by the English Shakespeare Company, involving the two parts of *Henry IV* and *Henry V*, ran from November 1986 to March 1987; the full *Wars of the Roses*, with *Richard II*, the adapted *Henry VI* plays and *Richard III* added, toured from December 1987 to July 1988, and from September 1988 to April 1989. *The Plantagenets* opened at Stratford in September – October 1988 and transferred to London in March 1989.

71 See Bogdanov and Pennington, *The English Shakespeare Company*, pp. xi–xiv.

72 Ibid., p. 24.

73 Ibid., pp. 43–4.

74 Ibid., p. 3.

75 For the text and a full account of the production see Tom Lanoye and Luk Perceval, *Schlachten!: nach den Rosenkriegen von William Shakespeare* (Salzburg and Hamburg: Salzburger Festspiele, Deutsches Schauspielhaus in Hamburg, 1999).

76 Michael Coveney, *Daily Mail*, 31 March 2000.

77 Raysor (ed.), *Coleridge's Shakespeare Criticism*, I, 125.

78 David Jays, 'This Island Now', *RSC Magazine* 19 (Summer 2000), 6–11.

3 WAR IMAGINED

1 Although Nick de Somogyi rightly stresses the widespread awareness in 1590s Britain of the impact and effects of war, he cites one authority who calculates that only 0.13 per cent of the population between 1585 and 1603 would have been sent for service abroad: see *Shakespeare's Theatre of War* (Aldershot and Brookfield, VT: Ashgate, 1998), p. 4.

2 Samuel L. Leiter, *Shakespeare Around the Globe* (New York, Westport, CT and London: Greenwood Press, 1986), p. 241.

3 OED notes that 'puzzle' as substantive is later than the verb, appearing first about 1612, but for Shakespearean vocabulary that is well within the range of possibility.

4 Richard Dickins, *Forty Years of Shakespeare on the English Stage*, [London, 1906], p. 128.

5 Déprats, 'Shakespeare in France', 390.

6 Here, and throughout (except where otherwise indicated) when I make reference to specific dramatic effects in the Barton–Hall *Wars of the Roses*, I am referring to the BBC Television transmission produced by Michael Barry, directed by Michael Hayes, broadcast in April 1965.

7 So described by B. A. Young reviewing *1 Henry VI* in *Financial Times*, 13 July 1977.

8 References to the ESC *Wars of the Roses*, here and throughout, are drawn from the seven-part video recording made in Swansea in 1989: full details in the Bibliography where it is listed under 'Archival materials'.

9 In the BBC Television Shakespeare version the original lines were retained, but Brenda Blethyn had to address the thin air of non-existent spirits.

10 Fenner's Talbot, according to one critical reviewer, was 'stranded by the production between ramrod military comedy and parental tragedy': see Martin Hoyle, *Financial Times*, 11 February 1989.

11 Robert Cushman, *The Observer*, 17 July 1977.

12 For an overview of the debate between new historicists and cultural materialists, see Graham Holderness' Introduction to *Shakespeare's History Plays: Richard II to Henry V*, New Casebooks (Basingstoke: Macmillan, 1992), pp. 1–34.

13 Photographs of Clive Swift, who played Cade in the original theatre production, suggests that he was not made so physically unattractive.

14 B. A. Young, *Financial Times*, 12 July 1977.

15 Robert Cushman, *The Observer*, 17 July 1977.

16 Thomas Nashe, *Pierce Penniless his Supplication to the Devil [...] and Selected Writings*, ed. Stanley Wells (London: Edward Arnold, 1964), p. 64.

17 *Henry VI Part 2*, The BBC TV Shakespeare (London: BBC, 1983), p. 19.

18 See Ian McKellen, *William Shakespeare's Richard III* (London, New York, Toronto, Sydney and Auckland: Doubleday, 1996), for the screenplay by Ian McKellen and Richard Loncraine.

19 See Paul Jorgensen, *Shakespeare's Military World* (Berkeley and Los Angeles: University of California Press, 1956).

4 THE EMERGENCE OF CHARACTER

1 Harold Bloom, *Shakespeare: The Invention of the Human* (New York: Riverhead Books, 1998), pp. 43–50, 64–73.

2 Ibid., pp. 45, 46.

3 Alan Sinfield, *Faultlines: Cultural Materialism and the Politics of Dissident Reading* (Oxford: Clarendon Press, 1992), p. 62.

4 Warwick's most recent biographer shows that the title (*regum creator*) was given to him in a Latin history by John Major in 1521, but that it was first deployed in translation by Samuel Daniel and did not achieve currency until the eighteenth century. See Michael Hicks, *Warwick the Kingmaker* (Oxford: Blackwell, 1998), pp. 3–4.

5 Lily B. Campbell (ed.), *The Mirror for Magistrates* (Cambridge University Press, 1938), Tragedy 16, lines 82–4.

6 G. K. Hunter, 'The Royal Shakespeare Company Plays *Henry VI*', *Renaissance Drama* 9 (1978), 93.

7 Saccio, 'The Historicity of the BBC History Plays', p. 210.

8 Campbell (ed.), *Mirror for Magistrates*, Tragedy 29.

9 A partial exception was Terry Hands' 1977 production of the *Henry VI* plays in which Henry (Alan Howard) and Margaret (Helen Mirren) were represented as deeply and mutually in love.

10 Jean E. Howard and Phyllis Rackin, *Engendering a Nation: A Feminist Account of Shakespeare's English Histories* (London and New York: Routledge, 1997), p. 82.

11 'this kynges tyme [*The pitifull life of kyng Edward the v*] with some parte of kyng Richard the .iii. as shall apere by a note made at that place was written by syr Thomas More' (Bullough, III, 252 n. 1).

12 The relationship between the two texts in the construction of the reputation of Richard III is usefully outlined by Charles Ross, *Richard III* (London: Eyre Methuen, 1981), pp. xxii–xxxi.

5 CURSES AND PROPHECIES

1 Wilbur Sanders, *The Dramatist and the Received Idea* (Cambridge University Press, 1968), p. 101.

2 The critical debate over the issue of providence is helpfully outlined by Ronald Knowles in the Introduction to his Arden edition of *King Henry VI, Part II* (London: Arden Shakespeare, 1999), pp. 41–67.

3 Henry Ansgar Kelly, *Divine Providence in the England of Shakespeare's Histories* (Cambridge, MA: Harvard University Press, 1970). The case against Tillyard, made effectively throughout the book, is usefully summed up in the 'Conclusion', pp. 297–306.

4 This idea is most fully developed in Phyllis Rackin, *Stages of History* (London: Routledge, 1990), but for the reflection of Elizabethan historiographical debate in the plays see also Holderness, *Shakespeare Re-cycled*, and Pugliatti, *Shakespeare the Historian*.

5 Keith Thomas, *Religion and the Decline of Magic* (1971; Harmondsworth: Penguin, 1973).

6 Ibid., p. 91.

7 Marjorie Garber, in elucidating this concept, cites Jacques Derrida's 'prior past that is still to come': see ' "What's Past is Prologue": Temporality and Prophecy in Shakespeare's History Plays', in Barbara Kiefer Lewalski (ed.), *Renaissance Genres* (Cambridge, MA: Harvard University Press, 1986), p. 307.

8 See headnote to *I Henry VI*, 1.1 in the New Cambridge Shakespeare edition.

9 Philip Brockbank, 'The Frame of Disorder – "Henry VI" ', in John Russell Brown and Bernard Harris (eds.), *Early Shakespeare*, Stratford-upon-Avon Studies 3 (London: Edward Arnold, 1961), p. 77.

10 Thomas, *Religion and the Decline of Magic*, pp. 461–514.

11 Henry Howard [Earl of Northampton], *A defensative against the poyson of supposed Prophesies* ... (London: John Charlewood, 1583).

12 See *DNB* entry on Henry Howard, Earl of Northampton (1540–1614).

13 Howard, *A defensative*, sig. E3.

14 The square brackets around the speech prefixes represent the convention adopted in the printed text of *Wars* to indicate that these were not the speakers in the original text; italics are used for lines written by Barton.

15 Barbara Hodgdon, *The End Crowns All: Closure and Contradiction in Shakespeare's History* (Princeton University Press, 1991), p. 94.

16 Lanoye and Perceval, *Schlachten!*, p. 221. The lines are in English in the original, according to the principle by which at this stage of the sequence the

language has degenerated into a mongrel mixture of German and American-gangster-film English.

17 Campbell (ed.), *Mirror for Magistrates*, Tragedy 18, line 89.
18 Quoted in Sprague, *Shakespeare's Histories*, p. 112.
19 *Richard III*, ed. Hammond, 1.3.119n.
20 David Scott Kastan, *Shakespeare and the Shapes of Time* (London and Basingstoke: Macmillan, 1982), p. 23.
21 Hodgdon, *The End Crowns All*, *passim*.
22 Rackin, *Stages of History*, p. 65.
23 Burns, Introduction, *King Henry VI Part 1*, pp. 67–8.
24 R. W. Chambers, *Man's Unconquerable Mind* (London: Jonathan Cape, 1939) p. 254.
25 See Bullough, III, 233–7 for the possible influence of Legge on Shakespeare's *Richard III*.
26 *Agamemnon*, 1672–4 in Aeschylus, *Oresteia*, trans. David Grene and Wendy Doniger O'Flaherty (Chicago and London: University of Chicago Press, 1989). All further quotations are from this translation.
27 For a full discussion of the debate on these issues see Anthony J. Podlecki, *The Political Background of Aeschylean Tragedy* (Ann Arbor: University of Michigan Press, 1966), pp. 63–100.
28 Edwards, *Threshold of a Nation*, p. 113.

6 LOOKING BACK

1 Andrew Gurr, in his Introduction to the New Cambridge Shakespeare edition of *Richard II*, dates it to 1595 and suggests that the *Henry VI – Richard III* plays 'were probably never performed as a sequence until [Shakespeare] was settled with the Chamberlain's Men, the company he joined when it was formed in mid 1594', pp. 3–4.
2 Graham Holderness has argued this point of view most fully in *Shakespeare's History* (Dublin: Gill and Macmillan, 1985), and in *Shakespeare Re-cycled*.
3 See John Wilders, *The Lost Garden: A View of Shakespeare's English and Roman History Plays* (London and Basingstoke: Macmillan, 1978).
4 See Gurr's note at 1.2.13 and his Introduction, p. 29, for an illustration of Edward III in an imitation Jesse tree from the title page of John Stow's *Annales of England* (1592).
5 See Bullough, III, 359.
6 Though Clifford Rose was playing the part at the point in the run when I saw the production in September 2000, reviewers' descriptions suggest that this was equally the style of Alfred Burke originally cast in the role.
7 The text quoted here is from the 1587 second edition of Holinshed, which Shakespeare used throughout as his main source; the passage is nearly, but not quite, identical in the 1577 edition reproduced in the illustration for the sake of the picture of Shrewsbury that accompanies it.
8 See Kristian Smidt, *Unconformities in Shakespeare's History Plays* (London and Basingstoke: Macmillan, 1982).

9 See prompt-book at Shakespeare Centre Library, Stratford.
10 See, for example, Daniel, who tries to give the king the benefit of the doubt in not having intended to break his oath:

> We will not say nor thinke O *Lancaster*,
> But that thou then didst meane as thou didst swere
> Upon th'Evangelists at *Doncaster*.
>
> (Bullough, III, 441)

11 Holderness, *Shakespeare's History*, pp. 42–3.
12 See the fine psychoanalytic reading of Harry Berger Jr, for whom the line 'Laud be to God' 'rings with a strange and wry tonality. I hear resignation in it, and relief, and an ironic recognition that he will at last get what's coming to him.' *Making Trifles of Terrors: Redistributing Complicities in Shakespeare*, ed. Peter Erickson (Stanford University Press, 1997), p. 250.

7 HYBRID HISTORIES

1 F. P. Wilson, *Marlowe and the Early Shakespeare* (Oxford: Clarendon Press, 1953), p. 106.
2 See for example the questioning of Wilson's statement by G. K. Hunter in *English Drama 1586–1642: The Age of Shakespeare* (Oxford: Clarendon Press, 1997), p. 161.
3 See Robert Greene, *The Scottish History of James the Fourth*, ed. Norman Sanders (London: Methuen, 1970), p. 2 for a reproduction of this title-page of the British Museum copy of the 1598 edition.
4 George Peele, *King Edward the First (1593)*, ed. W. W. Greg (Oxford: Malone Society Reprints, 1911). It has to be said that the play is preserved in an extremely poor text.
5 See Giorgio Melchiori, *2 Henry IV*, New Cambridge Shakespeare edition, Introduction, pp. 9ff.
6 Sir Philip Sidney, *An Apology for Poetry* ed. Geoffrey Shepherd (Manchester University Press, 1973), p. 135.
7 See prompt-book, Shakespeare Centre Library, Stratford.
8 Quoted in Samuel Schoenbaum, *William Shakespeare: A Compact Documentary Life* (Oxford University Press, 1977), pp. 195–6.
9 Ibid., p. 193.
10 Ibid., p. 196.
11 For a discussion of these name changes, see Herbert Weil and Judith Weil, Introduction to the New Cambridge Shakespeare edition of *1 Henry IV*, pp. 5–6. See *2 Henry IV*, 2.2.0 SDn. for reference to 'Sir John Russell' surviving in the Quarto text.
12 See Melchiori, *2 Henry IV*, Introduction, p. 11 n. 5.
13 Anne Barton, *The Names of Comedy* (Oxford: Clarendon Press, 1990), p. 109.

14 For an argument supporting this order see A. R. Humphreys, *1 Henry IV*, Arden edition (London: Methuen, 1960), pp. xiii–xiv.

15 I have retained this traditional spelling of the character's name, even though Andrew Gurr, in the New Cambridge Shakespeare edition of *Henry V* from which I quote, has emended it to Llewellyn. While I can see the logic of the change, argued by Gurr in his Introduction, p. 63, it seems to me to represent too great a defamiliarisation of the name.

16 See Melchiori, *2 Henry IV*, Introduction, p. 12.

17 *The Merry Wives of Windsor*, ed. Giorgio Melchiori (London: Arden Shakespeare, 2000), 1.1.3–5. All further quotations from the play are taken from this edition, cited parenthetically in the text.

18 Prompt-book, Shakespeare Centre Library, Stratford.

19 Herbert Weil and Judith Weil, Introduction, *1 Henry IV*, p. 47.

20 See Pugliatti, *Shakespeare the Historian*, p. 108.

21 See David Wiles, *Shakespeare's Clown: Actor and Text in the Elizabethan Playhouse* (Cambridge University Press, 1987), pp. 116–20.

22 Melchiori, Introduction, *Merry Wives of Windsor*, p. 84 n. 1.

23 T. J. King, *Casting Shakespeare's Plays: London Actors and their Roles, 1590–1642* (Cambridge University Press, 1992), Tables 50–2, 62–3.

24 Wiles, *Shakespeare's Clown*, p. 116.

25 See *The Famous Victories of Henry the Fifth* Sc. II, l, in Peter Corbin and Douglas Sedge (eds.), *The Oldcastle Controversy* (Manchester and New York: Manchester University Press, 1991).

26 See Michael D. Bristol, *Carnival and Theater: Plebeian Culture and the Structure of Authority in Renaissance England* (New York and London: Methuen, 1985), pp. 182–3.

27 John Dover Wilson calls the Falstaff of *Merry Wives* 'his simulacrum, the pretender to his name', in *The Fortunes of Falstaff* (Cambridge University Press, 1943), p. 51; Harold Bloom declares 'that the hero-villain of *The Merry Wives of Windsor* is a nameless imposter masquerading as the great Sir John Falstaff', *Shakespeare: The Invention of the Human*, p. 315.

28 Pugliatti, *Shakespeare the Historian*, p. 147.

29 Wiles, *Shakespeare's Clown*, 132.

8 CHANGE AND IDENTITY

1 Graham Bradshaw, *Misrepresentations: Shakespeare and the Materialists* (Ithaca and London: Cornell University Press, 1993), p. 116.

2 Stephen Greenblatt, *Shakespearean Negotiations* (Oxford: Clarendon Press, 1988), pp. 48–9.

3 See Christopher Allmand, *Henry V*, 2nd edn (New Haven and London: Yale University Press, 1997), pp. 50–1.

4 J. I. M. Stewart, *Character and Motive in Shakespeare* (London: Longman, 1949), p. 138.

5 C. L. Barber, *Shakespeare's Festive Comedy* (Princeton University Press, 1959), p. 218.

6 *Stratford-upon-Avon Herald*, 2 May 1975.

7 John Barber, *Daily Telegraph*, 25 June 1975.

8 B. A. Young, *Financial Times*, 25 June 1975.

9 *Heinrich 4*, 5.2, in Lanoye and Perceval, *Schlachten!*, p. 87.

10 Howard and Rackin, *Engendering a Nation*, p. 165.

11 The stage effects described here and throughout are those in the Zurich version of the production I saw in June 2000.

12 Erich Auerbach, *Mimesis: The Representation of Reality in Western Literature*, trans. Willard Trask (1953; New York: Doubleday Anchor, 1957), p. 284.

13 Prompt-book in Shakespeare Centre Library, Stratford.

14 Tillyard, *Shakespeare's History Plays*, p. 279.

15 Cited by A. R. Humphreys, Introduction, *2 Henry IV*, Arden Shakespeare (London: Methuen, 1966), p. xxii.

16 See Richard David, 'Shakespeare's History Plays: Epic or Drama', *Shakespeare Survey* 6 (1953), 129–39.

17 Harold Jenkins, *The Structural Problem in Shakespeare's 'Henry the Fourth'* (London: Methuen, 1956).

18 G. K. Hunter, '*Henry IV* and the Elizabethan Two-Part Play', *Review of English Studies* 5 n.s. (1954), 236–48.

19 Prompt-book, Shakespeare Centre Library, Stratford.

20 Irving Wardle, *The Times*, 25 April 1975.

21 Greenblatt, *Shakespearean Negotiations*, pp. 49, 48, 52–3.

22 Leonard F. Dean, '*Richard II* to *Henry V*: a Closer View', in Thomas P. Harrison et al. (eds.), *Studies in Honor of DeWitt T. Starnes* (Austin: University of Texas Press, 1967), p. 46.

23 William Hazlitt, *Characters of Shakespear's Plays* (London: R. Hunter, C & J. Ollier, 1817), pp. 204–5.

24 Edward Dowden, *Shakspere: A Critical Study of his Mind and Art* (London: Henry S. King, 1875), pp. 210, 215.

25 Tillyard, *Shakespeare's History Plays*, pp. 309, 317.

26 Jonathan Dollimore and Alan Sinfield, 'History and Ideology: The Instance of *Henry V*', in John Drakakis (ed.), *Alternative Shakespeares* (London and New York: Methuen, 1985), p. 226.

27 Beauman, *The Royal Shakespeare Company's Production of Henry V*, p. 54.

28 William Shakespeare, *Henry V*, a screen adaptation by Kenneth Branagh (London: Chatto & Windus, 1989), p. 24.

29 Ibid., p. 73.

30 Greenblatt, *Shakespearean Negotiations*, p. 63.

31 Gurr, Introduction, *Henry V*, p. 13.

32 Beauman, *The Royal Shakespeare Company's Production of Henry V*, p. 120.

33 Prompt-book, Shakespeare Centre Library, Stratford.

34 Gurr, Introduction, *Henry V*, pp. 18–23.

CONCLUSION

1 Hodgdon, *The End Crowns All*, p. 76.
2 Annabel Patterson, *Reading Holinshed's Chronicles* (University of Chicago Press, 1994).
3 Greenblatt, *Shakespearean Negotations*, p. 1.
4 Rackin, *Stages of History*, p. ix.
5 Tennenhouse, *Power on Display*, p. 11.

Bibliography

ARCHIVAL MATERIALS

Birmingham Central Library: Birmingham Repertory Theatre prompt-books, theatre records.
British Film Institute, London: *An Age of Kings*, BBC Television production, 1960, 15 episodes on video.
Huntington Library, San Marino, California: Pasadena Playhouse theatre collection.
Shakespeare Institute, University of Birmingham, Stratford: BBC TV Shakespeare, 1978–1983, *Richard II–Henry V, Henry VI–Richard III*, 8 videos.
Shakespeare Centre Library, Stratford: Shakespeare Memorial Theatre, Royal Shakespeare Company prompt-books, theatre records; *The Wars of the Roses*, BBC TV broadcast 1965 on video.
Trinity College, Dublin, Department of English: *The Wars of the Roses*, English Shakespeare Company, Portman Classics Production, 1990, 7 videos VRL 60–66.

EDITIONS OF SHAKESPEARE

These are editions other than those normally cited in the book which are listed under the note on 'Texts' at the beginning.

Complete Works, ed. Stanley Wells and Gary Taylor (Oxford University Press, 1986).
1 Henry IV, New Arden, ed. A. R. Humphreys (London: Methuen, 1960).
2 Henry IV, New Arden, ed. A. R. Humphreys (London: Methuen, 1966).
1, 2, 3 Henry VI, ed. John Dover Wilson (Cambridge University Press, 1952).
1, 2, 3 Henry VI, New Arden, ed. Andrew Cairncross (London: Methuen, 1962–4).
King Henry VI Part I , ed. Edward Burns (London: Arden Shakespeare, 2000).
King Henry VI, Part II, ed. Ronald Knowles (London: Arden Shakespeare, 1999).
Henry VI Part 2, The BBC TV Shakespeare (London: BBC, 1983).
King John, New Arden, ed. E. A. J. Honigmann (London: Methuen, 1954).

King John, Oxford Shakespeare, ed. A. R. Braunmuller (Oxford University Press, 1989).

The Merry Wives of Windsor, New Arden, ed. H. J. Oliver (London: Methuen, 1971).

The Merry Wives of Windsor, ed. Giorgio Melchiori (London: Arden Shakespeare, 2000).

Richard II, The BBC TV Shakespeare (London: BBC, 1978).

Richard III, The BBC TV Shakespeare (London: BBC, 1983).

Richard III, New Arden, ed. Anthony Hammond (London: Methuen, 1981).

OTHER PRINTED MATERIALS

Theatre reviews, already cited in the Notes, are not included here. Anonymous works have been alphabetised under the first substantive word of the title: thus, A most pleasant comedie, intituled, a knacke to knowe a knave *under K for* knacke.

Aeschylus, *Oresteia*, trans. David Grene and Wendy Doniger O'Flaherty (Chicago and London: University of Chicago Press, 1989).

Alexander, Peter, *Shakespeare's Henry VI and Richard III* (Cambridge University Press, 1929; repr. New York, Octagon Books, 1973).

Allmand, Christopher, *Henry V* (New Haven and London: Yale University Press, 2nd edn, 1997).

Auerbach, Erich, *Mimesis: The Representation of Reality in Western Literature*, trans. Willard Trask (1953; New York: Doubleday Anchor, 1957).

Barber, C. L., *Shakespeare's Festive Comedy* (Princeton University Press, 1959).

Barton, Anne, *The Names of Comedy* (Oxford: Clarendon Press, 1990).

Beauman, Sally, *The Royal Shakespeare Company: A History of Ten Decades* (Oxford University Press, 1982).

  The Royal Shakespeare Company's Production of Henry V (Oxford: Pergamon Press 1976).

Berger, Harry Jr, *Making Trifles of Terrors: Redistributing Complicities in Shakespeare*, ed. Peter Erickson (Stanford University Press, 1997).

Berry, Edward, *Patterns of Decay: Shakespeare's Early Histories* (Charlottesville, VA: University Press of Virginia, 1975).

Bloom, Harold, *Shakespeare: The Invention of the Human* (New York: Riverhead Books, 1998).

Bogdanov, Michael, and Michael Pennington, *The English Shakespeare Company: The Story of 'The Wars of the Roses' 1986–1989* (London: Nick Hern Books, 1990).

Bradshaw, Graham, *Misrepresentations: Shakespeare and the Materialists* (Ithaca and London: Cornell University Press, 1993).

Bristol, Michael D., *Carnival and Theater: Plebeian Culture and the Structure of Authority in Renaissance England* (New York and London: Methuen, 1985).

Brockbank, Philip, 'The Frame of Disorder – "Henry VI" ', in John Russell Brown and Bernard Harris (eds.), *Early Shakespeare*, Stratford-upon-Avon Studies 3 (London: Edward Arnold, 1961), pp. 73–99.

Bulman, J. C., and H. R. Coursen (eds.), *Shakespeare on Television: An Anthology of Essays and Reviews* (Hanover and London: University Press of America, 1988).

Campbell, Lily B. (ed.), *The Mirror for Magistrates* (Cambridge University Press, 1938).

Chambers, E. K., *The Elizabethan Stage*, 4 vols. (Oxford: Clarendon Press, 1923). *William Shakespeare: A Study of Facts and Problems*, 2 vols. (Oxford: Clarendon Press, 1930).

Chambers, R. W., *Man's Unconquerable Mind* (London: Jonathan Cape, 1939).

Colynet, Anthony, *The True History of the Civil Warres of France, betweene the French King Henry the 4. and the Leaguers. Gathered from the yeare of our Lord 1585. vntill this present October 1591* (London: Thomas Orwin for Thomas Woodcock, 1591).

Corbin, Peter, and Douglas Sedge (eds.), *The Oldcastle Controversy* (Manchester and New York: Manchester University Press, 1991).

Correspondence between Schiller and Goethe, trans. L. Dora Schmitz, 2 vols. (London: George Bell, 1877).

David, Richard, 'Shakespeare's History Plays: Epic or Drama', *Shakespeare Survey* 6 (1953), 129–39.

Dean, Leonard F., '*Richard II* to *Henry V*: a Closer View', in Thomas P. Harrison et al. (eds.), *Studies in Honor of De Witt T. Starnes* (Austin: University of Texas Press, 1967), pp. 37–52.

Déprats, Jean-Michel, 'Shakespeare in France', *Shakespeare Quarterly* 32 (1981), 390–2.

de Somogyi, Nick, *Shakespeare's Theatre of War* (Aldershot and Brookfield, VT: Ashgate, 1998).

Dickins, Richard, *Forty Years of Shakespeare on the English Stage*, [London, 1906].

Dollimore, Jonathan, and Alan Sinfield, 'History and Ideology: The Instance of *Henry V*', in John Drakakis (ed.), *Alternative Shakespeares* (London and New York: Methuen, 1985).

Doran, Madeleine, '*Henry VI, Parts II and III*': Their Relation to the '*Contention*' and '*The True Tragedy*' (Iowa City: University of Iowa, 1928).

Dowden, Edward, *Shakspere: A Critical Study of his Mind and Art* (London: Henry S. King, 1875).

Edwards, Philip, *Threshold of a Nation* (Cambridge University Press, 1979).

Foakes, R. A., and R. T. Rickert (eds.), *Henslowe's Diary* (Cambridge University Press, 1961).

Garber, Marjorie, ' "What's Past is Prologue": Temporality and Prophecy in Shakespeare's History Plays', in Barbara Kiefer Lewalski (ed.), *Renaissance Genres* (Cambridge, MA: Harvard University Press, 1986), pp. 301–31.

Greenblatt, Stephen, *Shakespearean Negotiations* (Oxford: Clarendon Press, 1988).

Greene, Robert, *The Scottish History of James the Fourth*, ed. Norman Sanders (London: Methuen, 1970).

Hall, Peter, and John Barton, *The Wars of the Roses* (London: BBC, 1970).

Hazlitt, William, *Characters of Shakespear's Plays* (London: R. Hunter, C. & J. Ollier, 1817).

Hicks, Michael, *Warwick the Kingmaker* (Oxford: Blackwell, 1998).

Hirst, David L., *Giorgio Strehler* (Cambridge University Press, 1993).

Hodgdon, Barbara, *The End Crowns All: Closure and Contradiction in Shakespeare's History* (Princeton University Press, 1991).

Holderness, Graham, *Shakespeare's History* (Dublin: Gill and Macmillan, 1985).

Shakespeare Re-cycled: The Making of Historical Drama (Hemel Hempstead: Harvester Wheatsheaf, 1992).

Holderness, Graham (ed.), *Shakespeare's History Plays: Richard II to Henry V*, New Casebooks (Basingstoke: Macmillan, 1992).

Howard, Henry, [Earl of Northampton], *A defensative against the poyson of supposed Prophesies . . .* (London: John Charlewood, 1583).

Howard, Jean E., and Phyllis Rackin, *Engendering a Nation: A Feminist Account of Shakespeare's English Histories* (London and New York: Routledge, 1997).

Hunter, G. K., *English Drama 1586–1642: The Age of Shakespeare* (Oxford: Clarendon Press, 1997).

'*Henry IV* and the Elizabethan Two-Part Play', *Review of English Studies* n.s. 5 (1954), 236–48.

'The Royal Shakespeare Company Plays *Henry VI*', *Renaissance Drama* 9 (1978), 91–108.

Jenkins, Harold, *The Structural Problem in Shakespeare's Henry the Fourth* (London: Methuen, 1956).

The First Part of Ieronimo. With the Warres of Portugall, and the life and death of Don Andraea (London: Thomas Pavier, 1605).

Jorgensen, Paul, *Shakespeare's Military World* (Berkeley and Los Angeles: University of California Press, 1956)

Kastan, David Scott, *Shakespeare after Theory* (New York and London. Routledge, 1999).

Shakespeare and the Shapes of Time (London and Basingstoke: Macmillan, 1982).

Kelly, Henry Ansgar, *Divine Providence in the England of Shakespeare's Histories* (Cambridge, MA: Harvard University Press, 1970).

King, T. J., *Casting Shakespeare's Plays: London Actors and their Roles, 1590–1642* (Cambridge University Press, 1992).

A most pleasant comedie, intituled, a knacke to knowe a knave (London: Richard Jones, 1594).

A pleasant conceited comedie, called, a knacke to know an honest man (London: Cuthbert Burby, 1596).

Knutson, Roslyn L., 'Henslowe's Naming of Parts: Entries in the *Diary* for *Tamar Cham*, 1592–3, and *Godfrey of Bulloigne*, 1594–5', *Notes and Queries* 228 (1983), 157–60.

Lanoye, Tom, and Luk Perceval, *Schlachten!: nach den Rosenkriegen von William Shakespeare* (Salzburg and Hamburg: Salzburger Festspiele, Deutsches Schauspielhaus in Hamburg, 1999).

Leiter, Samuel L., *Shakespeare Around the Globe* (New York, Westport, CT and London: Greenwood Press 1986).

McKellen, Ian, *William Shakespeare's Richard III* (London, etc.: Doubleday, 1996).

Malone, Edmond, *A Dissertation on the three parts of King Henry VI* (London: Henry Baldwin, 1787).

Marlowe, Christopher, *Complete Works*, 5 vols. (Oxford: Clarendon Press, 1987–98).

Nashe, Thomas, *Pierce Penniless his Supplication to the Devil . . . and Selected Writings*, ed. Stanley Wells (London: Edward Arnold, 1964).

Odell, George C. D., *Shakespeare from Betterton to Irving*, 2 vols. (London: Constable, 1921).

Peele, George, *King Edward the First (1593)*, ed. W. W. Greg (Oxford: Malone Society Reprints, 1911).

Podlecki, Anthony J., *The Political Background of Aeschylean Tragedy* (Ann Arbor: University of Michigan Press, 1966).

Pugliatti, Paola, *Shakespeare the Historian* (Basingstoke: Macmillan, 1996).

Rackin, Phyllis, *Stages of History* (London: Routledge, 1990).

Raysor, T. M. (ed.), *Coleridge's Shakespeare Criticism*, 2 vols. (London: Constable, 1930).

Ross, Charles, *Richard III* (London: Eyre Methuen, 1981).

Sanders, Wilbur, *The Dramatist and the Received Idea* (Cambridge University Press, 1968).

Sarlos, Robert K., 'Dingelstedt's Celebration of the Tercentenary: Shakespeare's Histories as a Cycle', *Theatre Survey* 5 (1964), 117–31.

Schelling, Felix E., *The English Chronicle Play* (New York: Macmillan, 1902).

Schlegel, A. W., *A Course of Lectures on Dramatic Art and Literature*, trans. John Black (London: Bohn, 1846).

Schoenbaum, Samuel, *William Shakespeare: A Compact Documentary Life* (Oxford University Press, 1977).

The First part of the Tragicall raigne of Selimus, sometime Emperour of the Turks, and grandfather to him that now raigneth (London: Thomas Creede, 1594).

Shakespeare, William, *An Age of Kings* (New York: Pyramid Books, 1961).

　Henry V, a screen adaptation by Kenneth Branagh (London: Chatto & Windus, 1989).

　The Plantagenets (London: Faber & Faber, 1989).

Shaughnessy, Robert, *Representing Shakespeare: England, History and the RSC* (New York etc.: Harvester Wheatsheaf, 1994).

Shoup, Gail Leo, 'The Pasadena Community Playhouse: Its Origins and History from 1917 to 1942', Ph.D. dissertation, UCLA, 1968.

Sidney, Sir Philip, *An Apology for Poetry*, ed. Geoffrey Shepherd (Manchester University Press, 1973).

Simpson, Richard, 'The Politics of Shakespeare's History Plays', *New Shakspere Society Transactions* 1 (1874), 396–441.

Sinfield, Alan, *Faultlines: Cultural Materialism and the Politics of Dissident Reading* (Oxford: Clarendon Press, 1992).

Smidt, Kristian, *Unconformities in Shakespeare's History Plays* (London and Basingstoke: Macmillan, 1982).

Sprague, Arthur Colby, *Shakespeare's Histories: Plays for the Stage* (London: Society for Theatre Research, 1964).

Stewart, J. I. M., *Character and Motive in Shakespeare* (London: Longman, 1949).

Swander, Homer D., 'The Rediscovery of *Henry VI*', *Shakespeare Quarterly* 29 (1978), 146–63.

Taylor, Gary, 'Shakespeare and Others: The Authorship of *Henry the Sixth, Part One*', in J. Leeds Barroll (ed.), *Medieval and Renaissance Drama in England*, VII (London and Toronto: Associated University Presses, 1995), pp. 145–205.

Tennenhouse, Leonard, *Power on Display: the Politics of Shakespeare's Genres* (London: Methuen, 1986).

Thomas, Keith, *Religion and the Decline of Magic* (1971; Harmondsworth: Penguin, 1973).

Tillyard, E. M. W., *Shakespeare's History Plays* (1944; Harmondsworth: Penguin, 1969).

Tynan, Kenneth, *Curtains* (London: Longman, 1961).

Wells, Stanley, and Gary Taylor with John Jowett and William Montgomery, *William Shakespeare: A Textual Companion* (Oxford: Clarendon Press, 1987).

Wilders, John, *The Lost Garden: A View of Shakespeare's English and Roman History Plays* (London and Basingstoke: Macmillan, 1978).

Wiles, David, *Shakespeare's Clown: Actor and Text in the Elizabethan Playhouse* (Cambridge University Press, 1987).

Wilson, F. P., *Marlowe and the Early Shakespeare* (Oxford: Clarendon Press, 1953).

Wilson, J. Dover, *The Fortunes of Falstaff* (Cambridge University Press, 1943).

Wilson, J. Dover, and T. C. Worsley, *Shakespeare's Histories at Stratford 1951* (London: Max Reinhardt, 1952).

Yeats, W. B., *Essays and Introductions* (London: Macmillan, 1961).

Index